More praise for *Divide* or *Conquer*

"*Divide or Conquer* is intelligent, riveting, and useful. Smith reveals a new approach to understanding how management teams work, what can go wrong, and what to do to make it right."

> —Amy Edmondson, Novartis Professor of Leadership and Management, Harvard Business School

"Smith brings a wealth of experience working with leadership teams to understanding and addressing relationships that effect a company's success. Her account of Abraham Lincoln gives the inspiration, insights, and tools leaders need to take their teams to a new level of performance."

> —Stephen N. Kahane, MD, MS, CEO and Chairman, AMICAS, Inc.

"One of the best books available on building a new team or regenerating an old one. Beautifully written."

> —Chris Argyris, James Bryant Conant Professor, Harvard Business School

"This book can save your sanity . . . The cases are terrifically instructive. It helps to learn how even the brilliant can be blinded and mess up!"

> —Susan Perrine, MD, Chief Scientific Office and Vice President, Clinical Affairs, HemaQuest Pharmaceuticals Inc.

"Smith is legend among Boston's social entrepreneurs for her insights into the sometimes thrilling, sometimes dysfunctional human relationships that are at the heart of any enterprise. In *Divide or Conquer,* Smith has put together in one accessible volume her vast intelligence about the usually unspoken, informal dimensions to relationships among leaders—and the ways these bonds can either sabotage or accelerate the success of an organization. I plan to share this book with all of our senior leaders at Citizen Schools."

> —Eric Schwarz, President and CEO, Citizen Schools

"Smith shows us how to salvage struggling relationships or turn good relatinships into great ones. Extraordinarily insightful and refreshingly new."

—Vanessa Kirsch, President and Founder, New Profit Inc.

"All leaders should keep a copy of this book handy. Using in-depth case studies, it shows you how to strengthen relationships *and* ensure good decision making."

—Ralph Biggadike, Professor, Columbia University, Graduate Business School

"Diana Smith's book reveals how relationships at the top can create winning performances or topple even the greatest organizations. Through clear, concise, and witty writing, she offers great hope by showing how our most important relationships can be changed and improved."

—Johann Koss, Four-time Olympic Gold Medalist; President and CEO, Right to Play International

DIVIDE *or* CONQUER

Divide **or** Conquer

*How Great Teams Turn
Conflict into Strength*

Diana McLain Smith

PORTFOLIO

PORTFOLIO
Published by the Penguin Group
Penguin Group (USA) Inc.
375 Hudson Street, New York, New York 10014, U.S.A.
Penguin Group (Canada), 90 Eglinton Avenue East,
Suite 700, Toronto, Ontario M4P 2Y3, Canada
(a division of Pearson Penguin Canada Inc.)
Penguin Books Ltd, 80 Strand, London WC2R 0RL, England
Penguin Ireland, 25 St. Stephen's Green, Dublin 2,
Ireland (a division of Penguin Books Ltd)
Penguin Books Australia Ltd, 250 Camberwell Road,
Camberwell, Victoria 3124, Australia
(a division of Pearson Australia Group Pty Ltd)
Penguin Books India Pvt Ltd, 11 Community Centre,
Panchsheel Park, New Delhi – 110 017, India
Penguin Group (NZ), 67 Apollo Drive, Rosedale, North Shore 0632,
New Zealand (a division of Pearson New Zealand Ltd)
Penguin Books (South Africa) (Pty) Ltd, 24 Sturdee Avenue,
Rosebank, Johannesburg 2196, South Africa

Penguin Books Ltd, Registered Offices:
80 Strand, London WC2R 0RL, England

First published in 2008 by Portfolio,
a member of Penguin Group (USA) Inc.

1 2 3 4 5 6 7 8 9 10

Excerpt from "Trouble Man" words and music by Marvin Gaye.
© 1972 (renewed 2000) Jobete Music Co., Inc. and
Twentieth Century Music Corp. All rights controlled and
administered by EMI April Music Inc. All rights reserved.
International copyright secured. Used by permission.

Illustration credits appear on page 281.

LIBRARY OF CONGRESS CATALOGING-IN-PUBLICATION DATA
Smith, Diana McLain.
Divide or conquer : how great teams turn conflict into strength / Diana McLain Smith.
p. cm.
Includes bibliographical references and index.
ISBN-13: 978-1-59184-204-0
1. Teams in the workplace. 2. Interpersonal relations. 3. Interpersonal communication. I. Title.
HD66 .S65 2008
658.4'022—dc22   2008005993

Printed in the United States of America
Set in ITC Galliard

To my husband, Bruce Patton
For everything

Contents

APPENDICES

Preface

A house divided against itself cannot stand.

—Abraham Lincoln

ll teams rise and fall on the strength of their relationships. Secretary of Defense Donald Rumsfeld and his top generals; Larry Summers and the faculty at Harvard University; Carly Fiorina and the Hewlett-Packard board; Michael Ovitz and Michael Eisner at Disney; Steve Jobs and John Sculley at Apple; Abraham Lincoln and his wartime cabinet: as far back as Agamemnon and Achilles on the beaches of Troy, relationships within teams have determined the fate of leaders and their enterprises.

Even so, relationships go largely unnoticed. We analyze group dynamics; we size up team members; we even consider the larger context within which teams operate. But we don't take a close look at the relationships that turn a bunch of people into a single team.

No one today would dispute the idea that relationships matter. Flatter hierarchies, tighter interdependencies, efforts to move decision making down in organizations all depend on the quality of people's relationships. Yet despite their obvious importance—perhaps because of it—relationships remain largely a mystery. We know *that* relationships matter, but not exactly *why* or *how*. And so, despite our best efforts to create collaborative, high-performing teams or flatter, more flexible organizations, many still look as territorial and hierarchical as ever.

In this book, I use stories from my own work and public sources to bring relationships to the foreground and peer inside them, so you can better understand how they work, develop, and change—and then use that understanding to build relationships flexible and strong enough to create and sustain an exceptional team.

DIVIDE *or* CONQUER

There are these two fish swimming along, and they happen to meet an older fish swimming the other way, who nods at them and says, "Morning, boys, how's the water?" And the two young fish swim on for a bit, and then eventually one of them looks over at the other and goes, "What the hell is water?"

—David Foster Wallace, "The Capital T Truth"

1
Introduction

Every team is only as strong as its weakest relationships. How well and how quickly teams make decisions, inspire innovation, tackle performance problems, or learn from mistakes depends on the strength of relationships within a team. Some relationships give teams the courage to face tough truths and make bold changes. Others kill every new idea or initiative within their reach. Still others plod along somewhere in between, causing little trouble but failing to inspire or sustain stellar performance. Without a doubt, individuals and group dynamics figure in all this, but all that figuring takes place in the context of relationships.

After 20 years of studying and advising leaders, I've come to believe that a team's performance, even a firm's, turns on the quality of its most important relationships.

The Real Sticking Point

In retrospect, this conclusion was inescapable. On many occasions I'd witnessed organizations falter—not because leaders failed to grasp the need to change or to design the right strategy or to inspire the troops or to appreciate the importance of culture, but because relationships within their teams prevented them from doing what they needed to do to succeed.[1]

Though I'd long suspected this, the top team at Elite Systems convinced me.[2] Touted by the press as one of America's great manufacturing firms, Elite's performance first stalled, then plummeted after competitors entered the market with knockoff products at much lower prices. Two years later, the firm's top team faced choices so fundamental they challenged its most basic beliefs and threatened its identity as a leader in product design. Quite understandably, the executives struggled.

As consultants to the team, my partner and I figured we could best help by gathering data on politically charged strategic questions, facilitating team deliberations, and developing people's knowledge of strategy, team dynamics, and negotiation. After a year and a half, I think it's fair to say we failed.[3] Despite everyone's hard work and best efforts, the team couldn't move quickly enough to turn around the firm's performance. In the end, the board felt it had no choice but to take action, and it did, firing the CEO and half his team. Needless to say, my partner and I went out with them, as we should have.

"It's the Relationship, Stupid!"

Afterward, I decided to take a closer look at what had prevented the team from moving fast enough to improve Elite's performance. As I pored over transcripts from over 50 meetings, tape-recorded over 18 months, I began to see the basic flaw in our approach. We were so intent on building the team, facilitating decision making, and developing individual leaders that we completely overlooked the real sticking point: relationships within the team.

Yet the closer I looked, the more obvious it became. Three sets of relationships had made it impossible for the team to move fast enough or well enough to succeed:

▶ The relationships among executives from competing business units;
▶ The relationships between those most central and those more peripheral to debates;
▶ The relationships between the CEO and members of his team.

In the first set, executives from different business units repeatedly got caught in what they called "point-counterpoint debates" about the cause of and the cure for the firm's deteriorating performance. The two executives who dominated this debate, Frank Adams and Ian McAlister, couldn't have been more different. One headed up the firm's newest and fastest-growing subsidiary, the other the firm's struggling core business. One was brash and quick, the other measured and reflective. One believed that the market should shape the products you make, the other believed that the products you make should be strong enough to shape the market. One appealed to facts and figures, the other to values and beliefs. Unable to resolve their differences— forget about *using* them—they began to accuse each other of trying to protect his turf or to promote his own business. The two went nowhere fast.

> *Relationship: The way in which two or more people or organizations regard and behave toward each other.* [4]

In the second set of relationships, leaders peripheral to the debate watched and waited as those caught up in it argued back and forth, back and forth. Over time, the silence of this peripheral majority led those embroiled in the debate to discount their inputs any time one of them waded in. Angered by the rebuff, those on the periphery withdrew even

"And now at this point in the meeting I'd like to shift the blame away from me and onto someone else."

further, making it impossible for them to alter the point-counterpoint debate that was stalling progress.

Finally, hoping to resolve differences the team couldn't, the CEO periodically stepped in and imposed a solution to get things moving. But this only strained his initially strong relationship with the team members, many of whom faulted him for violating his espoused commitment to collaboration and team autonomy. Now caught himself, the CEO grew more distant, creating a leadership vacuum that exacerbated the team dynamics and further strained his relationship with the team.

In the end, these three sets of relationships killed the team. With the first set polarizing debates, the second reducing the team to a handful of players, and the third destroying the CEO's ability to exert his leadership, the team didn't stand a chance.

The Waiting Game: When You Win, You Lose

No one in the room was blind to these dynamics. Everyone felt their corrosive effects, even complained about them regularly. Trouble was, no one seemed able to change them, at least not in any enduring way. They kept bumping up against the same problem: they were all looking to someone else on the team to change his or her behavior before they changed their own.

It was the old prisoner's dilemma. Worried that any change they made might be misunderstood or exploited by others, no one wanted to risk it.[5] What's more, they all shared the same conventional wisdom: convinced the other guy was the problem, they focused on getting him to change rather than changing themselves (see box). With no one willing to make the first move, they all got caught in a waiting game that made it hard for anyone to change.

Conventional Wisdom

• Because your behavior upsets me, you must be the cause of my upset. Since you're the cause, you should change.

• My telling you that you're the cause and that you should change is all you need to effect change.

• If you don't then change, you must not *want* to change or you *just don't get it.* (It's *not* a sign that my behavior is part of the problem.)

• If you continue to act in ways that upset me, then I need to try harder to *make* you change. (It doesn't mean I'm trying the wrong things.)

• Because I'm now trying harder and harder, and you're still not changing, you must be uninfluenceable. (It's not a sign that I am uninfluenceable.)

• Given that you're uninfluenceable, there's nothing else I can do.

• Given there's nothing else I can do, then there's nothing else I *will* do. As far as I'm concerned, the relationship is over—whether I leave or stay.

That Trapped Feeling

From years of observing teams, I had long understood how one person's actions—say, an accusation or a threat—could provoke reactions (indignation or outrage) in another that would lead him to act in ways (stonewall or counterattack) that would cause the first person to react further.[6] But now, as I studied what happened at Elite, I could see how these patterns, left to escalate, had made even the most irrational actions look downright reasonable, even inevitable, to the person acting. Over time, this sense of inevitability had made everyone on the team feel trapped in relationships that were no longer of their own making. And while no one liked the impact these relationships were having on the team, no one had a clue how to change them.

And there's the rub: once patterns of interaction take on a life of their own, relationships seem to operate independently of anything we do or want or intend. If they go well, everything else goes well. If they go poorly, everything else goes to hell. Which one happens, most of us chalk up to a chemistry too mysterious to decode and too difficult to change.

It need not be that way.

To Change the Game, You Have to See the Game

Relationships are such an integral part of everyday life they're like the air we breathe—or the water those fish swim in every day. Until something unpleasant or unexpected happens, we give them little notice; even then, we're often at a loss as to what to do. We can spot difficulties easily enough and feel their effects even more easily, but few among us can pinpoint their cause; still fewer know what to do about it. Like a firm's culture, relationships are part of the informal side of organizational life—the soft stuff that's hard to see, grasp, or change.

The purpose of this book is to shed a new light on old relationship conundrums. It reflects over two decades' worth of clinical research on teams operating at the top of organizations across sectors. That research convinced me of two things: first, that relationships have an informal structure that can be mapped and changed, and second, that relationships may be the single most underutilized lever for transforming the performance of teams and organizations.

This is especially true for relationships that operate along *organizational fault lines*—interfaces where coordination is as essential as it is difficult: research and marketing at Merck; manufacturing and design at Herman Miller; the president and the faculty at Harvard; business units competing in the marketplace; executive and legislative branches at the federal and state levels; and top management and middle management everywhere. At each interface, interests collide and conflicts erupt. Whether people can put these conflicts to work[7]—so they create value rather than destroy it—depends on the nature and the quality of their relationships.

This is where most of us find ourselves at a loss. Even the best ideas about teams or interpersonal dynamics often fail to bring relationships into the foreground, where we can see how they work and how they break down.[8] As a result, we may know *that* a relationship's in trouble, but we don't know *how* to change it, at least not in any reliable or lasting way.

This Book Can Help

Given the right tools, it's possible to build relationships flexible and strong enough to sustain stellar performance in teams—both over time and under pressure. This book helps by giving you ideas and tools for:

▸ Understanding relationships
▸ Transforming relationships
▸ Making change practical

Because two-person relationships are the DNA that shapes how a team operates and evolves, the book's three parts focus on these basic building blocks.[9] The first part of the book explores how relationships work and develop; the second, how you can change them over time; and the third, how to make that change practical. Let's look at what you'll find in each part.

Part 1: Understanding Relationships

When it comes to the *formal* side of a relationship—defining roles, clarifying responsibilities, allocating decision rights, calculating financial rewards—we have lots of tools. But when it comes to the *informal* side—the chemistry between people, the balance of give and take, the sense of connection or animosity they feel—we have only our intuition to guide us. Yet it is the interplay between these two sides of a relationship that determines its fate.

The first part of the book casts a light on the informal side of a relationship—what it looks like, how it develops, and why it breaks down under pressure. It opens with the story of the breakup between Steve Jobs and John Sculley at Apple in the 1980s, tracing the relationship's life and death and its impact on the firm (Chapter 2). In the next chapter, I use the story of a divisional CEO and her next-in-command to reveal the underlying anatomy of a relationship and to uncover powerful leverage points for change (Chapter 3). The last chapter tells the story of a fast-growing professional-services firm to show why some relationships grow stronger and others more fragile with time (Chapter 4). These three stories—and the tools they introduce—will help you understand and change the course of your own relationships.

Part 2: Transforming Relationships

The reason most people change so slowly, or not at all, isn't because you can't teach old folks new tricks (you can), but because we expect them to change independently of the relationships in which they operate. The same goes for teams, even organizations: we expect them to change independently of the relationships that make them up. Trouble is, the vast majority of people will wait for their peers to make the first, second, even the third move. And when it comes to their superiors, well then, the wait will be more on the order of a hundred moves. Meanwhile, a lot of time is a-wasting. People and teams will change a lot faster if they do two things: focus on their relationships, and make them flexible and strong enough to support change at all levels—from the individual to the team to the overall organization.

To show you how, this part of the book recounts how two leaders transformed their relationship over the course of three stages. In the first stage, they disrupted patterns of interaction that were getting in their way (Chapter 5). In the second, they invented patterns flexible enough to pick up the pace of change (Chapter 6). In the third, they reset the basis of their relationship so those new patterns could take hold (Chapter 7). As their story illustrates, each stage gives way to the next, with each creating more significant and lasting change than the one before it.

Part 3: Making Change Practical

When the best-laid plans go awry, it's usually because they're disconnected from the very realities they're supposed to address. Sure, all of us
want better relationships in our teams, but what team can afford to invest
the time, money, and energy to create them? To make change practical,
you need more than a theory of change; you need tools for making
change happen in the real world.

This part of the book gives you the tools you'll need to make changes
while getting things done. The first chapter shows you how to focus and
sequence your efforts so you can create the biggest impact with the least
amount of effort (Chapter 8). The next chapter introduces three strategies you can use to strengthen relationships while attending to business
(Chapter 9). The last chapter offers principles and practices you can use
to stay motivated enough to make changes in relationships over time
(Chapter 10).

Coda: Relational Sensibilities

Any time you talk about relationships, or teams, or organizations, it's
easy to forget that *people* create and sustain them. People matter. They
make choices—mostly unconscious choices—about how to operate in relationships. By cultivating what I call *relational sensibilities,* people can
naturally build relationships that bring out the best in others *and* in
themselves.

Perhaps no one illustrates this ability better than Abraham Lincoln. In
Lincoln's leadership of a nation at war, we can discern seven pairs of sensibilities. Together these sensibilities made it not only possible but natural for Lincoln to turn enemies into friends. To illustrate these sensibilities
and demonstrate their power, I look at Lincoln's Second Inaugural Address, in which he attends to the shattered relationship between the
North and the South. After identifying the sensibilities at work in Lincoln's speech, I explore how we might cultivate them in ourselves and in
each other.

Who This Book Is For

This book is for anyone committed to building an exceptional team, and for those who can help them: consultants, coaches, and academics. If you want to create a great team, then you need to understand how the relationships within that team work, develop, and change. This book gives you a navigational system with which to see and traverse—with far greater intelligence—that often unpredictable and sometimes treacherous terrain called relationships.

PART I

Understanding Relationships

Purpose: To show how relationships work, develop, and break down, so you can make your own relationships strong and flexible enough to master the shifting challenges you'll face.

Synopsis: Some relationships grow more *brittle*, others more *resilient*, with time. Which of these takes place depends on the interplay between the *formal* and *informal* sides of a relationship. When people ignore the informal side of a relationship, they're more apt to view any troubles they face from an *either/or perspective*. This perspective escalates conflict, harms relationships, and destroys value. In contrast, when people understand the underlying *anatomy* of a relationship, they're more apt to view any troubles they face from a *relational perspective*. This perspective puts conflict to work in the service of learning and change, allowing people to strengthen their relationships over time.

Taking Action: Under pressure, everyone reverts back to an either/or perspective. To shift perspective in the heat of the moment, you need to develop the ability to *reflect* and *reframe*—first alone, then with others. These companion abilities help people cool down when things get hot, so they can use any troubles they face to strengthen their relationships.

2
The Life and Death of a Relationship

I now had what the self-help books called baggage, which I would carry around for the rest of my life. The trick was to meet someone with similar baggage, and form a matching set, but how would one go about finding such a person?

—David Sedaris[1]

More than 20 years have passed since Steve Jobs and John Sculley's much-publicized breakup at Apple. Yet it still serves as a cautionary tale. In two short years, their celebrated camaraderie turned into an antagonism so great it escalated hostilities between divisions, put the firm at risk of a takeover, and sent Steve Jobs into a 12-year exile, from which the firm has only recently recovered. How these leaders went from soul mates to adversaries in such a short time shows how relationships, even those touted as a perfect match, can self-destruct under pressure, leaving a firm to pay the formidable price of a failed relationship.

When the Jobs and Sculley relationship fell apart, most people chalked it up to personalities: Jobs was too volatile, Sculley too cautious. Others cited circumstances: mounting competitive pressures put otherwise kindred spirits at odds.[2] Still others said their chemistry wasn't right: they may have seemed the perfect match, but Sculley was way too corporate, Jobs too iconoclastic. While each explanation holds merit, all overlook the most intriguing and instructive aspect of what happened: the way their relationship developed over time.

Only by understanding how relationships form, develop, and die can you see *why* people form ill-fated matches, *why* certain personalities clash, and *why* some relationships break down so quickly and completely under pressure. And only by understanding how relationships form, develop, and die do you stand a chance of altering the course a relationship takes. By looking closely at how the Jobs and Sculley relationship developed over the course of three stages, we can extract timeless lessons about the life and death of a relationship—and its impact on the firm.

Stage 1: How a Relationship Forms

When someone joins a team, everyone spends a good deal of time defining their formal roles in relation to each other. In some cases, they'll spend anywhere from weeks to months negotiating everything from tasks to responsibilities to financial rewards to decision rights. Unbeknownst to all involved, as these negotiations unfold, another deal is being struck: people are also defining their informal roles by signaling to each other through their interactions the emotional responsibilities they'll each assume, the psychological rewards they'll each need, and the interpersonal rights they'll each claim.

It is the interplay between these two deals that sets the foundation of a relationship. By paying attention to both deals, you're much more likely to get a relationship off to a good start. Conversely, as the Jobs and Sculley relationship shows, when you ignore the informal deal you strike, you're much more likely to get into trouble, and you're much more likely to be stunned and amazed when you do.

The Story: The Perfect Match

When Steve Jobs and John Sculley first met at a January 1983 dinner following a private preview of Apple's new Lisa computer, their mutual attraction was obvious to everyone.[3] One Apple chronicler, Frank Rose, tells the story of that midwinter evening in New York:[4]

After an hour or so they went downstairs, where Sculley's limousine was waiting to take them to the Four Seasons for dinner. It was a car that seemed as big as an airplane, with a bar and a TV and a driver named Fred, all on call twenty-four hours a day. . . . They swept down Park to Fifty-Second . . . and pulled up at the discreetly canopied entrance to the Four Seasons. Sculley led them into the travertine anteroom, up the stairway to the reservations desk, past the enormous Picasso stage curtain, and into the stark opulence of the Pool Room.

Over dinner the unlikely chemistry between Jobs and Sculley became readily apparent. Despite their obvious differences in age and background—Sculley was strictly Ivy League and corporate, having graduated from Brown University and the Wharton School and having spent most of his professional life at Pepsi; Jobs, seventeen years his junior, had dropped out of Oregon's funky little Reed College during his freshman year—they somehow clicked. It was almost as if each tapped something unrealized in the other. There was a cool, crisp professionalism to Sculley that Jobs respected, a utopian fervor to Jobs that Sculley found intriguing. Sculley was a man who knew how to run a multimillion-dollar enterprise. Jobs was a kid who proved he could change the world. Put them together. . . .[5]

Earlier that same day, the differences between Sculley and Jobs were as apparent as their affection was at dinner. While Jobs was jumping up and down with enthusiasm for his spanking-new product, Sculley held back. *He* was looking at the product through the eyes of a corporate executive at the helm of a traditional company in an industry where winning depended more on cost efficiencies and marketing know-how than on product innovation. Says Rose:

. . . he didn't take to it wholeheartedly. He was cautious. He had reservations. He wasn't sure that this new technology, dazzling as it was, would have much impact at a big corporation like Pepsi, because it didn't have the IBM logo. No one ever got fired, the saying went, for buying an IBM.[6]

To this side of Sculley, Steve Jobs gave no notice. All he saw was a savvy, ingenious marketer, whom he alone described as "very charismatic."[7] After all, Sculley was the one who had revived the Pepsi Generation campaign in the late sixties, spurring unprecedented growth for the next six years. By 1978, Pepsi Cola was surpassing Coke in sales for the first time in the firm's eighty-year history.[8] Perhaps at Apple, Sculley could do the same thing—invent the Apple Generation. That would certainly advance Jobs's vision of changing the world by resetting the balance of power between the individual and the institution. One person, one computer: that was his motto. Since Apple's inception, he'd dreamed of bringing power to the people, as the saying from the sixties went. Only, he was going to do it by putting an Apple computer in the hands of every person. With Apple cofounder Steve Wozniak gone and CEO Mike Markkula anxious to move on, the decision whether to hire Sculley was largely up to Jobs. And it looked to him as if Sculley had all the right stuff.

Two months later, the deal was done. In April 1983, Sculley accepted the offer to join Apple as its new president[9] and passed up the once-in-a-lifetime opportunity to succeed his mentor, Donald Kendall, as chairman of PepsiCo. To make the jump more palatable, Apple agreed to give the forty-four-year-old Sculley a $1 million salary along with a promised $1 million bonus, a $1 million severance package (in case things didn't work out),[10] an option to buy 350,000 shares of stock, a $2 million loan to buy a Tudor-style house in the California hills,[11] and $1.3 million for Sculley's Greenwich (Connecticut) home to save him the trouble of selling it.[12]

Although no small amount in 1983, the money is not what sealed the deal. Nor was it the opportunity to lead a company that was growing at a breakneck pace. No, what sealed the deal was the bond they'd forged out of their mutual attraction to power. For Sculley, Jobs held the awe-inspiring power to change the world; for Jobs, Sculley held the key to unbounded corporate power. It was a heady match, says Frank Rose, seducing them both and preoccupying everyone else:

> For weeks they had been gazing worshipfully at each other, finishing each other's sentences, parroting each other's thoughts. It was as if

they were on a perpetual honeymoon which they had to share with a great many unruly children. . . . The summer honeymoon between Steve and John was the talk of the company. The two were insepara- ble. John was listening and learning, and the person he was learning from was Steve. . . . He seemed so in awe of Steve—his brashness, his charm, his charisma—that he saw everything through Steve's eyes. . . . But the infatuation wasn't one-sided. It was almost like a father-son relationship in which the two adopted each other.[13]

But theirs wasn't just any father-son relationship. As Sculley later wrote: "I felt that part of my role was to nurture Steve from a prince to a king, so he would someday be able to run the company he cofounded."[14] That first summer, they were so absorbed with each other that they failed to see what those around them feared most—that their father-son indul- gences might demolish a useful, if delicate, balance of power within the firm. Says Rose:

In the original triumvirate—Scotty [Mike Scott] as president, [Mike] Markkula as chairman, and Jobs as visionary—Jobs's brash enthu- siasms had been leavened by Scotty's stern hand and Markkula's per- suasive manner. . . . Sculley's arrival changed all that. John made Steve his partner, not realizing that Steve had never been a partner in running Apple before. Suddenly there were no restraints. Sculley un- leashed him, and Steve unleashed what was an astonishing spectacle. People began to liken it to Godzilla being let out of his cage.[15]

But Sculley saw no trace of a monster in the hyperkinetic Jobs. He didn't understand there was a reason no one had ever granted Jobs un- checked access to power. Nor did he see what he later came to believe: that Jobs was often "stubborn, uncompromising and downright impos- sible."[16] All he saw was a prince entitled to inherit the throne of the king- dom he'd cofounded. Similarly, Jobs didn't see in Sculley what others saw: a cautious leader unlikely to make the bold moves that were second nature to Jobs. Nor did he see what he later came to believe: that Sculley wasn't really a leader but a "manager," preoccupied with control and unwilling to provide Jobs the support he needed. At the time, all he saw was a powerful, supportive benefactor committed to helping him realize his dreams.

What the Story Teaches Us

The one characteristic that marks the beginning of all relationships headed for trouble is obliviousness to the informal side of a relationship. Like most executives, those negotiating Sculley's entry into the firm focused on business matters. They discussed ideas for growing the business; they debated how Apple's technology might change the world; they talked roles and responsibilities; they negotiated compensation. And in the end, they came up with a deal so full of potential upside and so buffered against downside risk that Sculley couldn't refuse.[17]

What they didn't do was take a close look at the relationship between Sculley and Jobs. Sure, everyone could see the two were enamored with each other, but no one questioned why they'd clicked so quickly and so completely. While some found their instant intimacy unsettling and others worried that each was not seeing the other for who he really was, no one could say why or do much about it. All they could do was chalk it up to chemistry and leave it at that.

Most of us do the same thing. When people click or clash, we chalk it up to chemistry and leave it at that. But it is possible to identify and analyze the seemingly mysterious ingredients that go into the makings of a relationship. As this book shows throughout, given the right tools, it is possible to understand what happens when a relationship forms and anticipate what might happen next. For now, let's look more closely at what happened with Jobs and Sculley in this first stage.

Understanding what happens when a relationship forms. We all bring to relationships our own characteristic ways of interacting with others given our *behavioral repertoires*.[18] Built out of experience, these repertoires are organized around key themes, such as power, conflict, control, or success. When we negotiate the informal terms of a relationship, these themes give rise to patterns of interaction, through which we signal to each other:

▶ the *emotional responsibilities* we'll assume ("I've *gotta* help this guy!") and those we'll reject ("No way I'm doing that!")—regardless of formal roles.

▶ the *interpersonal rights* we'll claim ("You can't treat me that way!") and those we'll relinquish ("Don't worry about it")—regardless of any formal deal.

▶ the *psychological rewards* we'll want to receive ("Just once I wish she'd give me a pat on the back!") and those we'll be willing to give ("You did a great job. Thanks.")—regardless of financial rewards.

When people first meet, their themes intersect to give rise to distinctive patterns of interaction. Acting like DNA, these themes shape the way a relationship's patterns of interaction evolve over time, defining the formal and informal sides of a relationship.[19] One strand of DNA defining the relationship between Sculley and Jobs was a shared preoccupation with power, leading each of them to see in the other a form of power he coveted. Before Sculley joined Apple in the spring of 1983, the effusive Jobs saw in the more cerebral Sculley the corporate power he needed to change the world. Dazzled by the limousine, the chauffeur, and the opulence of the Pool Room, Jobs paid little attention to Sculley's more reserved, controlled side. To Jobs, the "charismatic" Sculley must have seemed more thoughtful than controlled, more sophisticated than reserved. And given how low-key Sculley acted, it must have been hard to imagine that he'd ever pose much of a threat.[20] As to how Sculley made it to the top of a highly competitive—some might say cutthroat—firm like Pepsi, Jobs apparently gave little thought, perhaps assuming it was due to his marketing talents. All Jobs saw was a perfect match.

Similarly, Sculley saw in Jobs a brilliant visionary with the power to change the world. Like Jobs, Sculley paid little attention to the behaviors he later found so unacceptable, even though they too were evident right from the start. Jobs's jumping up and down at the unveiling of Lisa, his unpredictable emotional outbursts, his caustic ridicule of Apple's competitors all must have seemed part of an otherwise attractive package—rough edges that could be smoothed out over time. Just how that smoothing out would occur, well, that too was assumed rather than anticipated. All Sculley saw was an opportunity to do more than sell sugared water for the rest of his life.[21] With Jobs's help, he was going to change the world.

Anticipating what might happen next. Two themes in Jobs's and Sculley's repertoires not only failed to form a matching set, they downright clashed: Jobs's well-known disdain for institutional authority (you could say he built the firm and its products upon this disdain),[22] and Sculley's corporately honed preference and talent for institutional control (to which his tenure at Pepsi was a tribute).[23] As Frank Rose recounts:

> [Sculley] liked to tinker with structure. Maybe it was his architectural training, maybe just his natural cast of mind, but he was always thinking about how things fit together. Jobs's thinking tended to be more intuitive, emotional, and visionary; Sculley was more a systems man, rational and analytical. Form and process were what interested him.[24]

Had anyone paid attention to these differences, they might have given more thought to how they might play out over time.

As it was, no one asked what might happen should Sculley seek to impose the kind of corporate controls at Apple he'd imposed at Pepsi. Nor did they ask what might happen should Jobs bristle under that control. Intent on finding a seasoned executive to counterbalance and contain Jobs's more intuitive, even impulsive leadership style, Apple's board didn't think through how all this counterbalancing and containing would occur.

Nor did they anticipate the events their relationship might set in motion or the effect those events might have on the firm's delicate balance of power.

Stage 2: How a Relationship Develops

In the second stage of development, people renegotiate their formal and informal roles, as initial impressions give way to more stable interpretations and people come to know each other for "who they really are."

These more stable interpretations—what I call frames—inform people's negotiations about who should do what *and* turn early patterns of interaction into more stable informal structures. Though hard to discern without the proper tools, these structures give relationships their distinctive character (dominating boss and deferring subordinate).

Those who pay attention to how the informal side of a relationship develops during this stage understand that what they see is what they'll get, giving them room to maneuver if they don't like what they get. Those who ignore the informal side, as Sculley and Jobs did, believe that what they see is the only way it is, leaving them disillusioned and trapped.

The Story: The Road to Disillusionment

Six months before Sculley joined Apple, Jobs had gotten approval from Apple's board to build his own factory for the Macintosh and to get it up and running before turning it over to Del Yocam, Apple's VP of manufacturing. Several months after Sculley's arrival, sometime in the fall of 1983, Sculley knew he had a problem: Jobs didn't want to turn manufacturing over to Yocam. Instead, Jobs pitched another idea: let Yocam keep the Apple II division and the Dallas factory, and let Jobs keep the Macintosh division and its new Fremont plant.[25]

After some thought, Sculley took to the idea, figuring it would allow him to solve two problems at once: Jobs's desire to take operational control of Macintosh, and his own desire to gain greater control of Apple.[26] Jobs would get his chance to run something, and Sculley would have two profit-and-loss centers to manage the same way Pepsi, Taco Bell, and Pizza Hut were managed at PepsiCo. But Apple wasn't Pepsi, Sculley wasn't Kendall, and Jobs wasn't Sculley. And so, in an effort to solve two problems with one redesign, Sculley inadvertently created a much bigger and eventually fatal problem, wedging himself between Jobs-as-boss (in his role of chairman) and Jobs-as-subordinate (as the head of Macintosh). Equally problematic, he distanced himself from the operations of the company while drawing Jobs in closer to them. This placed Sculley in the untenable position of depending on Jobs not only for his technical expertise but also for his knowledge of day-to-day operations.

"It was a mistake," Sculley later wrote. "I became more remote from the business. . . . He really had more knowledge about what was going on in the business than I did because all the information was coming up through the product divisions. They had all the power. The corporate staff basically became an impotent group."[27]

This decision, although later regretted, made sense in the context of the two men's relationship at the time. It was autumn 1983. Their summer honeymoon was just ending. They were turning their attention to building "insanely great products" and growing a "phenomenal firm." They were also building their relationship on the foundation set over the summer. During that time, Sculley had taken on the informal task of turning a prince into a king. Now, in an effort to fulfill that role, he was continually coaching, cajoling, and chastising Jobs into behaving properly. Early on, Sculley was full of confidence. All Jobs needed was experience, the kind of experience a prince can only get by running his own province.[28] Besides, Jobs was more than accommodating. If anything, he was acting like an adoring young kid, relenting when cajoled, expressing regret when chastised, and repenting each time Sculley coached him to rein in his sometimes rude, occasionally cruel, always emotional outbursts.

Six months later Sculley regretted what he'd done. In his memoir he cites the precise moment when things took a turn for the worse. It was May 1984, only a year into Sculley's tenure at Apple. At a celebratory dinner arranged by Jobs as a tribute to his friend and mentor, Sculley stood up to thank the group and to praise Jobs. He began by speaking glowingly of their relationship, saying they'd developed a friendship, not just a partnership. And then, pausing for effect, he looked across the room at Jobs and declared: "Apple has one leader, Steve and me." Later on, Sculley would say of these words: "I didn't yet know it, but my statement proved to be a turning point."[29]

Within weeks of that dinner, Sculley began to worry that he was losing his grip on the management of the company. He watched with concern as Jobs's power increased after he decided to fold the Lisa prod-

uct line into the Macintosh group to create two distinct lines of business.[30] He noticed how Jobs was trying to influence all matters of business,
not just those related to product development. Even more worrisome,
Sculley also sensed that he was losing purchase on his relationship with
Jobs. His coaching, cajoling, and chastising no longer had much effect, if
it ever did. While Jobs kept promising to behave, he never seemed to
make good on those promises. "For the first time," Sculley wrote, "I felt
as if I was losing control."[31]

That feeling only intensified during a meeting with a group of Xerox
executives a few months later. When Sculley first arranged the meeting, he knew Jobs had little respect for the company,[32] but he persuaded
Jobs that acquiring a firm like Xerox would accelerate Apple's growth
and put it within shooting distance of IBM. With images of a defeated
IBM dancing in his head, Jobs agreed to the meeting and promised to
behave. Yet, once in the meeting, Jobs couldn't or wouldn't contain himself. Within minutes, he was telling Xerox representatives: You're doing
it wrong, just doing it completely wrong. Sculley recounts what happened next:

> Adams [head of Xerox's computer systems group] bristled, and things
> went downhill from there. Glavin [vice chairman of Xerox] glanced
> across the table at me and rolled his eyes.
>
> "Now let's step back and talk about this," I hopelessly interjected.
>
> But Steve couldn't hold back. A pained look appeared on his face
> as the words came tumbling out of his mouth.
>
> "I really shouldn't say this," he said. "But I'm going to say it. You
> guys don't have any idea what you're doing."
>
> Within fifteen minutes or so, it was clear we were going to accom-
> plish nothing. So I pulled Bill Glavin aside and suggested that we call
> off the session and perhaps regroup at a later date. The meeting quickly
> ended and Steve and I left the room. I was incredulous.
>
> "Steve," I asked, "why did you do that? I thought we had an agree-
> ment that you were going to control yourself."
>
> "I'm sorry, but I couldn't help myself," he said contritely in a little
> boy's voice. "I went to Xerox PARC and saw that they had all the

great people and they were doing all the great things and they just didn't see it. . . . I just couldn't control myself. I'm sorry."

Steve and I never rescheduled the meeting with Xerox.[33]

During this same time, Jobs's doubts about Sculley were also taking shape. Things weren't going so well for Macintosh. While Apple's profitability was soaring, Mac sales for September were less than two-thirds of what they'd projected. Jobs felt like a failure. Stunned and upset, he walked around, head down, asking those around him the price he'd have to pay for his failure.[34] But according to Rose, Jobs's self-scrutiny quickly gave way to blame, most of it directed at Sculley:

> The reason Macintosh wasn't more profitable, Jobs was convinced, was that the company . . . wasn't supporting it. Take distribution. He had gone to Sculley with his vision of 747s loading up computers at the factory gates, but other people were trying to block him on it. . . . He wanted to fire all those people and close down their warehouses and go with Federal Express right away. . . . Sculley was hedging. He wanted to appoint somebody to study it. Jobs saw no need for study. . . . And so he was beginning to question Sculley's performance. He was beginning to wonder why the CEO he'd picked wasn't providing the leadership he needed.[35]

Jobs *must* have been mystified. Until then, Sculley had been his most avid ally, opening doors to corporate power everyone else had kept shut. Now, much to Jobs's consternation, Sculley's only response was to caution him *to slow down, to study the problem.* He couldn't believe it. Instead of helping him stave off failure, Sculley was actually blocking him! For the first time, he questioned Sculley's more measured, studious approach to leadership. Perhaps Sculley *wasn't* the key to power after all. Perhaps he was just another ineffectual authority who didn't get it and had no right to tell him what to do.

What the Story Teaches Us

Sculley made three fateful decisions during this stage; later on, he regretted all three. First, after creating two separate divisions—one for the Mac, the other for Apple II—he decided to give Jobs operational control of Mac. Next, much to the chagrin of those working on Lisa (Jobs called them "bozos"), he decided to fold the Lisa line into the Mac division, expanding the division's scope and Jobs's power. Finally, to signal that Jobs did in fact have operational control of the Macintosh division, he changed Jobs's title from vice president to executive vice president. Together, these choices moved Jobs closer to the operations of the company, gave Jobs more formal power, and wedged Sculley between Jobs-as-boss and Jobs-as-subordinate.

When people make bad design choices, it's often a sign that they're caught in informal structures that make unwise choices look smart. Sculley's choices, as bad as they were, flowed naturally from the pattern of interaction established during the first stage. Right from the start, Sculley indulged Jobs without holding him accountable, while Jobs admired Sculley without empowering him as Pepsi's Kendall had. Within this relational context, it made sense for Jobs to ask for a division of his own and for Sculley to give it to him.[36] Their informal dealings had led them to see each other in a particular light and to expect certain things from each other, turning their early pattern of interaction into a more enduring structure. Let's take a look at how that structure evolved, then consider its effects.

How an informal structure takes shape. After Sculley put Jobs in charge of Macintosh, he started paying closer attention to the impact Jobs had on him and others, noticing that:

> [Jobs] could inspire people, and he could make them sweat. . . . At one moment, he could drain all your self-esteem. At the very next, he could praise you, offering just a few complimentary crumbs that somehow made all the angst worthwhile.[37]

While this kind of behavior would never be tolerated at Pepsi, Sculley accepted it. "Steve was unique," he explained. "People made exceptions for him. They held him to the standard of a young, smart kid; they didn't really view him as an adult.[38] Besides, Sculley added:

When he looked at me, it was a look of admiration, a what-can-I-learn look that was terribly gripping. In Steve's eyes I couldn't do anything wrong.[39]

Perhaps even more gripping, Sculley saw himself in Jobs:

None of Steve's behavior alarmed me, maybe because I so clearly saw my younger self in him. People had often found me difficult to deal with during my early days at Pepsi, too. I never verbally attacked anyone, but I insisted on only the best from them, as Steve did. So I tried to coach Steve the way Chuck Mangold coached me at Pepsi.

This way of seeing Jobs led Sculley to stop short of holding him accountable for his impact. He figured he could coach and cajole Steve into behaving more constructively.

"You've got to learn to hold back some things," I told him. "All you're going to do is cause a lot of unnecessary frustration which isn't constructive."

Treating his mentor as an indulgent father figure who could do nothing wrong, Jobs responded by relenting, regretting, and repenting.

"You're right," he said. "I know it. Keep talking to me, you're absolutely right. I know I shouldn't do that."[40]

If we now step back for a moment and look at the data presented so far, we can see the outlines of a structure take shape. If we were to map that structure, it would look something like Figure 1.

As the map shows, Sculley's actions invite and reinforce the very behavior in Jobs that he later finds so unacceptable: he repeatedly makes exceptions for Jobs and never holds him accountable. Jobs, in turn, acts

Figure 1: An Informal Structure Takes Shape

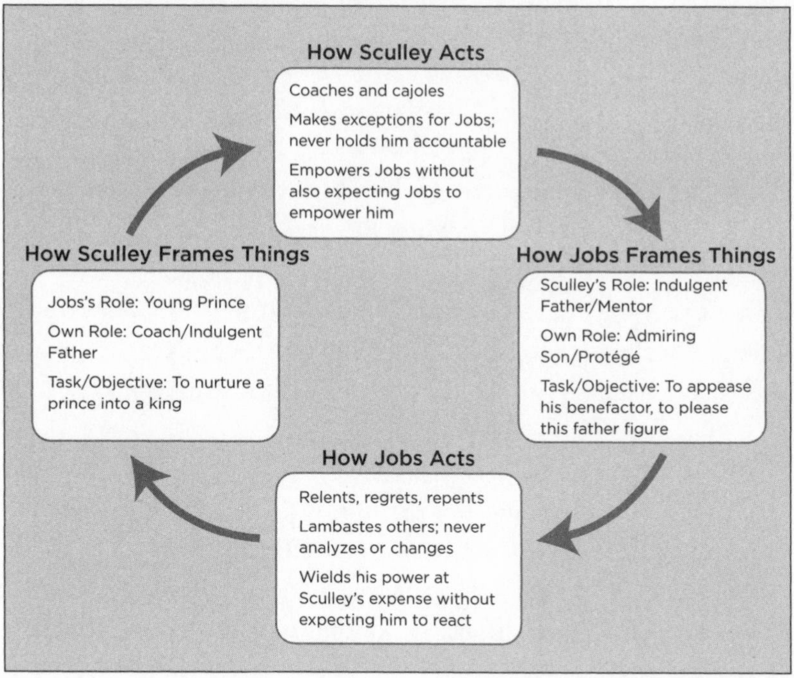

How Sculley Acts

Coaches and cajoles

Makes exceptions for Jobs; never holds him accountable

Empowers Jobs without also expecting Jobs to empower him

How Sculley Frames Things

Jobs's Role: Young Prince

Own Role: Coach/Indulgent Father

Task/Objective: To nurture a prince into a king

How Jobs Frames Things

Sculley's Role: Indulgent Father/Mentor

Own Role: Admiring Son/Protégé

Task/Objective: To appease his benefactor, to please this father figure

How Jobs Acts

Relents, regrets, repents

Lambastes others; never analyzes or changes

Wields his power at Sculley's expense without expecting him to react

in ways that invite Sculley to exert the very control he hates: he regrets but never examines his behavior or its impact. At the same time, both of them do things that empower Jobs—even if it's at Sculley's expense. It doesn't occur to either one of them that Sculley might come to feel so threatened that he will feel the need to reassert his power—even if it's at Jobs's expense.

As problematic as these interlocking actions are, they follow logically from the way each man *frames* his informal role in relation to the other. Seeing their roles one way and not another, Jobs and Sculley take on some tasks and not others, making some actions seem obvious, others irrelevant. *It's these less conscious informal roles that lock patterns into place, turning them into more stable structures.* And it's these structures that make unwise choices look smart. Only later, when Sculley's decisions end up undermining his control, does Sculley see what he couldn't see then: that he had let power flow unchecked from himself to Jobs. And only later, when Sculley seeks to reassert his power, does Jobs see what he couldn't see then: that Sculley wanted far more control and power than Jobs ever wanted to give him.

Had Sculley and Jobs had such a map in hand at the time, they would have seen that they were locking themselves into a structure that could end up harming them *and* Apple.

How informal structures evolve. The turning point in the two men's relationship takes place when the two meet with the executives from Xerox. After that meeting, an "incredulous" Sculley realizes that Jobs can't or won't control himself, and a contrite Jobs senses he's in trouble. To see how these shifts occur and how they affect the evolution of their relationship, let's take a closer look at what happened:

▸ Before the meeting, Sculley takes his usual approach to Jobs, cajoling him into attending the meeting with the Xerox executives by appealing to his ambition to overtake IBM. Jobs responds to Sculley's cajoling by doing what he usually does: relenting. Despite his disrespect for Xerox, he agrees not only to come to the meeting but also to behave himself.

▸ At the meeting, Jobs violates his agreement by launching into an emotional harangue, accusing the executives of getting it wrong, *all wrong*.

▸ As soon as the meeting ends, Sculley asks Jobs the same question he'd asked him countless times before: "Why did you do that?" Only, this time, he adds in utter frustration, "I thought we had an agreement that you were going to control yourself."

▸ Sensing Sculley's disappointment and mounting frustration, Jobs appeals for forgiveness, explaining that he *couldn't* control himself, that the folks at Xerox *made* him do it.

This sequence of events marks a subtle but irrevocable shift in how Jobs and Sculley see each other. Jobs's inability to keep his agreements or to take responsibility for his actions signals to Sculley that he may be unable or unwilling to control himself. For the first time, Sculley sees just how unruly a prince Jobs can be, leading him to take on a new role and a new task: that of a disapproving parent, intent on controlling an unruly charge who can't or won't control himself.

At the same time, the frustration permeating Sculley's question signals to Jobs that Sculley wants more than an answer. He wants Jobs—no, he *expects* Jobs—to follow through on his agreements. Sensing this shift, Jobs also takes on a new role and task: that of a contrite little boy intent on eliciting the forgiveness he needs to retain Sculley's indulgence.

By mapping this sequence, we can see why this moment is such a turning point. *It marks a structural shift.* As Figure 2 shows, once Sculley casts Jobs in the role of an unruly prince, he himself must take on a new role— that of a disciplinarian whose task is to *get* Jobs to behave. In that role and with that task, some actions make more sense than others. No longer believing that Jobs can control himself, Sculley stops coaching and cajoling him and starts challenging, confronting, and criticizing him. Adapting to this shift, Jobs no longer sees Sculley as an indulgent father but as a disapproving one, leading him to take on the role of a contrite little boy intent on retaining Sculley's indulgence. Since his prior actions aren't quite up to this new task, Jobs must adopt new ones, which he does. He stops relenting and repenting and starts apologizing and begging for forgiveness.

Figure 2: An Informal Structure Evolves

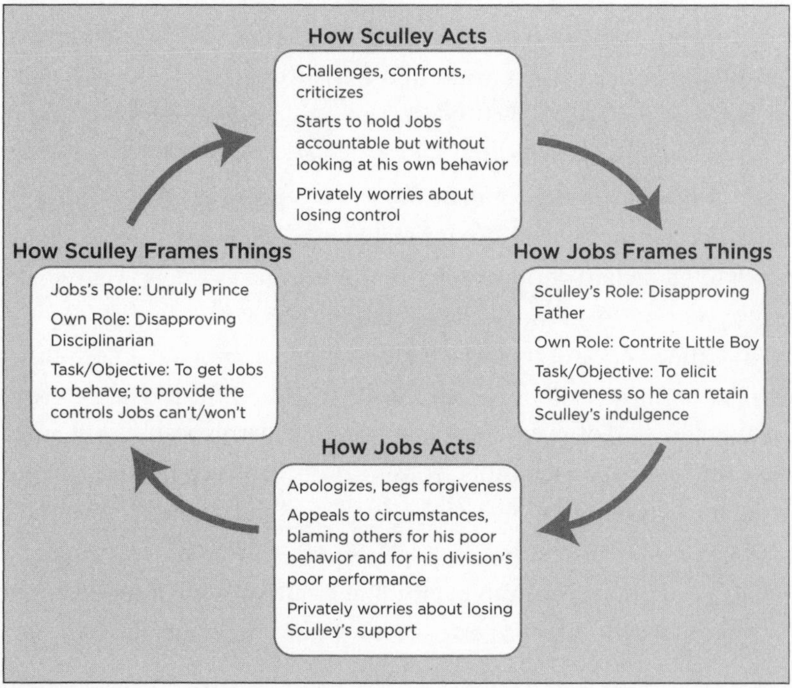

How Sculley Acts

Challenges, confronts, criticizes

Starts to hold Jobs accountable but without looking at his own behavior

Privately worries about losing control

How Sculley Frames Things

Jobs's Role: Unruly Prince

Own Role: Disapproving Disciplinarian

Task/Objective: To get Jobs to behave; to provide the controls Jobs can't/won't

How Jobs Frames Things

Sculley's Role: Disapproving Father

Own Role: Contrite Little Boy

Task/Objective: To elicit forgiveness so he can retain Sculley's indulgence

How Jobs Acts

Apologizes, begs forgiveness

Appeals to circumstances, blaming others for his poor behavior and for his division's poor performance

Privately worries about losing Sculley's support

These new ways of seeing and interacting lead the original structure to evolve, creating a new variation on the old theme of power. Only, this variation prevents them from getting what they want from each other. While they both sense a worrisome shift, they each assume that the other is causing it, making it impossible for them to change course.

What they can't see is what the map so clearly shows: that they're each eliciting from the other the very responses that worry them the most. The more critical and controlling Sculley becomes, the more Jobs apologizes, blames others, and appeals to circumstance; and the more Jobs apologizes, blames others, and appeals to circumstance, the more critical and controlling Sculley becomes. By the end of this stage, they're left with nothing but a paradox: the more their relationship develops, the more fragile it becomes.

Stage 3: How a Relationship Dies

As Sculley continues to challenge, confront, and criticize Jobs, an increasingly perplexed Jobs realizes that his apologies will no longer elicit the indulgent responses to which he's grown accustomed. Soon he starts to bristle under Sculley's control, doing what he wants without Sculley's knowledge or approval. This only angers Sculley, who feels less and less able to control the organization he's designed.

In this new relational context, the power they originally found so appealing in each other takes on a threatening cast. From here on, Sculley scurries to gain control of the firm, while Jobs seeks the power he needs to resist, putting them on a direct collision course.

When they finally do collide, under the pressure of a failing business, their relationship breaks down and comes to an end. By looking closely at what happens in this third stage, you can see why their relationship ends so abruptly and why they can't revive it. Let's return to their story, then analyze the way it ends.

The Story: Things Fall Apart

By the end of 1984, just after Jobs and Sculley appeared on the cover of *BusinessWeek* as "Apple's Dynamic Duo,"[41] it was clear that Macintosh was in trouble. It was selling well enough to universities, but it wasn't moving anywhere else.[42] As inventory piled up each day, people like Debi Coleman, who ran manufacturing at Macintosh, and Roy Weaver, vice president in charge of distribution, knew something was wrong. But those at the top didn't seem to notice. It didn't occur to them that Apple had been growing not so much because of its insanely great products, or because it was beating the competition, but because the market was growing.[43]

"We had no reason to suspect that our success would not carry us in our race into the next year," Sculley later wrote. "If anything, 1985 seemed to promise as much or even more for us than any other year in the company's history."[44]

Like Sculley, everyone was focusing on the good news: profits for the quarter ending December 28 had leaped almost eightfold to a record $46.1 million. Sales had more than doubled to a record $698.3 million.[45] No one had a clue that Apple's world was about to crumble.[46]

A critical new product, Macintosh Office, was late. The Apple II division was at war with the Macintosh division. Jobs's cofounder and long-time friend Steve Wozniak was leaving the company for the second and last time, as were many other executives. IBM was cutting into Apple II sales with a discounted PCjr. Shipments had slowed. Unsold computers were lining the shelves of Apple dealers. The press was scrambling for gossip and forecasting the company's demise. The impact on Sculley and Jobs's relationship wasn't good. As Sculley recalls:

> Inside Apple, we were increasingly absorbed by finger-pointing and infighting. The long, meandering chats and intellectual debates about how technology would change the world became far more basic. For the first time since Steve and I had met, we found ourselves entrenched on opposite sides of major issues.[47]

The operative word here is "entrenched"—and not just on the business issues. Their views of each other had also hardened. By this point, Jobs was certain he'd made a mistake in hiring Sculley,[48] and Sculley was equally convinced that he'd created a "monster."[49]

Soon they found themselves agreeing on less and less and fighting more and more.[50] Every time Sculley asked Jobs to account for Macintosh's disappointing results, Jobs would blame Sculley.[51] And every time Jobs told Sculley how to solve the distribution problem, Sculley would tell him to *stay out of it, and let the task force handle it*.[52] Others around them couldn't help but notice the mounting tension. Increasingly worried, they paid less attention to the business and more attention to the interpersonal chaos swirling around them. And no wonder: Sculley, ordinarily cerebral and controlled, was visibly upset. In one meeting, after discovering that one of Jobs's direct reports hadn't heard of an upcoming divisional review, he finally blew. Says Apple chronicler Frank Rose:

> After two years as an emotional cipher, [Sculley] suddenly switched to an "on" state. He was screaming, cursing, pounding the table. He'd scheduled a formal performance review for all the different divisions of the company, and Steve had never told his staff about it? He couldn't believe it. Well, there was going to be one, and if her boss didn't show up for it he would be fired.[53]

Incidents like this began to pile up, distracting everyone within shooting distance. Sculley's administrative assistant threatened to resign, the animosity between the two making it impossible to get things done. By March, the business was failing fast. Excessive inventory forced them to close all four of their California manufacturing plants for a week. Analysts on Wall Street were cutting their estimates of their earnings. Their stock was in a free fall. Rumors of a takeover were everywhere.[54] They were desperate, and it was time to come to Jesus. Frank Rose recounts what happened next:

> The beginning of the end came on a rainy night in March, the night John finally confronted Steve. He wasn't eager to go through with it.

But Jay Elliot [Apple's VP of HR] had been pushing for a meeting, because he thought it was time that the two of them shared their feelings with each other. For John that meant telling Steve that he was dissatisfied with how he was running Macintosh. . . . Steve and his minions had grown openly contemptuous . . . not just of the Apple II division but of corporate Apple as well—'Corportino,' Debi [Coleman] called it. More and more Corportino was being challenged to justify its own existence. This meeting was considerably overdue.[55]

For the next several hours, they "shared their feelings" about the worsening situation:

John was willing to acknowledge that he hadn't been running things as aggressively as he might have, but he also had to say that Steve hadn't given him the opportunity. Steve was always interfering. That's how the finger-pointing began. Why was Mac in such trouble? Steve claimed it was because John wasn't keeping on top of the inventory situation, wasn't taking care of the distribution issue, wasn't taking charge of finance, wasn't providing the leadership to run the company. John said it was because the product wasn't right, because they didn't have the software and the office products to make it work. Maybe he had been too far removed from operations, but now he was going to take charge, and he wanted somebody else to run Macintosh.[56]

As happens at many such meetings, the fact that they were finally being honest with each other obfuscated the fact that they were being dishonest with themselves. At no point did either of them look at his own role in creating the situation he found so unacceptable. By focusing only on the other's shortcomings, it didn't occur to either of them that they were both right: the products *were* late; distribution *was* a disaster; each of them *had* made it harder for the other to succeed. Sculley *was* abdicating his leadership; Jobs *was* creating too much divisiveness. In the end, all they could see was what the other guy was doing to screw things up.

After the meeting ended, Sculley stepped out into the rain, convinced he had no choice. "There was nothing else to do," he recalls thinking. "I

had to remove Steve as general manager of the Macintosh division." He
went on to add:

> It was a painful decision because I knew the cost was high. Steve would
> pay the price of a job that he liked; I would pay the price of our friend-
> ship because I knew it could never survive this. For days I wracked my
> mind for an alternative. But I knew I wasn't doing what I was hired
> to do. My responsibility was to the shareholders, the board, and the
> employees.[57]

The next two months were consumed with countless meetings—some
with the board, some with the executive staff, others with the two of
them, either alone or with another executive. In each meeting people
tried desperately to redeem the situation. Several, including Sculley, asked
Jobs to take on a nonoperational role. But Jobs refused, his heart set on
leading the operations of the company. Jobs suggested that Sculley become chairman and leave him to run the company. But Sculley refused,
not wanting to become a figurehead. Jobs then suggested that they divide the firm up, so they could each lead a separate division. But Sculley
no longer had any confidence in Jobs and didn't want to share power
with him. With no options left, a depressed but not yet defeated Jobs
made a last-ditch effort to come out on top, secretly lobbying the executive staff and the board to throw Sculley out.

His efforts failed. In a meeting held late in May 1985, all but one
executive staff member lined up behind Sculley. Later that same week,
the board voted to remove Jobs as executive vice president of the Macintosh division. Only Jay Elliot refused. He didn't want to support either
of them. Disgusted by their failure to settle their differences, he told
them:

> . . . they were both being self-indulgent with their little power strug-
> gle. They were too wrapped up in themselves to care about the five
> thousand people who worked for the company. It was ridiculous, he
> told them, that they couldn't work this thing out. He wouldn't pledge
> his loyalty to either one of them; he was pledging it to Apple.[58]

But it was too late, and everyone knew it. Neither Jobs nor Sculley could find a way to make their relationship work. In their minds, no pleas—no matter how impassioned—could alter what had now become a basic "fact." Their relationship was over, and they could find no way to revive it. A few days later, Sculley asked Jobs to sign the papers that made it official.[59]

"Well," [Steve] said meekly, obviously hurt, "I guess that's it."
"I'm sorry, Steve," I said. "I guess it is."
"Okay."
It was a brief conversation, an abrupt end to our relationship.

What the Story Teaches Us

By the time the Jobs and Sculley relationship broke down, their degrees of freedom were so constrained that they could only imagine one solution: get rid of the other. It never occurred to them that they might change the way they saw and interacted with each other, even though that's what got them into trouble in the first place. But what if it had occurred to them? They probably would have rejected the idea. And who could blame them? They would have had to invest a lot of time and energy to turn around their relationship, and there was no guarantee that that investment would pay off. And then where would they and the firm be? Sculley was right. He was responsible to the shareholders, the board, and the employees. He had no choice.

And that's the point. When people ignore the informal side of their relationships, they're more apt to create ones that leave them little choice. By the second stage of their relationship, Jobs and Sculley had created a structure that significantly reduced their degrees of freedom; by the third stage, that structure had eliminated their freedom altogether. Let's take a look at how the third stage of their relationship unfolds.

Nearing the end. By the time Sculley and Jobs reach the third stage in their relationship, they have moved from idolizing to demonizing each other. At this point Sculley no longer sees Jobs as the rightful heir to Apple's throne, but as a "monster,"[60] unable to stay out of things and incapable of controlling himself.[61] For his part, Jobs no longer sees Sculley as an indulgent, supportive mentor committed to his vision, but as an ineffective manager, intent on controlling him and undermining the values that had made Apple great.[62]

Seeing each other in this more toxic light, Jobs and Sculley treat each other accordingly, either fighting or distancing. Unable to agree on much of anything, they blame each other for their troubles and outrightly refuse to do what the other no longer requests but demands.[63] This new structure leads their relationship to take on a whole new look and feel: looking more like mortal enemies than the perfect match, they feel compelled to fight to the death.

By mapping the evolution of their structure into this third stage, you can see just how far their relationship has come and just how toxic the structure underlying it has grown:

Figure 3: An Informal Structure Grows Toxic

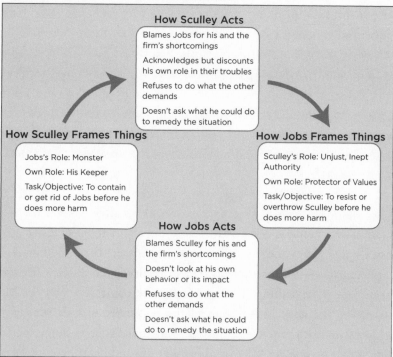

Sealing their fate. Not until the very end do Sculley and Jobs sit down, ostensibly to share their feelings. By then, however, it's too late. Given how toxic the structure underlying their relationship has become, there's no longer any room for learning—only for accusations.

Why was Mac in such trouble? Jobs claimed it was because Sculley wasn't keeping on top of the inventory, wasn't taking care of the distribution, wasn't taking charge of finance, wasn't providing the leadership to run the company. Sculley said it was because the product wasn't right, because they didn't have the software and the office products to make it work.[64]

Throughout this discussion, there are no surprises, only reiterations of past positions. Neither asks the other about the behavior that bothered them so much. Nor does either provide any incentive for answering such a question, had it been asked. By now, any questions would be met with the suspicion that any answer given would be used to prove a case against them. Indeed, that's all they are doing now: proving their case. Neither shows any interest in understanding how their relationship went wrong or how they might set it right. That's why, at the meeting's end, Jobs leaves more convinced than ever that hiring Sculley was the biggest mistake of his life, and Sculley leaves confirmed in his belief that he has no choice but to remove Jobs.

A few days later, Sculley gives the board a choice: remove Jobs from Macintosh, or he will resign. The board, as constrained by the men's relationship as they were, feels it has little choice but to remove Jobs, and so they do—at which point, Sculley and Jobs confront yet another choice: whether to end their relationship or reboot. Initially they try to reboot, casting about for formal roles they both can live with. But neither can imagine how anything will work given the state of their relationship. It doesn't occur to anyone, except perhaps Jay Elliot,[65] that it is their informal relationship—not their formal one—that needs redesigning. By then, the outcome is inevitable, and their relationship comes to an abrupt end.

Creating baggage. After their relationship ends, neither Sculley nor Jobs seems to learn much from its demise. While Sculley's memoir offers a remarkable chronicle of the relationship's life and death, you never get the sense that he fully understands his role in either.[66] While he speaks of creating a monster, he never seems to figure out how. This is largely because he never scrutinizes the role he played in creating a relationship that harmed him, Jobs, and the firm.

"It's not enough that we succeed. Cats must also fail."

Unlike Sculley, Jobs rarely says anything in public about his relationship with Sculley. But in 1995, with Apple still struggling and Jobs still in exile, he did briefly touch on what happened in an interview with *Smithsonian*. In that interview, he demonstrates the same unawareness and the same behavior that undercut his leadership, the firm, and his relationship with Sculley. Asked why Apple had failed to thrive after his exit, he answers:

John Sculley ruined Apple and he ruined it by bringing a set of values to the top of Apple which were corrupt and corrupted some of the top people who were there, drove out some of the ones who were not corruptible, and brought in more corrupt ones and paid themselves collectively tens of millions of dollars and cared more about their own glory and wealth than they did about what built Apple in the first place—which was making great computers for people to use.[67]

Unaware that they'd both played a starring role in creating a relationship that failed them and their firm, the only thing they could take out of their relationship was the same thing David Sedaris took out of his: what the self-help books called baggage.[68]

Key Points

All relationships develop at a formal and informal level. At a formal level people define and redefine their formal roles, including responsibilities, decision rights, and rewards. At an informal level people define and redefine their informal roles: the emotional responsibilities they'll assume and assign, the interpersonal rights they'll claim and relinquish, and the psychological rewards they'll want to give and get.

All relationships develop over a series of stages, as people adapt to each other and the circumstances around them. Some adaptations are better than others. Jobs and Sculley's adaptations generated vicious cycles that gave rise to structures that reduced their degrees of freedom until they had none left. In two action-packed years, they moved from idolizing to demonizing each other, acting in ways that brought out the worst in both of them. By the time they discussed their troubles, their views were so entrenched they were impervious to change, making it impossible for them to create a different future. In the end, they *had* to call it quits.

It need not be this way. As the next chapters show, with the right tools, it's possible to see, map, and change the informal side of a relationship so it grows stronger, not weaker, over time.

3
The Anatomy of
a Relationship

[S]ome key part of human activity—whether it is something as simple as pounding out a Morse code message or as complex as being married to someone—has an identifiable and stable pattern.

—Malcolm Gladwell[1]

Once a relationship gets into trouble, it can be awfully hard to get out. We're so riveted on the other person—on divining his motives or on avoiding his impact—that we don't take a close look at what we ourselves are doing to create a relationship neither of us wants. Sure, we may think hard about what we're trying to do and how hard we're trying to do it, or we may recall what the other person did and how it made us feel. But for the most part, all we see are the constraints others are imposing on us, while remaining blind to the constraints we're imposing on them. Unaware, we wait for others to make life easier for us while we make it harder for them to make it easier for us. In the end, like Sculley and Jobs, we're left with little choice: either end the relationship or settle for one that doesn't work.

When people get to the point where their difficulties "must" be addressed, most of them have long since reached conclusions about each other—*he's a wimp, she's a control freak*—and most have spent months, perhaps even years, trying to get the other person to behave differently:

How can I get him to step up and act like a leader? How can I get her to let go? But just locating the problem inside the other person and attributing it to immutable traits won't get anyone to do *anything.*

To change the course of a relationship, people need to slow down and look at what they're actually feeling, thinking, and doing with each other, so they can see that they're not nearly as helpless as they think they are. To illustrate, this chapter uses the story of the relationship between a divisional CEO and her next-in-command to introduce a framework you can use to map relationships and uncover powerful leverage points for change.

The Story: Dangerous Times at SafetyNet

Three years ago, Christina Bellanti was a woman on a mission. When she first joined Secureware,[2] a software company that sells security products for computer networks, it was as CEO of the firm's largest but worst-performing division, SafetyNet. A tall, energetic woman in her early forties, Chris was the quintessential entrepreneur, utterly convinced that she could turn around the division's flagging performance and establish it as the industry leader in security products worldwide. She was right. Eighteen months later SafetyNet was one of the most profitable divisions in the firm, and Chris was setting her sights on becoming the industry leader.

She had only one problem. She needed a second-in-command who could help her grow the division more quickly than ever. Always on the lookout for emerging young talent, she thought she'd spotted the right stuff in Peter Thompson, a brilliant project manager in his early thirties from another division. Over the course of a year, Peter had been assigned to several projects in Chris's division. While working together, Peter had come to admire Chris's charismatic leadership and passion for SafetyNet's products, while Chris had come to respect Peter's unusually sharp intelligence and dedication. After their third project together, Chris thought Peter might be just the guy who could help her turn SafetyNet into a world-class firm.

The Beginning of a Beautiful Friendship

When Chris broached to Peter the possibility of his joining her as the division's COO, Peter agreed to meet with her to explore the opportunity further. Over two dinners that went late into the night, Peter, intrigued but noncommittal, sat back and listened as Chris regaled him with stories about SafetyNet's recent success and talked about her vision for its future. Peter was impressed. Chris had all the effusiveness, passion, and vision that his own CEO lacked, and her division was growing faster than any other in the company. Even better, this could be his chance to move into a real leadership position.

At the end of their third dinner, they relaxed back into their chairs, the waiter handing them each a snifter of cognac. Then, leaning forward as if to confide in Peter, Chris said, "I need a partner, someone who shares my vision and has the technical savvy to help me turn it into a reality." Pausing for a moment, she then added, "I feel in my gut that that partner is you."

Peter felt flattered but cautious. He wanted to make sure that this really was the leadership opportunity he was looking for. Leaning back in his chair, he asked what kinds of opportunities the new role would offer: Would he have free rein in managing the top team? How much time and counsel would Chris give him? How would decisions get made? Would he be able to influence them?

The more they talked, the better the match looked. Chris felt confident that she could rely on Peter's calm demeanor and analytic sharps to complement her own less systematic and more intuitive approach, while Peter thought he had a lot to learn about leadership from Chris.

After an hour, Peter broke into a warm smile, and by the evening's end, they'd sealed the deal. Peter agreed to manage the top team and help drive the division's growth; Chris agreed to coach Peter on his leadership and to help him realize his ambitions within the firm.

As they left the restaurant and stepped into the night, Chris quipped, "I think this is the beginning of a beautiful friendship."

The Plot Thickens

A few months after Peter joined the division, a small incident occurred that signaled a subtle but important shift in their relationship. Early one day Chris and Peter decided to call a meeting of the division's top team to discuss the sales numbers Peter had delivered to Chris that morning. Everyone filed into the conference room with coffee in hand, relaxed and joking—everyone, that is, except Peter, who knew Chris was disappointed in the numbers. Quiet and tense, Peter took his seat, looking over at Chris, who was busy rifling through a pile of spreadsheets. While Peter waited for her to start the meeting, as she usually did, Chris continued to sort through the spreadsheets, ignoring him.

After a few moments, Peter turned to Chris. "So how would you like to proceed?"

Looking up for the first time, Chris shot back, "Rather than ask me, why don't you take the lead and tell us how you'd like to proceed?"

Surprised and embarrassed, Peter took a moment to compose himself, then went ahead and proposed an agenda. An hour and a half later, the meeting ended with no one giving much notice to how it began—except Peter and Chris. They both knew something out of the ordinary had just happened, but they weren't quite sure what it was or what it meant.

Later on, Peter said of the incident, "In the overall scheme of things what Chris did wasn't a big deal. But it *was* mystifying and embarrassing to be confronted that way in front of the group." What happened next? "I let it go. But I did have this lingering doubt: it wasn't the first time I'd seen Chris overreact; it was just the first time she'd directed it at me."

Looking back, Chris said of the same incident, "It was a bad day. Just as people were taking their seats, I noticed an error in the numbers Peter had given me, and I was checking to see if it would affect the overall picture. The whole time, I could feel Peter looking at me, expecting me to start the meeting, when I've been waiting for him to step up and lead the meetings as the COO. In that moment, I found his passivity especially irritating and I let it show. I don't like it, but there it is."

After the meeting a somewhat sheepish Chris approached David, the head of sales, to ask if she'd been too harsh with Peter. In a measured tone, David said circumspectly, "Let's put it this way: I wouldn't have felt so good if you had done that to me."

"No, I guess not," Chris said, then turned to go in search of Peter.

A few minutes later she found him standing by the coffee machine in the corporate kitchen. "Look, I'm sorry about this morning," she said. Then, in a mildly accusatory tone, she added, "I feel uncomfortable when people defer to me. I really want you to step up and take more leadership. I respect your opinion, and I want to hear it. But I feel like you're always asking questions and waiting for me to take the lead. I really want you to start taking more initiative."

Relieved by the apology, Peter decided to overlook the implied criticism. "I understand. No problem," he replied. "I'll try to weigh in more." What he didn't say was that he had an uneasy feeling. He wasn't so sure how Chris would react if he took her up on her request and exercised more leadership.

Though the next few months went by without a major incident, the truce they'd struck wasn't wholly satisfying, either. More cautious about asking Chris for advice or testing his ideas with her, Peter wasn't learning as much. And Chris, who continued to tease opinions out of an even more hesitant Peter, got the uncomfortable feeling that, while technically sharp, Peter might turn into more of a burden than a partner who could take initiative.

The Plot Sickens

Several months later, at another team meeting, Chris and Peter grew convinced that things had taken a turn for the worse. Right before that meeting, Chris was upset to learn from her lead engineer, Donna Petersen, that their most important new product, due for release in a month, might have a serious defect. Only a week earlier Chris had met with Secureware's CEO, Katie Lang, to assure her that Netsafe was on track and the delivery date on schedule. A lot was riding on this product, Lang reminded her, from commercial success to people's reputations—"yours and mine included," she added. Supremely confident, Chris had just reassured her that there was nothing to worry about. Everything was going according to plan.

Now, as she took her seat at the conference table, it looked like everything was going to hell. Netsafe's delivery date was at risk, and the product itself might be a bust. Anxious to get to the bottom of the problem, Chris turned to Donna. "Tell me exactly what you found."

"Well, it's not exactly clear," she began, then went on to describe in great technical detail how she'd uncovered the problem. As Chris listened, she tapped her pencil on the table, all the while wishing that Donna would hurry up, get to the point, and tell her whether the problem could be fixed and by when.

Peter, a software engineer by training, wasn't in such a hurry. As he listened to Donna's account, he found himself thinking, *This just doesn't sound right. It just doesn't add up to a major glitch.* He wanted to know more. "Donna, I'm curious about something," he said, coming in as she was finishing up. "Under what conditions does this problem actually occur?"

"Hang on a second," Chris interrupted. "Curiosity aside, I'd like to know if we can have *any faith* in what we've been telling people about this product!"

Not sure what to say or to whom, a startled Donna froze while others looked furtively over at Peter, then down at the table. No one, including Peter, said a word.

Frustrated by the silence, Chris came in again. "Well, Donna, you're closest to it. What do you think? Can we have *any faith* in this product?"

After a moment's pause, Donna began, "Perhaps if we target the home market—"

"But we're not!" Chris interrupted. "We're targeting the corporate market!"

Donna glanced down at her hands as the rest of the team looked over at Peter, who was now so angry he could hardly speak. "Maybe I'm missing something," he finally said, his voice trembling. "But even if we can't fix it, doesn't it still meet current standards for the corporate market?"

Opening her mouth in exaggerated disbelief, Chris thought, *Is he serious? Settle for current standards when we've promoted Netsafe as the next big breakthrough?* Her frustration curdling into anger, she stood up, collected her papers, and turned to leave the room.

"I'm not going to tell people this product represents a breakthrough until I know that's the case! We've invested a lot of time and money in developing this software, and I want to know if it's going to deliver to our customers what we said it's going to deliver! Peter, I want you to get back to me tomorrow morning on what you plan to do about this."

As she left the room, Chris felt defeated. *God almighty! Peter just doesn't get it. You can't be an industry leader with products that meet current standards. What can he possibly be thinking? He's way too detached and passive to take this business to the next level.*

Peter said nothing as he filed out of the room with the rest of the team, but he was furious: *What an emotional tyrant! Her volatility is going to destroy the entire team's morale. These outbursts have got to stop!* Still, he was painfully aware that the division's future depended on this product. Putting his anger aside, he went to find Donna.

For the next six days and nights, the two of them worked with the engineering team until they finally located the problem and discovered a way to fix it. When Peter told Chris the good news, she offered only a cursory thanks, which he accepted with a nod.

The following day, an exhausted Peter met David, the head of sales, for lunch. "No offense, pal," David said, pulling out a chair for Peter as he arrived, "but you look horrible."

"I've got no idea what she thinks she's doing," Peter said as he sat down. "But whatever it is, it isn't working. She's really pissing me off!"

David raised his eyebrows but said nothing in the hope that Peter might say more.

"We can't just sit back, David, and let her moods dictate. She's browbeating the whole team! I've got to do something." Then, shaking his head, he added, "*We've* got to do something."

"I couldn't agree more," David said. "Her outbursts are impossible. She's totally unprofessional. But what are we supposed to do? The woman's a *nut*." For the next hour, they commiserated, telling each other stories about how difficult Chris was.

By the end of lunch, they knew something had to be done but they didn't know what, so the next few months passed as the previous few had. Every time Chris did something that struck Peter and David as more emotional than the situation warranted, they'd get together and vent their frustration.

Meanwhile, back at the office, Chris also knew something had to be done. Increasingly isolated, she felt more and more burdened by responsibilities she now had to shoulder alone. *I guess if you want a friend, you should get a dog,* she told herself. *I'd hoped Peter would help me lead the division, not sit around waiting for me to tell him what to do. He's behaving like such a kid; I can't rely on him to do anything.* The only way to keep her enthusiasm above the waterline, she concluded, was to look outside the division for collaborators she could count on.

Nearing the End

Six months later a series of incidents brought things to a head. The division, under CEO Katie Lang's increasing scrutiny, had recently committed to a strategy that required unprecedented discipline and focus, something Chris was finding more difficult by the day. At almost every meeting of the leadership team, Chris would talk about the next new project they should pursue, while Peter would think, *Is she serious? We can't take this on! It's clearly off strategy, and it makes absolutely no economic sense!*

Convinced that expressing any doubts would only set Chris off, Peter kept them to himself. Instead, each time Chris raised an idea, he'd work hard to gently steer her away from it. "I'm confused," he would say. "Maybe I'm missing something, but this opportunity doesn't look like it's on strategy, at least not to me." Or: "Yes, we could do that, but I don't think we have anybody available right now to pursue it." Or when really pressed: "I'm not sure this is something we can do right now, given our capacity constraints. But let me look into it, and perhaps we can talk later on." Only they never did.

Chris got the message loud and clear despite Peter's efforts. *He thinks this is a bad idea but isn't telling me. What a wimp!* Too discouraged for words, Chris's only response was a pouting silence, which Peter took as further evidence of her emotional instability. *Is she actually sulking?* he'd ask himself as he'd watch discouragement cross Chris's face. *All I did was suggest that we might not be able to do every project that pops into her head. What a nut!*

Now after almost every meeting Peter would seek David out and vent, in an effort to shore up his flagging spirits. "The team's getting spread too thin," he'd say. "We're not going to be able to deliver against our objectives if this keeps up."

David, who could always be counted on to commiserate, finally told Peter, "Look, Chris isn't going to be happy unless she's doing something new that takes her outside the division. If you raise this with her, she'll just get angry. There's nothing you can do. Leave it alone, or look for something else. That's what I'm doing."

Two months later, after David announced his departure, Peter had had enough. He knew a tough conversation was long overdue, but he'd always had some reason to put off what now seemed inevitable. No longer seeing any other choice, he went to Chris's office.

"What's up?" Chris asked, signaling with her hand for him to take a seat as she hung up her phone. Then, turning her back to Peter to check her e-mail, she asked, "How goes it?"

Peter cleared his throat. "Not so good. For the past few weeks, I've been giving my job here a lot of thought, and I think it may be time for me to move on. I don't think I've been that effective leading the team, and I'm not sure there's much more for me to learn or do here."

Chris sighed audibly. "I can't say I'm terribly surprised." Then, turning to face Peter, she asked, "Have you made up your mind?"

"Pretty much," Peter hedged. "I'm certainly leaning in that direction. But maybe we should talk about it before deciding what makes sense."

"If you feel it would help," Chris offered, with little confidence it would. "I've got to run now. But why don't we put some time aside early next week to talk about it."

*"I'm looking for a 'yes man', who can
say 'no' without sounding negative."*

Mapping the Anatomy of a Relationship

After talking about it, Chris and Peter decided that they wanted to do more than just air their grievances. They wanted to look at how they'd gotten into trouble to see whether they could get out. For years, Lang and others at the top of Secureware had invested in relationships, and they'd encouraged their division heads to do the same. At Lang's suggestion, they asked for my help, and the next week, the three of us sat down to take a look at what had happened. As I listened to their accounts, I used the framework shown in the box on page 50 to make sense of what I heard.[3] That framework helped us uncover and map the four elements that combined to give their relationship its distinctive character. The following pages illustrate what we learned, starting with their interlocking actions and reactions.

The Anatomy Framework

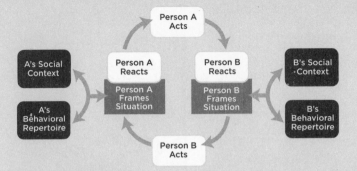

All relationships have an informal structure. You can use the Anatomy Framework to see and alter the four interlocking elements that make up that structure:

1. **Actions and Reactions.** Actions refer to what someone actually says and does, while reactions refer to what someone actually thinks and feels in response to what the other person says and does, each person's actions making the other person's reactions more explicable (see the white boxes in the diagram and the way they reinforce each other).

2. **Frames.** The interpretations embedded in our reactions, making some actions seem obvious, others impractical (see the gray boxes behind "Person A Reacts" and "Person B Reacts").

3. **Social Contexts.** The contextual backdrop—formal roles, time constraints, historical events—against which some triggering event occurs, prompting the need to respond (see the black boxes with the two-way arrows running into "A Frames" and "B Frames").

4. **Behavioral Repertoires.** The largely unconscious *experiential knowledge* and *interpretive strategies* that define the range of responses people have at their disposal for framing and acting in different social contexts, once triggered by some event (again, see the black boxes with the two-way arrows running into "A Frames" and "B Frames"). As the arrows suggest, people's behavioral repertoires both shape and are shaped by their *social contexts*. Together the two govern the way people frame situations, leading them to react and act toward each other in some ways and not others.

If our interlocking frames and actions are the engine that drives a relationship, our social contexts—along with our behavioral repertoires—provide the fuel that keeps that engine going. These four elements combine to give a relationship its distinctive character, one we intuitively recognize but have difficulty seeing or changing.

1. Interlocking Actions and Reactions

If you look closely at Peter and Chris's interactions, you can see that those interactions formed a pattern right from the start. When they first met over dinner, Chris's talk and body language filled the space around her. She leaned forward; she regaled Peter with one story after another about SafetyNet's success; she made sweeping claims about the division's future; she waxed enthusiastic about what a powerful partnership they'd make; and she asked Peter very little about what he wanted or what he thought. Peter's talk and body language stood in stark contrast. He reserved judgment; he leaned back; he asked Chris about the COO role without ever expressing his own preferences; he listened to her answers in silence; he quietly analyzed what she said; and the few times he responded, he chose his words with great care. If Chris's actions filled up the space around her, Peter's created a vacuum.

This basic pattern of interaction, established at their first dinner and reestablished in the room with me, escalated over the next year and a half. In each of the incidents that followed, their actions and reactions reinforced each other, Chris's emotional declarations filling the space and Peter's analytic quiet making it easier for Chris to do so. At first, this was no big deal. If anything, they considered their differences an asset. Only under pressure—when their differences clashed and no longer seemed so benign—did doubt emerge and, later on, despair set in. Here's how:

Looking at what happened. In the first incident, disappointing sales numbers, coupled with the pressures of time, combine to put Peter's "calm demeanor" and Chris's "passion" on a collision course that culminates in Chris's snapping and Peter's surprise and embarrassment. For the first time, Chris and Peter get the uneasy feeling that the very characteristics they'd found so attractive in the other might actually become a problem.

The second incident moves the relationship into a more ominous zone. Anxious to fix a defect jeopardizing an important new product, Chris is shocked by Peter's "curiosity" and lack of urgency. Worried that neither he nor Donna will come up with an answer quickly enough, Chris engineers an interpersonal takeover, determining who talks about what and when. In response, Peter gets so furious he fears losing his temper. Cautiously entering the conversation, he takes pains to qualify his challenge ("Maybe I'm missing something") and to couch his views as a question ("Doesn't it still meet current standards for the corporate market?"). But all this does is suggest to Chris that she's the only one truly concerned about the defect, leading her to get angry and leave. Afterward, the two seek solace elsewhere, Chris going outside the division and Peter turning to David. This last move, designed to relieve their upset, only alienates them further.

By the time the final series of incidents occurs, they're so far apart that they resort to game playing: Peter repeatedly challenges Chris's initiatives while acting as if he's not, and Chris speaks volumes through her uncharacteristic silences. In the end, when Peter finally goes to Chris, they can only halfheartedly agree to seek advice on whether to call it quits.

Analyzing what happened. After Peter and Chris recounted their version of the events, it was clear that they each saw only half the picture—the very half the other didn't see:

▶ Both Peter and Chris were aware of their own reactions and what the other was doing to provoke them.

▶ But neither Peter nor Chris was aware of the other's reactions or what they themselves were doing to provoke them.

It's this *asymmetrical awareness* that leads interactions to take on a life of their own, independent of the people who create them.[4] Neither could see what they were doing or its impact on the other.

To expand their awareness, we used their accounts to "map" how they were *both* acting and reacting, helping them see something they couldn't imagine before: their difficulties were a product of a joint venture (see Figure 4). As the map made evident, each of them—through their actions and reactions—was helping to create and maintain a pattern neither of them wanted or intended.

What they couldn't see or understand is why *this* pattern and not another took shape. To answer that question, we had to peel the onion

Figure 4: Interlocking Actions and Reactions

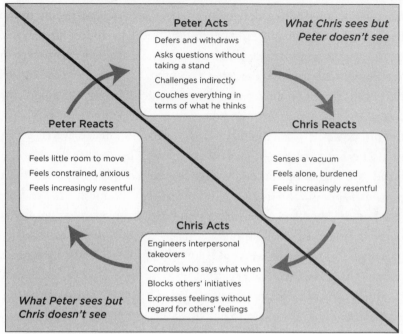

back further, looking at how they framed each other and the situation such that some actions seemed obvious while others never entered their minds.

2. Interlocking Frames

Neither Chris nor Peter liked the way they were acting or the results they got. Yet they would be the first to resist any suggestion that they behave differently. If you suggested to Peter that he might take more initiative or raise his concerns earlier, he'd say it was out of the question. He *couldn't* do that. It was impossible. Chris would erupt, things would get worse, and the team and the division would pay the price. Similarly, were you to suggest to Chris that instead of taking over, she ask more of Peter or the team, she'd say *that* was out of the question. You couldn't count on Peter when the chips were down. He was a wimp, a kid.

The way Chris and Peter made sense of each other—or *framed* each other, as I call it—held such emotional power and created such insidious self-fulfilling prophecies that neither could see things any other way.[5] Each was, in effect, being held captive by their interlocking frames. Seeing things one way and not another, they could do only one thing—the very thing that reinforced the other's framing. If they were going to break free of the pattern they'd created, they were going to have to take a closer look at how they were framing things.

This, however, is anything but easy. We're all so skilled at framing that we don't go through some methodical step-by-step analytic process. Rather, we size things up in a matter of milliseconds without giving it a moment's thought. So quick is this process that we don't experience it as first thought, then feeling. Instead, everything happens all at once. What we see, feel, and think all flows together to create a unified experience of a particular moment. If we could slow this process down, though, and look at it as it unfolds, we'd see that we're always selecting some things for attention while ignoring others, and we're always organizing these things into some story line that tells us what's going on and what we should do about it.

To uncover how Chris and Peter were framing things, I used their in-the-moment reactions to look at how they were framing (1) the different situations they faced; (2) themselves in relation to others in those situations; and (3) the goals or tasks they felt compelled to pursue as a result. By taking each in turn, we were able to see how their frames intersected, turning an early pattern of interaction into a more enduring structure.[6]

Framing the situation. As Chris saw it, when push came to shove she couldn't rely on Peter or on the team. *Look at the way they handled the product defect,* she'd say. *They acted as if nothing was wrong. They just don't get it!* Every one of Chris's accounts focused on the ways in which people had let her down when she needed them most: the product was a mess, the division was in trouble, her reputation was at stake, and *no one cared but her!* This way of framing the situation left Chris in a tough spot: with the division at risk and her team unreliable, taking over wasn't only reasonable, it was a practical necessity.

Though Peter made different things out of the "same" situation, his framing was equally compelling, at least to him. What stood out most for Peter was the situation's volatility and the potential for his team or him to get hurt. When Chris took over the discussion of the product defect, Peter fastened his attention on Chris's emotionally wrought interruptions and noticed how they were immediately followed by the team's silences and averted glances. Assuming the former caused the latter, Peter never considered that Chris might also be feeling vulnerable, or that the team's silences might also be contributing to Chris's upset. Seeing the situation as volatile, even dangerous, Peter was also in a tough spot: the only thing he could do—at least in his mind—was avoid an explosion.

Framing roles in relation to each other. Though we all think of ourselves as having a unified "self," we actually possess a large stock of what psychologists call "self-concepts."[7] While some of these are more stable and central to our identity than others, all of them are exquisitely sensitive to circumstance.[8] Take the young up-and-comer who casts himself in a slightly deferential role with a boss he admires, and you'll soon see this same young man puffing out his chest with his own admiring subordinate. In each case, he assumes for himself—and assigns to others—a role to play, always doing one in relation to the other, given the situation he sees.

Peter and Chris are no different. *Each of them assumed a role relative to the one they assigned to the other.* In the same moment that Peter cast Chris in the role of an emotional tyrant—with the power to determine what happened in a volatile situation—he took on the role of a threatened subject whose fate lay in her hands. Someone else might have created an altogether different role relationship, one that had nothing to do with either volatility or power. As it was, the role Peter assumed and assigned to Chris gave him little choice but to retreat, which encouraged Chris to see herself as the only one who could make things turn out right.

And that's exactly how she saw it. Preoccupied with others' unreliability in a threatening situation, Chris took on the role of the only adult among a bunch of recalcitrant kids. This way of seeing herself in relation to Peter and the team left her little choice but to fill the many voids she saw. Yet this only heightened her sense of burden—first fueling, then justifying her outbursts—which only encouraged Peter to cast her in the role of an emotional tyrant. And so on it went.

Framing goals. Once we frame a situation and our role relative to others, some goals or purposes[9] spring to mind, while others would never occur to us.[10] In most complex social situations, it's not uncommon for several goals to come to mind all at once, some of them clashing. Hence the adage: he wants to have his cake and eat it too. When conflicting goals spring to mind, we usually feel caught, at which point the best we can do is find or craft a strategy that satisfies each goal well enough to get by.

Such was the case with Peter and Chris. We might reasonably conclude from what Peter felt, thought, and did that his primary goal was to protect himself from intense conflict and emotion. This goal, which followed from his framing of the situation and his role relative to the roles of others, inclined Peter to keep his head down and to lie low. But if you look closely enough, you'll see that Peter also had another goal: protecting his team. He saw how quiet the team got, how they looked to him when Chris got upset. This secondary goal, unlike the first, inclined Peter to jump in, so he could help the team out. Thus faced with two conflicting goals—to protect himself *and* to protect his team—Peter could do only those things that would help him do a little of both.

That's why, instead of withdrawing or making suggestions directly, Peter asked questions to steer Chris in the "right" direction ("Might it make sense if we did this?"). And instead of staying completely silent or directly challenging Chris, he qualified anything she could possibly construe as a disagreement ("I may be missing something but . . ."). And instead of exploding or stifling his feelings, Peter couched them in intellectual or practical terms and cast them as questions ("But even if we can't fix it, doesn't it still meet current standards for the corporate market?"). Though designed to protect himself and his team—albeit unconsciously—each action had the unintended effect of confirming Chris's view of Peter as a wimp, which only prompted Chris to act more, not less, volatile.

We might surmise from what Chris thought, felt, and did that her primary goal was to reduce her reliance on others by taking control. This goal, which followed from her framing of the situation and her role relative to those of others, inclined Chris to be hypervigilant about others' reliability and to take over whenever she got the slightest hint of it. But just as Peter had a secondary goal, so did Chris: she wanted to avoid alienating anyone so they didn't become even more unreliable than they already were.

That's why instead of asking the group for help or exploring its apparent lack of concern, she engineered interpersonal takeovers, telling this person to be quiet, that person to talk ("Hang on a second," she'd say, interrupting. "I'd like to hear from . . ."). And instead of pointing out their lack of initiative or asking them to take more, she imposed her own view ("But that's not who we're targeting!"). And instead of expressing her upset directly or helping others understand why she was upset, she went outside the division for support and expressed her feelings only indirectly through her tone of voice ("I'm not going to tell people that this product represents a breakthrough until I know that's the case!"). Although Chris relied on these actions to take situations where she wanted them to go, they also took her in a direction she regretted: the more control she took, the more alienated others felt, making them act less, not more, reliably.

Implications. People aren't unidimensional, even if they sometimes seem so in our minds. Everyone has better or worse sides; everyone does their best to satisfy multiple goals—many of which conflict, most of which lie outside their awareness, and all of which follow from their framings of a situation. What's so tragic about the way Chris and Peter framed things is that it only made it harder for them to be at their best or to bring out the best in each other.

Worse, because they were equally convinced that what they saw was the way it was, they didn't realize that two other factors were also at play, shaping what they saw and how they saw it. These factors—their *social contexts* and their *behavioral repertoires*—make matters of interpretation look like matters of fact, locking frames into place. Let's take a look at each one of these factors and at how, left unnoticed, they conspire to seal the fate of any relationship.

3. Social Contexts

All events take place within a larger social context: those things outside ourselves that we must take into account, even if only peripherally, when interacting with others, such as limited resources, formal roles, organizational history, physical arrangements, formal structures, cultural norms, corporate politics. It's against this backdrop that events occur, prompting us to frame what's happening so we can act. In Chris and Peter's case, the two of them operated in a social context with both distinct and overlapping aspects. As Table 1 illustrates, those aspects that were distinct, shaded in gray, influenced how they saw those aspects that overlapped.

Consider the defect incident. Both Chris and Peter had to move quickly to solve a complex technical problem before it cost them the division's future and, by extension, their own. Both of them had a lot at stake. But what they had at stake differed, as did what they saw.

As divisional CEO, Chris was formally and ultimately accountable for the division's performance, which Secureware's CEO, Katie Lang, had just reminded her of a week earlier when she warned Chris that the future of the firm, not to mention their reputations, was riding on this product. During that meeting, Chris had reassured Lang that everything was fine. But now it looked as if it was anything but. Worse, by the time the second incident occurred, Chris's relationship with Peter had deteriorated so much that when she looked around the table that day, she saw no one in whom to confide her worries. All she saw was a COO whose quiet curiosity stood in stark contrast to her own anxieties. For fifteen minutes, she listened to Donna's detailed technical account of the defect, though nothing in her current or prior roles helped her understand the implications. Yet that's exactly what this situation was requiring her to do.

Peter, who was operating in a slightly different context, couldn't help but see the same meeting differently. As COO, he'd had very little contact with Lang, and none at all the previous week. In his role, Peter was accountable for managing the top team and for helping them get their products to market on time. He had to exercise this accountability in the context of a relationship with a boss whose actions were affecting the team's morale, a team that was looking to him. He noticed how tense

TABLE 1: Peter and Chris's Social Contexts		
	PETER'S CONTEXT	**CHRIS'S CONTEXT**
Current Role	SafetyNet's COO	SafetyNet's CEO
Accountabilities	Accountable to Chris for managing the team and getting products to market on time	Accountable to Lang, Secureware's CEO, for her division's overall performance
Historical Role/ Training	Engineer	Manager
Closest Contacts	SafetyNet's top team, David, other subordinates, Chris	Secureware's CEO, customers, division heads, subordinates, Peter
What's at Stake	Division's performance, his job, the team's morale/ performance	Division's performance, her job, SafetyNet's and her reputation
Political Atmosphere	Highly charged: a lot of dissatisfaction within division	Highly charged: a lot of competition among divisions
Nature of Problems	Ambiguous, technically complex	
Level of Uncertainty	High: causes and consequences of the technical problems are unknown	
Interpersonal Context	Significant stylistic differences, distant and emotionally charged	
Time	A lot of time pressure, product's due date in jeopardy	

people got every time Chris interceded; he saw the anxiety on their faces. And when he discussed what he saw with David, David only confirmed his views. What's more, when Donna launched into her technical account of the defect, Peter, unlike Chris, was able to listen not only as a manager but also as a software engineer. He had no problem grasping the details in her account or in spotting gaps. But absolutely nothing in his past or current roles had prepared him to exercise leadership in the face of such emotional and political complexity. Yet that is exactly what this situation was calling upon him to do.

Once Peter and Chris saw the table summarizing what they were up against, they were able to see for the first time that each of them was struggling with somewhat different demands and responding to somewhat different constraints. While that helped them empathize more, they would need more than empathy alone to break free of their interlocking frames. They'd need to understand what predisposed them to see things the way they did within those contexts.

4. Behavioral Repertoires

When it comes to framing, no one starts from scratch. Like the rest of us, Peter and Chris had built out of experience a large store of *experiential knowledge* with which to make sense of what was happening and a set of *interpretive strategies* with which to apply and revise that knowledge. Together these make up each person's *behavioral repertoire,* the range of interpretations and actions at one's disposal in any social situation.

Like all behavioral repertoires, Peter and Chris's were organized around a limited number of *key themes*—conflict, authority, success, loss, competence—each forged out of emotionally salient and often unsettling events. Every time Peter and Chris encounter each other, they have to navigate their repertoires, looking for the right explanation here or the appropriate action there. The trouble is that since these repertoires operate largely outside their awareness, Peter and Chris are unable to see, revise, or expand them fast enough to respond effectively to each other or to the circumstances around them.

To help them navigate their repertoires more intelligently and to expand them more quickly, we used "A Thinking Person's Guide to Behavioral Repertoires" (see Appendix A). With this guide, we were able to identify the interlocking themes and experiential knowledge each brought to their relationship. In Peter's case, we discovered that his relationship with Chris touched on two themes: conflict and emotion. Around these themes, Peter had developed a large stock of experiential knowledge—including theories, stories, values, and practical strategies. This knowledge allowed him to handle even the most threatening situations without giving them much thought. With the use of his theories, he recognized and categorized Chris's behavior as "volatile" and explained it in terms of her "nutty" personality. With the use of his stories, he fashioned a role for himself and gave one to others, all the while imagining what a more or less happy ending might look like. With the use of his value system, he took pride in his emotional restraint and condemned those, like Chris, who got upset. And with the use of his practical strategies, he found a number of ways to avoid conflict and dampen emotion.

What Peter's repertoire lacked, however, was a way of understanding conflict and emotion that underscored the upside of each. Although quick to concede that conflicts can generate learning, Peter had no way of explaining it and no strategies for making it happen. As a result, he couldn't see or handle conflicts any differently *even if he'd wanted to*. He also lacked a value system nuanced enough to distinguish between "good" and "bad" ways of approaching conflict and emotion—ways that, by his own standards, would cause "better" or "worse" things to occur. Similarly, his practical knowledge was full of action strategies for avoiding negative emotion, but he had no strategies for doing these things without making matters worse, and none that told him how to harness conflict or regulate emotion so it stayed in a productive range. When it came to making something good out of an emotionally laden conflict, he was completely at a loss.

Just as Peter came to see the themes at play in his responses to Chris, so Chris came to see what was at stake with Peter. Over the course of our work together, Chris identified two themes—reliability and control—around which she'd developed at least as much knowledge as Peter had around emotion and conflict. Around these two themes, Chris had a wide range of theories, stories, values, and strategies to draw on. But as comprehensive as this experiential knowledge was, much of it was geared toward a single end: avoiding dependence and ensuring control. As a result, whenever Chris thought things were spiraling out of control or people were letting her down, her first and last instinct was to take over. As you might expect, this limited her repertoire and prevented her from responding flexibly enough to handle Peter (or others) effectively. Only when she saw these limits and their associated costs did she reexamine what she "knew" about control and reliability—first with Peter, then with others.

A New Story to Tell

When Peter and Chris first recounted what had happened, they each focused on one side of the story—theirs. Only by bringing their two perspectives together could they see how their whole relationship worked, and only by seeing the whole could they understand how they had each created and sustained it.

Once they took this step, they decided to conduct a series of practical experiments to see if they could transform their relationship. In a surprising but necessary twist, Peter went first, taking the initiative to fill the vacuum he'd created in the past. This in itself was a useful disruption: it went against the grain of their historical pattern in which Chris constantly initiated and Peter either followed or subverted her lead. For the move to succeed, however, Chris had to respond in kind: instead of undermining or discounting Peter's efforts for fear of being let down, she had to learn to put her concerns to work by helping Peter help her in those moments.

A year later, the two of them had a very different story to tell. Instead of feeling trapped by their relationship, they had come to see it as a context for growth—one in which they could experiment more freely and explore the results of those experiments more openly. Not only did this accelerate their growth as leaders, it improved the morale and functioning of the top team so much that they were able to pick up the pace of growth in their division.

Key Points

Underlying all relationships is an informal structure. This structure includes four interlocking elements: actions, frames, contexts, and repertoires. If our interlocking frames and actions are the engine that drives the way people interact, our social contexts, along with behavioral repertoires, provide the fuel that keeps that engine running.

By mapping the underlying anatomy of their relationship, Chris and Peter could stand outside it and see what they couldn't see from the inside: their roles in creating a relationship they didn't want or intend. This increased their awareness of themselves and freed them to create a relationship that supported growth—their own and their division's.

4
The Key to Resilience

So prevalent are relationship troubles that most of us merely accept them as the way things are. Indeed, a 2002 *Time* magazine article went so far as to say, "Until recently, being driven mad by others and driving others mad was known as life."[1] The article, entitled "I'm OK. You're OK. We're Not OK," questioned whether it was wise to include "relational disorders" in the newest edition of a psychiatric diagnostic manual. What would happen, the author asked, to notions of personal responsibility? How could you ever hold anyone accountable for anything? After all, you can fire or sue a person, but not a relationship. Besides, he concluded, relationship troubles are simply a fact of life. You're better off keeping your eye on individuals, where blame can be clearly assigned and appropriately taken.

I doubt many people would disagree. There's already enough blame-shifting in organizations without adding another excuse: "It wasn't me. My relationship made me do it." But taking a relational perspective doesn't prevent people from taking re-

> *Resilience*
>
> • *ability to withstand or to recover quickly from difficult conditions*
>
> • *ability to recoil or spring back into shape after bending, stretching, or being compressed*[2]

sponsibility. When people focus on relationships, *they assume responsibility not just for themselves but for the relationships they together create and for the impact those relationships have on their firm*. Far from diluting responsibility, then, a relational perspective actually takes excuses off the table. No more "He made me do it." Instead, people together take responsibility for building relationships resilient enough to weather the troubles they'll face.

To illustrate, this chapter tells the story of a professional-services firm I'll call Merrimac.[3] Since its inception, the firm's leaders have invested heavily in building relationships strong enough to withstand the stresses and strains of a fast-growing company. By comparing the way Merrimac's leaders handled their troubles with the way Steve Jobs and John Sculley handled theirs, this chapter shows that resilience is a matter of perspective. It depends, above all else, on the ability to think complexly about stressful events, to see what each person is doing to create results no one likes, and to experience more than just anger when upset.[4] In the following pages, you'll see that, unlike Sculley and Jobs, the leaders at Merrimac were able to shift quickly from a simplistic, either/or perspective to a more complex, relational perspective—first by reflecting, then by reframing. These companion abilities made it possible for people to cool down before things got too hot, allowing them to strengthen their relationships over time.

The Story: Founding Friends

Twenty-five years ago, a band of friends fresh out of business school set out to build a professional-services firm like no other. They were convinced that by wedding stellar client service with innovative new content they could surpass other players currently dominating the industry. At the same time, they were committed to building a firm that put into practice ideals many firms espouse but few enact. They wanted to demonstrate—not just state—an uncompromising commitment to excellence, innovation, colleagueship, speaking the truth, learning, and professional growth.

For the founders of Merrimac, these ideals weren't mere niceties. They were essential to attracting and retaining the best talent and the best clients in an industry growing more competitive by the year. Hoping to build what they called an "elite organization," CEO Dan Gavin and his cohorts joined together to realize their dreams.

Reality Sets In

Over the next eighteen months, the firm catapulted to success. Revenues exceeded expectations; its reputation for quality spread; it attracted exceptional talent; and its client list included some of the best companies in the world. Before the founders knew it, they were off and running, growing so quickly they could scarcely keep up.

The very pace of their growth let loose a stream of controversial issues, one right after the other: How should the firm be run? Whom should they hire? How should rewards be allocated? Who should be accountable for what? How should decisions get made and by whom? As people took different sides on each of these issues, tensions stretched the group to the breaking point.

At first, everyone papered over their differences, not wanting to jeopardize their success by raising them. But as time went on and problems festered, a kind of cold war set in, with people forming adversarial coalitions behind the scenes and working hard to disguise their growing animosity whenever they met. Before long, almost no one was telling the truth, learning came to a halt, and colleagueship broke down. Only eighteen months into the life of the firm, their dream was falling apart. Though revenues remained solid and product quality high, the environment around them was growing more toxic by the month.

By the third year, a dismayed but determined Dan Gavin decided to get help. After researching the field, he asked a highly regarded organizational consultant to help him and his cohorts look at what had happened and to advise them on what to do next. Today, many still credit that work with getting them through the first crisis in the firm's life. More than that, they credit it with establishing the shared belief that, as leaders, they were mutually responsible for the kinds of relationships they created and

"All those in favor say 'Aye.'"

     "Aye."   *"Aye."*   *"Aye."*

           "Aye."   *"Aye."*

for working through any tensions or conflicts that arose among them. While some founders believed this more than others did, it gave the group enough common ground to turn their collective attention to growing the firm.

And that's exactly what they did. Over the next ten years, they went after and served the best firms in the world; they opened offices on almost every continent and went from a firm of 150 professionals to over a thousand; they swelled their ranks every summer with eager young talent from top schools; they launched and acquired new businesses. By the late 1990s, they were bursting at the seams. They had taken a single company and grown it into a group of businesses. Now, with far more people, geographies, and businesses than leaders to manage them, they encountered their second developmental crisis.

Bringing the Next Generation Along

Even with excellent staff support, the founder-heavy executive team couldn't keep up with the pace of growth. The sheer scope and complexity of the business was fast outstripping their ability to manage the firm's operations. At an informal level, the firm's overdependence on Dan Gavin was wearing thin. Ever since the firm's inception, Dan had become the indisputable hub in the wheel of relationships that propelled the firm forward. No one knew more about people's lives; no one spent more time talking with folks about their careers; no one offered more motivation or inspiration. Now, with the number of people in the firm multiplying by the day, that wheel was slowing down, and the bonds of affection holding it together were starting to fray. It was time to take a few risks and bring the next generation of leaders along.

Perhaps that's why Dan took to the idea of Luke Turner leading Fast-Start, one of the firm's newer businesses. For many years Dan had seen great leadership potential in Luke's grasp of people and in his even-keeled response to business crises. As Luke's mentor, Dan had spent many an evening talking with Luke about his long-range goals, encouraging him to aim high and to take big risks. Dan's encouragement had endeared him to Luke, who admired Dan's quick, incisive intellect and felt indebted to Dan for his many kindnesses. More than colleagues, they considered themselves friends.

Now, the more Dan mulled over the idea of Luke leading FastStart, the more appealing it seemed. The fledgling unit needed a leader to bring costs under control and to spur growth, and Luke needed leadership experience to grow professionally. It made sense. Besides, by now Dan was as invested in Luke's success as he was in the business.

Though it took some selling to the firm's new board—some of the directors were as wary of new leaders as they were of new businesses—Dan convinced them to go along. True, Luke had never had profit-and-loss responsibility for a business unit, Dan told the directors, but few outside the founder's group had. If they were going to keep growing, he argued, they would need to take some risks on people. What happened next was emblematic of how the firm weathered its second major crisis.

Things Heat Up

A year after Luke took the helm, FastStart's results looked promising. In twelve months, Luke had successfully managed to cut unnecessary costs, reduce overhead, increase people's motivation, and improve revenue growth. Halfway into the second year, however, growth leveled off, and Dan began to worry. Ever sensitive to board politics, Dan knew that Luke and the new business were still politically vulnerable, as was he for having convinced the board to bet on Luke. Growing anxious that the inexperienced Luke wasn't moving fast enough to remedy the situation, Dan sent what Luke later called a "flaming" voice mail a week before the next board meeting:

> Luke, we've got a problem. You're not making decisions fast enough. You're being too bureaucratic and making too many decisions by committee. It's slowing down the whole company! I don't know whether you're risk-averse or just anxious, but it's a problem. Last year, you and I convinced the board to invest in your business unit and they bought it. Now you're not delivering. I'm going to a board meeting in a week, and I have no fucking idea what I'm going to tell them. They expect results, and we've got none to speak of. The sooner we can connect on this the better. [Click.]

When Luke first heard Dan's message, he was "mad as hell." This wasn't the first time he'd received this kind of message from Dan. Long at the center of the firm, Dan would frequently disappear for months at a time, focusing on one part of the business only to show up in another, using his laserlike attention to uncover problems. Ever anxious to see those problems solved, Dan would ask people what they were doing to address them—sometimes patiently, other times not. Right now, Dan was looking mighty impatient, and unfairly so from Luke's point of view.

Furious, Luke reached for the "respond" button. He was going to blast Dan for sending such a negative message. *How dare he say the unit isn't moving fast enough! We've done a lot—built a leadership team, launched new programs, improved profitability.* And with no thanks to Dan, he might add. For weeks, Dan had been too busy to return Luke's voice mails asking for guidance on how to move forward. If they were going too slow, well then, that was Dan's fault! *I'm all for moving fast,* Luke told himself, *but let's get real about what's going on here. If you returned my calls, I'd be glad to move faster!*

Cooling Down

Just before hitting the "respond" button, Luke caught himself: *Wait a second,* he thought. *What am I doing? That's not going to accomplish anything.* In his mind's eye, he imagined what would happen next: *if I retaliate in kind, Dan will only dig in further and nothing will get done, and then Dan will be right; we will be moving too slowly.*

In an instant, Luke realized how quickly his reactions could become part of the problem. Then, mulling over the year from Dan's perspective, he thought, *He's right. It would be better if he weren't so negative about our progress, but I can see how from his point of view we are moving too slowly.*

Luke again reached for the "respond" button, this time in a more temperate state of mind. "I'm with you," he told Dan. "I agree we need to move faster. I'll make sure we meet soon to talk about it. I have some thoughts on how I might speed things up, and I'd like to get yours."

When Dan heard Luke's response, he relaxed. Ever since sending the voice mail, he'd worried that Luke might get so defensive it would slow things down further. Now, listening to Luke's message, he felt instant relief, prompting him to wonder why he'd gotten so overwrought in the first place. If anything, he now thought, his own message was a bit "hysterical." Feeling chagrined, he took a moment to reflect on the source of his agitation. The next day, when he met with Luke, Dan shared his reflections before discussing the substance of the message:

> My voice mail made me realize that I have a sentimental as well as a practical interest in your taking on more leadership in the firm. When I see you including a lot of people in your decision making, I get anx-

ious it's going to slow you down and undermine your credibility. But I feel like I can't say anything, because I don't want to be seen as hovering, which of course I'm prone to do, since I'm so invested in your success. Hence the hysteria.

This dilemma, which accompanies many efforts to expand a firm's leadership, had tied Dan up in knots. By recounting it, Dan helped Luke see that his hysteria sprung from his feeling caught between an interest in Luke's success and a desire not to hover. This revelation gave Luke what he needed to help. "Actually, there was a part of the message that was very helpful," Luke told him. "Although you were rumbling me, you were very clear about what you needed. I'd have to be an idiot not to get it. 'Dan wants to go faster,' I thought. 'I want to go faster too. Let's go fast together.'"

If anything, Luke's problem wasn't that Dan was hovering, as Dan had worried. It was that he waited so long to express his concerns that all Dan could do was focus on the negative. This made sense to Dan, and it helped relax the dilemma that was keeping him from voicing his worries until they reached a hysterical pitch. At this point, the two struck a new deal: Dan agreed to raise his concerns earlier, while Luke agreed to make it easier by asking if he had any.

They were now free to turn their attention to how they might speed up progress. Here Luke agreed to modify his decision-making process, while Dan agreed to modify his tendency to go silent. Most important, in the weeks following the meeting, neither of them simply sat back and watched to see if the other guy changed. Quite the contrary—they helped each other out by reflecting on how they were doing and looking together for ways to do better.

No Easy Answers

Luke and Dan were not alone in their experience. As other managers outside the founding group stepped into leadership roles, they took on as part of their responsibilities the obligation to make their relationships work. This helped them immeasurably a year later, when a combination of industry forces and firm choices conspired to slow Merrimac's growth.

Figuring out which factors and what choices were causing the problem put the firm's leaders squarely at odds. Some believed the firm's strategy was at fault; others believed that they'd allowed "peripheral" investments to take their eye off of the core business; and still others thought that too much control had been left in the hands of too few for too long and that lingering dysfunctions among the founders had led revenues to lag and costs to rise.

At the same time, tensions within and among generations emerged over the future of the firm. Many people thought it was past time to decide what the firm wanted to be when it grew up. Did they want to remain a private company or to go public? And how should they divide the rewards of their successes? Should they offer liquidity to the older generation or more stock to the younger ones?

With no easy answers in sight and different people's interests at odds, resolution eluded them for months, raising fundamental doubts about the future of the firm and about one another.

At this point, many other firms might have fallen apart or smoothed over their differences for fear of doing so. But at Merrimac, the shared belief in working things through together served them well. Even though the volatile mix of issues chewed up precious time and energy, the firm's leadership was able to wrestle most of their disagreements to the ground while strengthening and repairing those relationships critical to the firm's future success. And while no constituency was completely happy with the ultimate outcome, the firm did succeed in transferring a significant amount of managerial, political, and economic power to the next generation without losing the old. Even so, a number of relationships within and across generations took a big hit. Whether the people in those relationships will be able to use what happened to grow as leaders and as partners, the jury is still out. Meanwhile I can say this: they stand a better chance than most. The next section explains why.

It's All a Matter of Perspective

No matter how aligned people are around some overarching goal—increasing profitability, reducing costs, accelerating product development—they'll disagree over how to achieve it. At Apple, Steve Jobs insisted that they could go a long way toward fixing their revenue shortfall by revamping distribution. John Sculley insisted that they could achieve the same goal by getting Mac Office to market. Sometimes people share the same overarching goal but clash over local goals—the amount of cost reduction needed, the rate of growth a business unit should target, how fast decisions should get made. In the end, this is where Dan and Luke ran into trouble.

Trouble, as the song goes, is as inevitable as death and taxes. But what you make of that trouble depends on how you see things. If you compare how Luke and Dan handled their troubles with how Jobs and Sculley handled theirs, you can see different perspectives at work: an *either/or perspective* and a *relational perspective*. These perspectives cast things in a very different light, leading some relationships to grow more resilient with time, others more fragile.[5]

The Either/Or Perspective

When events at Apple put pressure on Jobs and Sculley's relationship, they each assumed that the other was at fault: Sculley wasn't providing leadership, Jobs was constantly meddling in things that were none of his business. This assumption riveted their attention on what the other guy was doing and turned their attention away from what they themselves were doing. This escalated their already negative reactions, compromising their ability to think clearly. At this point they were each convinced that the other guy really was the cause of his difficulties. After all, he was *making* him do this or feel that. The idea that both of them—not one or the other of them—might be contributing to the difficulties never sprang to mind, although it did occur to others.[6] Equally certain that the other's behavior was causing some adverse effect (lack of leadership, tardiness), neither gave thought to the possibility that these effects might also be causing the other's behavior (interference, impatience). Instead, they each assumed that the other was acting the way he was because he was either *mad* (stubborn, unable to control himself) or *bad* (corrupt, cared more about wealth and glory).

These twin assumptions—"You alone are the cause of the problem" and "You are either mad or bad"[7]—make it natural for people to place blame and make accusations. This, of course, is what Sculley and Jobs did. In the months leading up to their come-to-Jesus meeting, they each complained about the other to like-minded peers, blaming the other for their difficulties and accusing him of wrongdoing. Only when they felt they had no choice did they confront each other, and even then, all they did was take their private accusations public—Jobs accusing Sculley of failing to lead, Sculley accusing Jobs of failing to give him the opportunity to lead.

These accusations, which focused on one side of the problem, had no influence on either one of them, making them feel as if they had no choice. They *had* to prepare airtight cases that would place institutional blame where they thought it belonged: on the other person's shoulders.

In addition to turning their relationship into a toxic-waste site, this either/or perspective made it impossible for Jobs and Sculley to resolve their substantive differences well or quickly. Each of them assumed that only one (or the other) of them could be right. They thus figured: if I'm right, then the other must be wrong. It didn't occur to them that they each might see things the other missed or that together they might see things in a more complex and useful light. Nor did it occur to them to ask the other what led him to see things the way he did. They already knew: *the other guy was either mad or bad!* The best they could do at this point—in fact, *all* they could do at this point—was make the same assertions and counterassertions over and over again in the desperate, if deluded, hope that they could get the other guy to *see things his way.*

Within this context, it's small wonder Sculley and Jobs staked out either/or positions, with Jobs *demanding* that Sculley solve the distribution problem and Sculley *ordering* Jobs to stay out of it and finish Macintosh Office. Unable to make headway under the conditions they'd unwittingly created, they took their dispute behind the scenes, where

THE KEY TO RESILIENCE   75

their either/or perspective led them to build narrow coalitions—Jobs within the Macintosh division, Sculley within corporate headquarters—in the hopes of advancing their own interests at the other's expense.

When the showdown finally came, they could see only another either/or choice: one or the other of them had to go. Either Jobs or Sculley. With that either/or choice in mind, they worked behind the scenes, lobbying board members to keep one and get rid of the other. With the board's choice now narrowed down to either Sculley or Jobs, it chose Sculley. The rest is history.

The Relational Perspective

Events at Merrimac weighed just as heavily on relationships at the top as they did at Apple, putting people at odds. In those moments, they grew anxious, frustrated, and defensive, blaming each other for their own shortcomings and resenting it when others did the same to them. Worse, instead of working these reactions through, they often went to like-minded peers, who were quick to sympathize and slow to challenge.

Obviously none of this sets Merrimac apart. What sets it apart is the ability of its leaders to shift to a more *relational perspective* when faced with substantive differences and relationship troubles. This perspective helps decision makers create options that balance competing interests and prompts them to look at what they're each doing to get in their own way.

You can see this perspective at work in how Luke and Dan handled their difficulties. Luke and Dan didn't believe, as Sculley and Jobs did, that one or the other of them was the sole cause of their difficulties. Instead, they assumed that they each must be doing something to make it harder for the other to be at his best. They also assumed that, far from being mad or bad, the other was doing the best he could given his capabilities and the circumstances he was up against. Sure, from time to time, they both ranted and raved about how the other guy was *making my life impossible,* but they each assumed that the other was largely unaware of his impact and that he had reasons for doing what he did—even if neither one of them yet understood what those reasons were.

This perspective made their relationship troubles easier to handle. It's a lot easier to discuss what's wrong in a conversation when you assume that you're each doing the best you can and that you could use the other's help to do better. That assumption allowed Dan and Luke to discuss Dan's "flaming" voice mail and to explore how they each might have contributed to results neither liked: Dan feeling caught in a bind, Luke having to contend with Dan's negativity, the board's impatience, the "slow" pace of decision making. Through these discussions, they were able to map—then work on changing—the patterns of interaction that were creating these results. This last step, which helped them see things they hadn't before seen, motivated them to learn from their troubles.

Their substantive disagreements were also easier to handle. Though equally confident of their views, neither assumed that he alone had a lock on The Truth, or that only one (or the other) could be right. Rather, they assumed that each of them saw things the other missed and missed things the other saw, requiring them to put their heads together to achieve some goal. Sometimes, when they put their heads together, they clashed. When that happened, each asked the other how he arrived at his views. And in answering, everything was game, from hard data and logic to softer feelings and needs, to subjective beliefs and interests. Since all these things went into their views, the two felt they might as well get them out on the table: Dan's sentimental and practical interest in Luke's success, Luke's need to hear Dan's concerns before they reached a fevered pitch, their different perceptions of the progress in Luke's unit, Dan's need to satisfy a board that wanted to see results, Luke's need to satisfy a leadership team that wanted a say in decisions. All the data in the world weren't going to solve differences that turned on their feelings, preferences, and values, and they knew it.

In plotting their course forward, both assumed that any solution they devised would have to work for the two of them. At one level that wasn't so hard, since they both wanted the same outcome—for Luke and his business to succeed. But Dan's most immediate concern was securing support from the board, while Luke's was keeping his team involved and motivated. So the real question was twofold: what was preventing Luke's team from moving faster, and how could they pick up the pace without jeopardizing the team's motivation? Far from limiting them to an either/ or choice, this question allowed them to generate a number of different possibilities: Luke making more decisions on his own, Dan making himself more available, Luke delegating some decisions to others, Dan raising his concerns earlier and offering more timely advice. With a number of options in hand, none of them mutually exclusive, they could more quickly turn their attention to figuring out how to make those options so. Later on, when their differences became far more fundamental and threatening, these earlier experiences helped: they didn't feel as compelled to do one or another thing; they knew they had options.

What You See Is What You Get

In the end, the only thing Jobs and Sculley's either/or perspective made of their differences was a mess. They lost credibility as leaders, burned through much-needed social capital, divided the firm, distracted the firm's leadership, and destroyed most of their political clout—especially in the case of Jobs, who only a year earlier had enough political power to make almost anyone do almost anything.[8] Over the course of two short years, their relationship destroyed far more value than it created, culminating in Jobs's exile and a decade-long decline in the firm's performance.

The relational perspective taken by leaders at Merrimac created different results. While they too faced fundamental disagreements, they were easier to handle. Each knew that he depended on the other to see things he missed *because of* their different experiences, values, interests, and beliefs. This made it more possible for them to use even their most basic differences to strengthen their relationships, while the strength of their relationships made it easier for them to handle their differences.

These perspectives—though presented as opposites—actually exist along a continuum (see Table 2). Like Jobs and Sculley, the leaders at Merrimac often lost perspective, seeing things in purely either/or terms and getting hysterical or mad as hell as a result. But unlike Jobs and Sculley, most of the leaders at Merrimac could shift perspective most of the time. By helping one another move up the continuum from a relatively simplistic

TABLE 2: Contrasting the Two Perspectives*		
	EITHER/OR PERSPECTIVE	**RELATIONAL PERSPECTIVE**
Relationship Troubles	Assume the other person is the problem: "You made me feel this or do that"; "you gave me no choice."	Assume you're both contributing to your difficulties: "We're each failing to bring the best out of the other."
	Assume the other is either mad or bad—that is, crazy, stupid, incompetent, or immoral.	Assume you're each doing the best you can, given your capabilities and circumstances.
	Blame each other (to his face or behind his back), while seeking support from like-minded peers.	Explore what you each did to contribute to results neither of you liked.
	Make an airtight case, proving the other person is to blame and punishing him for it.	Map and alter patterns of interaction that repeatedly create results neither of you like or want.
Substantive Disagreements	Assume one of you is right and the other is wrong.	Assume you each see things the other misses.
	Assume the rightness of your view is a matter of obvious fact, not interpretation.	Assume your different beliefs and interests will quite reasonably lead you to see things differently.
	Keep making assertions and counterassertions to get the other to agree or back down.	Say what leads you to see things the way you do and encourage the other to do the same.
	Garner support behind the scenes for your position, while undermining the other's.	Explore options in light of your interests, outcomes you both want, and data you both consider relevant.
	Build narrow coalitions that advance your own needs and interests at the expense of others, whether you intend it or not.	Build broad-based coalitions that seek to satisfy or balance, over time, the needs and interests of different constituencies and the firm as a whole.

*The shaded boxes describe the largely unconscious assumptions that govern the way people approach relationship troubles *and* substantive disagreements. The unshaded boxes describe the actions that follow from those assumptions.

either/or perspective to a more complex relational perspective, they were more able to spring back and recoup, allowing them to turn potentially vicious cycles of interaction into more virtuous ones. Since this is the key to resilience, let's take a look at how you can build it.[9]

Building Resilience

In the heat of the moment, cooler heads rarely prevail. The very phrase, *in the heat of the moment,* tells you why. You're *in* the moment, unable to stand back and look at what's happening. Your emotions are heating up and overwhelming your ability to think. And the moment itself, well, it's going by *really fast.* Before you know it, your automatic responses are kicking in and you're hot as hell.

Developing a High-Performing Cool System

Dan and Luke were able to recoup so quickly because over the years they'd built a high-performing "cool system" that allowed them to cool down when things got hot. According to psychologists Janet Metcalfe and Walter Mischel, all of us process events through two systems: a hot system and a cool system (see Table 3).[10] While the former includes all our hot buttons, which lead us to react quickly (to "go"), the latter

TABLE 3: Hot and Cool Systems	
HOT SYSTEM	**COOL SYSTEM**
Emotional	Cognitive
"Go"	"Know"
Simple	Complex
Reflexive	Reflective
Fast	Slow
Develops early	Develops late
Accentuated by stress	Attenuated by stress
Stimulus control	Self-control

Source: J. Metcalfe and W. Mischel, "A Hot/Cool-System Analysis of Delay of Gratification." *Psychological Review* 106, no. 1 (1999).

includes a more or less interconnected set of ideas, which help us think coolly about events (to "know").

The ability to access our cool system and to use it to good effect—to put our reactions in perspective so we can reason through an emotional topic with others—depends on two things: how developed our cool system is, and how well connected it is to our hot system. A well-performing cool system contains a large stock of ideas or "mental representations," which we draw on to think coolly about a wide range of events. The more these ideas are connected to our hot buttons, the easier it is to access our cool system whenever they get pushed. By reflecting and reframing, people can cool down together; over time this has the effect of developing the relationship's cool system and improving their access to it.

Cooling Down by Reflecting and Reframing

Recall the moment Luke got Dan's flaming voice mail. Despite feeling mad as hell, he was able to cool down relatively quickly and send a voice mail to Dan that cooled *him* down. First by reflecting, then by reframing—first alone, then together—the two were able to recall each other to their better selves *while* developing their ability to do better next time. With the aid of a tool called the Ladder of Reflection, Luke and Dan took the following six steps to cool themselves down and build their cool system (see Appendix B):[11]

▶ **Step One:** When a mad-as-hell Luke reaches for the "respond" button to blast Dan for being so negative, he stops himself just before hitting the button. What stops him is the ability to imagine what will happen next if he "goes," and acts on his first-blush reaction. In a matter of seconds, he "knows" that Dan will only dig in further; he knows that he (Luke) will do the same; and he knows that *nothing will get done*. The reason Luke knows these things is that he and Dan have spent time reflecting together on the patterns of interaction that get in their way. Chief among them is the pattern depicted in Figure 5 in which they dig in their heels and fail to convince each other of anything, except perhaps their unreasonableness. Some version of this map, one of several mental representations stored in Luke and Dan's collective cool system, springs to mind just as Luke reaches for the "respond" button, stopping him in his tracks.[12]

Figure 5: Recognizing an Unproductive Pattern

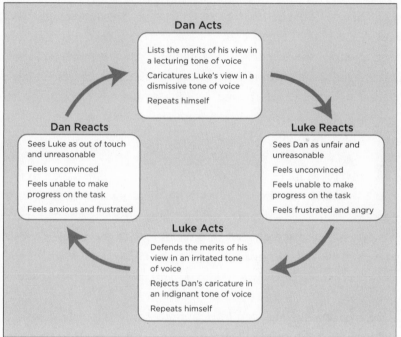

Step Two: As soon as Luke retrieves some version of this map, he's able to get the distance he needs to reframe what's happening.[13] No longer caught up in the moment, he's able to look back at what happened from the outside. While he had originally seen Dan's voice mail in purely stimulus-response terms—Dan *made* me angry—he's now able to entertain the idea that he might have played a role in Dan's upset. While he still doesn't like Dan's negativity, he no longer sees it as a product of Dan's personality alone, and he no longer sees himself as a victim of it. As we'll see later, this shift sets the stage for their reflecting together.

▶ **Step Three:** No longer as emotionally triggered, Luke is deep in thought and ready to look at Dan's assertions in a cooler frame of mind. This allows him to reassess his decision-making pace in light of Dan's concerns. While he still objects to Dan's caricatures of him as "bureaucratic" and "risk averse," he recognizes that he needs the board's support. If the board thinks he's going too slowly, as Dan suggests, then Dan is right to worry and Luke needs to listen up.

▶ **Step Four:** A more even-keeled Luke sends a temperate voice mail to Dan, signaling that he takes his concerns seriously without agreeing with his caricatures. The former recalls Dan to his better self; the latter suggests that Luke won't collude with Dan at his worst. The combination of the two prompts Dan to reflect on his "hysteria."

▶ **Step Five:** As a more thoughtful Dan reflects, he doesn't try to justify his "hysteria" by making a case for how "bureaucratic" or "risk averse" Luke is. Instead he looks *at* and *inside* himself, and comes to see that his practical and sentimental interest in Luke's success is competing with a desire not to hover. This gives him a sense of what led to his behavior: *unable to contain or to express his anxieties, he finally blew!*

▶ **Step Six:** In this final step in the sequence, Dan and Luke together reflect on what happened. Dan goes first. He doesn't do what Steve Jobs so often did: apologize for his behavior and leave it at that. Instead he shares his reflections with Luke so they can explore them together. This allows Luke to help Dan see that his fear of hovering is misplaced: he wants to hear Dan's concerns; he even finds them helpful. The only thing he finds problematic is Dan's negativity, which Luke can now trace to Dan's censoring concerns until they build up to the point of hysteria. This joint reflection leads them to see the situation and each other in a new light, allowing them to address their concerns better the next time.

By reflecting and reframing, first alone and then together, Dan and Luke are better able to address their substantive concerns while strengthening their relationship. These two cooling strategies work hand in hand, allowing them to use their emotions to think things through together. As they do so, they build their collective cool system by adding another map to it (see Figure 6). This map, based on what happened after Dan's voice mail, gives them a tool they can use to increase the odds of cooling down before doing something they regret.

Figure 6: Creating a More Productive Pattern

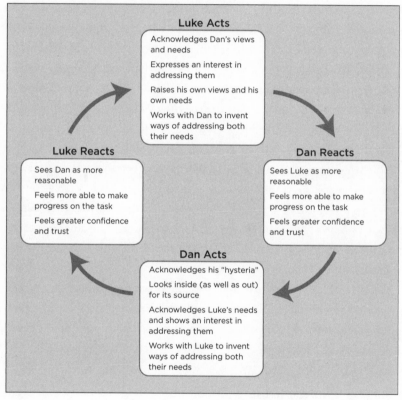

Luke Acts

Acknowledges Dan's views and needs

Expresses an interest in addressing them

Raises his own views and his own needs

Works with Dan to invent ways of addressing both their needs

Luke Reacts

Sees Dan as more reasonable

Feels more able to make progress on the task

Feels greater confidence and trust

Dan Reacts

Sees Luke as more reasonable

Feels more able to make progress on the task

Feels greater confidence and trust

Dan Acts

Acknowledges his "hysteria"

Looks inside (as well as out) for its source

Acknowledges Luke's needs and shows an interest in addressing them

Works with Luke to invent ways of addressing both their needs

Key Points

Relationship troubles are a fact of life. How you see and handle those troubles is a matter of perspective. The either/or perspective evident in the relationship between Jobs and Sculley oversimplified matters, blinded them to problems they needed to address, and reduced their degrees of freedom. The relational perspective evident in the relationship between Luke and Dan helped them see things they each missed and increased their degrees of freedom. Where the former perspective created vicious cycles that destroyed value, the latter created virtuous cycles that created or sustained value. Where the former led to greater blindness and brittleness over time, the latter led to greater understanding and resilience.

The best way to avoid waiting games—where each person waits for the other to calm down and see things his way—is for people to *help each other shift perspective, so they can regain their collective cool.* While shifting perspective won't make feelings go away, it will make it easier for people to use their emotions to think things through together.

To shift perspective, it helps to reflect and reframe, first alone, then together. Over time these two cooling strategies build a relationship's cool system by adding maps to that system that are tightly connected to the hot buttons triggered by stressful events. Once developed, that system makes it a lot easier to handle even the hottest topics and the most tumultuous troubles.

Taking a relational perspective goes against the grain of an either/or world, in which there are good guys and bad guys, evil empires and mighty kingdoms. In this respect, some may say the odds are against it. The next three chapters report on Merrimac's efforts to change those odds.

PART II

Transforming Relationships

Purpose: To show how a relationship changes and what that change produces, so you can decide whether to change your relationships, then take steps to change them.

Synopsis: Just as it takes time to build relationships, it takes time to change them, especially if you want that change to last. Moreover, change can't occur all at once: it can only proceed in stages. In the first stage of change, people disrupt patterns of interaction that are getting in their way. In the second, they create more satisfying patterns. In the third, they reset the foundation of their relationship, so new patterns can take hold. The overarching goal is the same throughout: to rebuild relationships so they're strong enough to withstand—and flexible enough to master—the shifting challenges people will face.

The Story: To illustrate how relationships change, we return to Merrimac to tell the story of CEO Dan Gavin and Stu Fine, one of the firm's most important leaders (see Chapter 4 for more on Merrimac). Though Dan and Stu had known each other for fifteen years, they'd never worked closely together. All that changed when Merrimac's leadership decided to pursue a new strategy. With the goal of turning the firm into a group of

TABLE 4: A Three-Stage Model of Relationship Change*			
STAGE	OBJECTIVES	STEPS	RESULTS
STAGE I **Disrupt**	• To disrupt patterns of interaction that are getting in your way. • To make your relationship more amenable to change.	1. Assess the relationship. 2. Map patterns of interaction. 3. Design action experiments.	• Able to disrupt patterns of interaction that trouble or puzzle you, making it easier to imagine a better future. • Willing and able to try new things. • Fall back into old patterns under *moderate* stress.
STAGE II **Reframe**	• To create more flexible patterns of interaction. • To accelerate the pace of growth and change.	1. Freeze frame. 2. Invent new frames. 3. Design frame experiments.	• Able to use upsetting moments to understand each other better. • Operate more freely within the relationship, picking up the pace of change and decision making. • Still prone to falling back into old patterns but only under *high* stress.
STAGE III **Revise**	• To reset the relationship's foundation so changes last. • To make growth and change sustainable.	1. Revisit past events. 2. Restructure outdated knowledge. 3. Return to the future.	• Able to respond more flexibly and effectively to each other and to the challenges you face together. • Treat the relationship as a context for your own and the firm's growth. • Able to recoup when you fall back into old patterns even under extreme stress.

* You can decide to stop at the end of any stage by considering two things: (1) how strong your relationship needs to be, and (2) how willing and able you are to continue. It's best not to decide in advance, but rather at the end of each stage, when you can make more informed choices. Chapter 8 discusses what should inform those choices.

companies in two years' time, the strategy depended on a handful of people stepping up to launch and grow new businesses. Dan was now looking to the highly regarded Stu to plow the way for others by turning his marketing team into its own business. Recognizing that the strategy's success depended on how well the two of them worked together, Dan and Stu decided to invest in making their relationship the best it could be.

Taking Action: At each step, I identify the actions you can take to get started on changing *your* relationships, and I let you know when you should get help. While it's best to take these steps with your partner, even if that's not possible, you can still go a long way on your own.

5
Disrupt Patterns of Interaction

The relationship—the pivotal point on which all else turns—is built (or undermined) in every interaction.

—Suzanne Clothier[1]

When a relationship critical to a firm's success could put that success at risk, it may be time for a change. Fifteen years into their relationship, Dan Gavin and Stu Fine suspected their time had come. For two years, the firm's top leadership had been transforming Merrimac[2] from a professional-services firm into a group of businesses that combined these services with innovative new products. CEO Gavin was now looking to Stu, the firm's marketing expert, to launch the firm's first product business. As one of the firm's most respected thought leaders, Stu had driven much of the firm's innovation, and he welcomed the chance to ensure that those innovations took root. At the same time, Dan and Stu both recognized that this new challenge would put a lot more pressure on their relationship. Stu knew he'd have to partner more closely with Dan, while Dan knew he'd have to rely more heavily on Stu. Whether their relationship was up to these tasks, neither could say for sure. To find out, they took three steps with my help:

Step 1:   Assess the Relationship
Step 2:   Map Patterns of Interaction
Step 3:   Design Action Experiments

As straightforward as these steps may seem, people face a funny kind of paradox before taking even the first one: *they know each other so well, they no longer know each other at all.* All they see are the caricatures in their heads—*he's so sensitive, she's so competitive.* The very efficiency these caricatures give, they also take away, because they make a person's underlying complexity—sure to emerge under stress—harder to understand or to handle. That's why, early on, the single most important thing people can do is *slow down and take a closer look at each other and at how their relationship works.* As you'll soon see, this helps people figure out where their relationship is up to the challenges it will face, and where it's not.

Step 1: Assess the Relationship

By conventional standards, most people— including Dan and Stu—would probably say their relationship was doing fine. They felt a good deal of trust; they were committed to making their relationship work; they didn't expect their interactions to be conflict-free; they shared an interest in producing results; and they

STEPS TOWARD CHANGE	
STAGE I **Disrupt**	Assess the Relationship
	Map Patterns of Interaction
	Design Action Experiments
STAGE II **Reframe**	Freeze Frame
	Invent New Frames
	Design Frame Experiments
STAGE III **Revise**	Revisit Past Events
	Restructure Knowledge
	Return to the Future

thought accountability was essential to achieving those results.[3] All things considered, many might say, if it ain't broke, don't fix it.

But like more and more leaders today, Dan and Stu held standards that were anything but conventional: they were far more interested in achieving excellence than in fixing things. The fact that they felt good about their relationship didn't tell them much. What they wanted to know was whether their relationship was strong enough to withstand the pressures they were about to face. To find out, they assessed how well their relationship was likely to handle two kinds of pressures: those bearing down on them from outside, and those bubbling up from within.

Assessing Outside Pressures: Demands + Constraints

Until now, Dan and Stu had built their relationship around their mutual love of ideas and their mutual respect for each other's talents. Although they interacted a lot, their fates had never been intertwined. But that context was now shifting, as Dan looked to Stu to help him implement the firm's group strategy by turning his marketing team into a separate business.

Like any new strategic challenge, this one posed its own set of demands and constraints (see Table 5).[4] On the demand side, Stu had to launch and lead a new business as quickly as possible; on the constraint side, his lack of experience was bound to affect how well and how quickly he did either. This, in turn, placed a demand on Dan: he would have to help Stu launch the business and develop into a general manager; on the constraint side, Dan's expertise was highly complex and largely intuitive, making it hard to transfer to others.

Demands and constraints invariably combine to create pressures that

TABLE 5: Outside Pressures on Stu and Dan	
DEMANDS	**CONSTRAINTS**
• Stu was charged with launching and leading a new business.	• Stu had no experience launching or leading a new business.
• Dan would have to help Stu launch the business and develop into a general manager.	• Dan's expertise was largely intuitive, making it hard to transfer quickly.
• They would have to depend on each other for their success like never before.	• Failure would be costly. As the first unit to be launched, it would serve as a model for others.
• They would have to confront and negotiate differences they could avoid in the past.	• Their negotiating styles were quite different. Dan relished a good debate; Stu hated them.
• They would have to move fast if the group strategy was going to look credible.	• Business building takes time, especially when you're building people's capabilities at the same time.

turn the heat up on relationships. When people don't take stock of those pressures, they're much more likely to turn against each other; conversely, when they do take stock, they're much more likely to turn together toward the challenges they face. By starting here, we increased the odds of Dan and Stu working together instead of at cross-purposes.

Assessing Inside Pressures: Hopes + Worries

To their relationship, Dan and Stu brought both hopes and worries (see Table 6). On the one hand, Stu worried that their relationship might grow stale if they didn't invest in improving it. On the other hand, Dan hoped that the decision to invest in their relationship might serve as a model for others. Both hoped that in the course of improving their relationship, they'd accelerate their own development, Dan wanting to change the way his anxiety comes out as anger, Stu wanting to handle tough disagreements more effectively, especially with CEOs. Last but not least, they both hoped the other would change those things that worried them the most: Stu's anxieties and sensitive zones; Dan's debating in ways that shut Stu down.

There's a healthy dose of self-interest in all this. It's as if they're thinking what most people think at this stage: *by investing in this relationship, perhaps the other guy will be less of a pain in the ass, and I'll be better off.*

That kind of thinking is what makes change worthwhile; without it, all you have is some vague notion of improving a relationship for its own sake. That's never enough. To make change of any significance, people need to have skin in the game; Dan and Stu's answers in Table 6 suggest they have some. What they say next suggests they have plenty.

TABLE 6: Inside Pressures Within Stu and Dan		
	WHAT DAN SAID	**WHAT STU SAID**
The Relationship	I want to turbocharge our relationship, move it from a good relationship to an excellent one. I'd like to make this relationship a model for investing in the top people in the firm.	Our relationship is important to me. Right now, it's at risk of going stale. I want to take what is a good relationship and turn it into an excellent one.
The Other Person	I'd like to help Stu with leadership issues that get in his way, like getting anxious about taking on new, controversial, or challenging tasks, and getting too upset when people touch on his sensitive zones.	I'd like to help Dan learn how to be more definitive and prescriptive without getting into the kind of debate behavior that can undermine his effectiveness and shut me and others down.
Themselves	I believe this work will help me reflect on and improve my own behavior. I know my anxiety often comes out as anger, which is not particularly constructive. So getting rid of that would be a good idea.	I want to learn how to put myself in a CEO's shoes, so I can understand how they think about things and what they find more or less helpful. I want to learn how to have constructive, tough disagreements without either shutting down or assuming too much responsibility.

Assessing a Relationship's Assets and Liabilities

When assessing a relationship, it helps to take stock of a relationship's assets and liabilities relative to the pressures that relationship is likely to face (see Table 7). This way people not only anticipate what might cause them difficulty under pressure, they also identify the assets they can use to deal with any difficulties that do arise.

TABLE 7: The Relationship's Assets and Liabilities		
	WHAT DAN SAID	**WHAT STU SAID**
Assets	I have genuine respect for Stu's character, integrity, and intellect. I believe his heart is in the right place in terms of fun, family, and our relationship. I believe Stu is capable of change and dedicated to learning, and that he can be more helpful to me than most people can.	I have a lot of time and patience for Dan. I'm extremely grateful to him for his support, counsel, and understanding over the years. I think Dan genuinely cares about me and doesn't just consider me an important economic engine. My faith in Dan's caring for me gives me courage and confidence to acknowledge and challenge some of my behaviors in his presence. I'm eager to change, and I don't think I can do it by myself. I also believe that our relationship is important to Merrimac. There are economic incentives to making this work.
Liabilities	It can be difficult to communicate with Stu in short-cycle time; it can take a long time to get things moving. There are things I do or say that have unintended effects on Stu. Sometimes without realizing it I raise Stu's anxiety level, hurt his feelings, or cause him to tune out. There's something about our relationship to which Stu tends to overreact.	There's a history of one-way learning in our relationship. I go to Dan with my thinking about a problem, and Dan then pronounces. Dan talks about situations, not about himself. I don't know or understand Dan very well, out of my own naiveté, lack of curiosity, or his "boss persona." As we work to change our patterns, I may come to resent the patterns more and not know how to talk to Dan about it well. Finally, we've fallen into a habit of joking about each other in stereotypical terms, which can also cause difficulties.

In taking stock of their assets, Dan and Stu recounted with ease all they had going for them, including a shared belief in their good intentions, mutual respect, a sense of caring, and confidence that they would learn from whatever risks they took.

But when it came to their liabilities, they struggled. Like most people, they could point to symptoms but not their cause. Dan knew it was difficult to communicate in short-cycle time with Stu, but he couldn't figure out why; he sensed that Stu overreacted to something in their relationship, but he didn't know what it was; he knew his behavior had unintended effects on Stu, but he didn't know what those effects were or what he did to create them. And despite Stu's professed confidence and trust in Dan, it troubled him that he didn't know Dan that well and that their relationship wasn't more reciprocal; he worried that their stereotyping, even in jest, might cause difficulty; and he could see how unnamed patterns, left intact, might breed resentment.

As is often the case at this point, Dan and Stu's assessment of their liabilities wasn't of much help. They sensed things—things that troubled them—but they couldn't give those things a name or explain their existence, let alone change them. Since this would put their success at risk, I helped them map those interactions that concerned them most.

TAKING ACTION
How to Assess Your Own Relationships

Now that you've seen how we assessed Dan and Stu's relationship, here's what you can do to assess your own.

• Identify a relationship that could make or break your success or that of your team, unit, or organization.

• Invite that person to join you in assessing the ways in which your relationship is making it easier *and* harder for each of you to succeed.

- Focus your attention not just on each other but on your relationship.

- Create a shared list of the challenges you'll have to master to-gether and the pressures they'll generate for each of you.

- Jointly assess the relationship's assets and liabilities relative to those challenges and pressures.

- If, based on the assessment, you both want to invest further, pro-ceed to Step 2. If you had trouble taking Step 1, get help before proceeding.

Step 2: Map Patterns of Interaction

This second step zeroes in on interac-tions that shed light on the concerns Dan and Stu raised in their assessment. To take this step, we used a tool I call the Ladder of Reflection to do three things: capture key interactions, describe them in concrete terms, and map the patterns underlying them (see Appendix B). This section describes how we took this step, so you can map any interactions that puzzle or trouble you.

STEPS TOWARD CHANGE	
STAGE I **Disrupt**	Assess the Relationship
	Map Patterns of Interaction
	Design Action Experiments
STAGE II **Reframe**	Freeze Frame
	Invent New Frames
	Design Frame Experiments
STAGE III **Revise**	Revisit Past Events
	Restructure Knowledge
	Return to the Future

Capturing Interactions

We already know from Dan and Stu's assessment that Dan is concerned about the amount of time it takes to communicate with Stu, his effect on Stu, and what he calls Stu's overreactions. We also know from Stu that the one-way nature of his relationship with Dan worries him, as does Dan's tendency to pronounce and to debate. To understand what they're doing to give rise to these concerns, we recorded their meetings as they went about their work together, and we waited until one of them illus-trated his concerns.[5]

It didn't take long.

Shortly after starting our work together, Dan and Stu confronted an issue that immediately put them at odds: how to negotiate a deal with a valued leader by the name of Hal Goldstein so he'd be motivated to stay and help launch Focuspoint, Stu's new marketing business. As Stu told it, he and Hal had reached an impasse on Hal's salary. In hopes of getting help from Dan, he recounted their negotiations to date and the concerns Hal had expressed.

After listening, Dan was convinced that their impasse didn't revolve around salary at all. Instead, he thought Hal was worried about becom-ing a "wage slave" whose salary would be forever tethered to the time he spent working rather than the value he created. Based on that view, Dan suggested that Stu promise Hal ownership in the new venture. But Stu, who was deeply wary of making promises he couldn't keep, didn't want to go in that direction. Without a legal structure in place, and with little understanding of how the ownership structure would work, Stu didn't trust that he or Dan would be able to deliver the goods. Let's listen in as they discuss what to do about Hal:[6]

Dan: One of the things I hear Hal saying is, "Wage slave! Wage slave! Wage slave!" If he said anything like that to me, I'd take out a venture-capital model and promise him some ownership in the firm, assuming he sticks around. And if it's cash now he wants, I'd tell him he can trade some of that ownership for cash now.

Stu: I don't want to go there.

Dan: Why not? He has to be adult about his decisions.

Stu: Dan, Dan. I don't have the same degree of certainty you do that there are going to be shares.

Dan: Why wouldn't you, Stu?

Stu: Because it depends on what goes on in your head and other things I don't know anything about.

Dan: I have a high degree of certainty. So if it depends on what's going on in my head, I have a high degree of certainty.

Stu: I'm making a representation to somebody else about what's in your head. I'm uncomfortable about that.

Dan: But in this case, to the extent my certainty fails to pan out over time, it can only benefit him. You're giving him money now for something that might not exist.

Stu: To be blunt, Dan, there are things you've said were going to happen which haven't happened, like, "There may be different kinds of directors" and things like that. So I'm very leery, because I know people will latch on to things. And, I'm bad at this stuff already, Dan!

Dan: [Looking and sounding annoyed] But Stu—

Stu: [Putting his hand up to form a stop sign] I'm just saying that, for me, if it doesn't happen, recouping will take me a century! I don't want to go there!

Dan: [Leaning forward] But Stu—

Stu: [Hand still up] I'm sorry. I'm a coward, but at least I know I'm a coward!

It's not every day you come across someone who makes an apologetic appeal to cowardice as a way out of a conflict. It's so self-deprecating it's disarming, which of course it's meant to be—which isn't to say that Stu is *consciously* trying to disarm Dan. Quite the contrary—he doesn't have to try. His response is so habitual—so intrinsic to his behavioral repertoire[7]—that it comes naturally. All he needs is the proper cue, which Dan's relentless persistence gives him. By the end of the exchange, all Stu wants is for Dan to back off, prompting him to do what he usually does under those circumstances: apologize and appeal to a character flaw—in this case, cowardice—after which Stu and Dan reach the same kind of impasse Stu reached with Hal.

Not good.

This brief exchange exemplifies one of the patterns that gets Dan and Stu into trouble. It's a classic. While the particulars may vary—one day they may talk about Hal, the next about products—the pattern itself will remain the same, repeating over and over until they disrupt it, which they won't be able to do until they can describe it.

Describing Interactions

When people look at interactions like the one between Dan and Stu, the first things that usually spring to mind are evaluations: "That went nowhere!" or "That was weird!" That's only natural. But it's not enough: it won't help you change what you see. To change patterns, you first have to see them, which means you have to describe what's happening in concrete terms, so people can connect your description to their behavior.[8] To do that, you must look closely at each step in an interaction and ask *What is this person actually doing?*

By asking this question, you focus attention on people's behavior instead of their motives (see Appendix B for more on this distinction). In other words, instead of speculating about what people are *trying* to do, you simply observe what they *are* doing. There's a reason for this. If you focus on motives—what people are *trying* to do—before describing what they *are* doing, you'll come up with speculations that are quite disconnected from actual behavior. This causes two problems. First, people won't be able to see the behaviors you think they need to change, making it less likely they'll change them. And second, they may wonder whether your speculations say more about you than them, leading them to discount your views. Although there *is* a time and a place for understanding what people are trying to do, it's not now but in the next stage.

To be most useful, descriptions should help people see what they're doing to contribute to those patterns that concern them the most. Take Dan's opening move, when he tells Stu:

> One of the things I hear Hal saying is, "Wage slave! Wage slave! Wage slave!" If he said anything like that to me, I'd take out a venture-capital model. He'd get some ownership in the firm, assuming he sticks around. And if it's cash now that he wants, I'd tell him he can trade some of that ownership for cash.

Different observers will inevitably describe this statement in different ways, which raises the question: which description should you choose?

For all practical purposes, the answer is pretty simple: the one that suits your purposes best. Our purpose here is to understand what Dan and Stu are doing to give rise to the concerns they each have about their relationship. Here you might recall that Stu is concerned about their one-way dynamic. "I go to Dan with my thinking about a problem, and Dan then pronounces" (see Table 7). Well, right here we have a great example of what that pronouncing looks like in action: we might describe Dan's opening statement as *pronouncing what he thinks the right answer is.* By describing Dan's statement this way, we help Stu see the behaviors that concern him while helping Dan see what he does to create the mystifying "unintended effects" he has on Stu (see Table 8).

Moving to the next step in the interaction, Stu responds to Dan's pronouncement: "I don't want to go there." Looking at this statement, you might reasonably say that Stu *rejects Dan's answer.* But notice: it's not any old rejection. Stu doesn't say why he rejects Dan's suggestion, nor does he build on it by saying what might make it more appealing. In this re-

"You're a partner now, Cosgrove. Partners don't do self-deprecation."

spect, it's not a mere rejection; it's an *outright rejection,* leaving little to no room for negotiation. This description draws our attention to the behavior that leads Dan to worry that Stu slows things down more than necessary (see Tables 6 and 7).

In the next step, Dan meets Stu's rejection and raises him one: "Why not?" he asks, before asserting, "He has to be adult about his decision." Although short, this two-pronged move is quite complicated. On the one hand, we might call it a question, because he starts off by asking why not. On the other hand, he doesn't wait for an answer but instead goes on to pronounce, "[Hal] has to be adult about his decision." It's this latter statement that makes the move so complicated, because it implies, "If you [Stu] believe that adults have to be adult about their decisions, then you would do what I propose." Since most of us believe that adults should be adults, it suggests that only unreasonable people would not do what Dan is proposing. In this way, Dan's move—the kind of move a debater might make—*challenges Stu to account for his resistance,* as if his resistance is, on the face of it, unreasonable.

This appears to frustrate Stu who, like most of us, probably believes that adults should act like adults; yet he still doesn't want to do what Dan suggests. And so he exclaims, "Dan, Dan" as if to stop him before going on to say, "I don't have the same degree of certainty you do that there are going to be shares." In this statement, Stu explains why he's rejecting Dan's suggestion, in effect saying, "I'll tell you why not. You're certain about something I'm not at all certain about." Here we might simply say that Stu is *explaining his concerns* or *raising a concern* about offering shares. But also notice what he's *not* doing: *He's not asking Dan to address his concerns.* He doesn't say, for example, "You have more certainty than I have about the shares. If I understood why, I might feel more comfortable doing what you suggest. What leads you to be so confident?" Instead Stu *raises a concern without asking Dan to address it.*

This last description, unlike the first two, describes not only what Stu *is* doing (raising a concern) but also what he's *not* doing (not asking Dan to address the concern). This kind of description is always tricky, because there are any number of things he's *not* doing: he's not checking his voice mail; he's not pacing the room; he's not yelling at Dan. How can we possibly know how to focus our attention? Once again, the answer is to rely on their initial assessments, where we discovered that Stu wants Dan to stop debating and start advising, and Dan wants Stu to move faster and to overreact less (see Tables 6 and 7).

As with all people, it's not just what they do that gets in the way of what they want; it's also what they don't do. And here's a great example. By not inviting Dan to address what troubles Stu about the idea, Stu gives Dan no room to put his troubles to rest, which requires Stu to persist to get Dan to address his concerns. But this only leads Dan to think Stu's overreacting, which requires Stu to persist further. And so on.

In the next step of the interaction, Dan responds by asking, "Why wouldn't you be [as certain as I am], Stu?" Here, you could say that Dan is asking a question. But that wouldn't say much about the *kind* of question he's asking, nor would it explain how the two get stuck. After all, Dan isn't asking just any question. He's asking *why Stu isn't already as certain as he is.*

That question is quite different from the more open-ended question, "What leads you to be uncertain, Stu?" If anything, Dan's question assumes that his level of certainty is the right standard, and it implies that Stu must justify why he isn't meeting it. In this sense, Dan's question doesn't open up an inquiry as much as it launches a debate, in which Dan is *debating the legitimacy of Stu's concerns.* This more nuanced description of Dan's question helps explain exactly how their interaction breaks down and what leads them to feel frustrated and worried.

Although the three of us continued to make our way through their interaction, by now you probably get the gist of what we did: we described their interaction in ways that helped us understand what behaviors gave rise to their concerns. Let's move on to how you can pull these descriptions together into a map that captures the pattern underlying their interaction.[9]

Mapping the Pattern

Mapping is a technique that helps you understand patterns of interaction that produce outcomes that neither person in a relationship consciously wants or intends. By using the template in Figure 7, you can portray in graphic form *how each person's actions help to elicit reactions that produce the next step in the sequence that makes up the interaction.*[10] This helps people see how their actions and reactions interlock to form an identifiable pattern, allowing them to step outside the pattern, see how it works, and imagine how it might work differently.

Figure 7: The Act-React Template

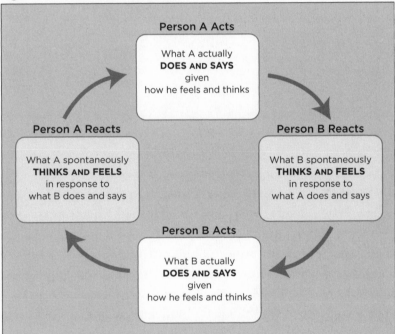

The map in Figure 8 uses this template to pull together and add to what we've learned so far. Included in the white boxes, labeled "Dan Acts" and "Stu Acts," are descriptions of what Dan and Stu did. Each action is described so that Dan and Stu can see what they're actually doing to give rise to the other's concerns. All of this is pretty straightforward.

Figure 8: Mapping Dan and Stu's Interactions

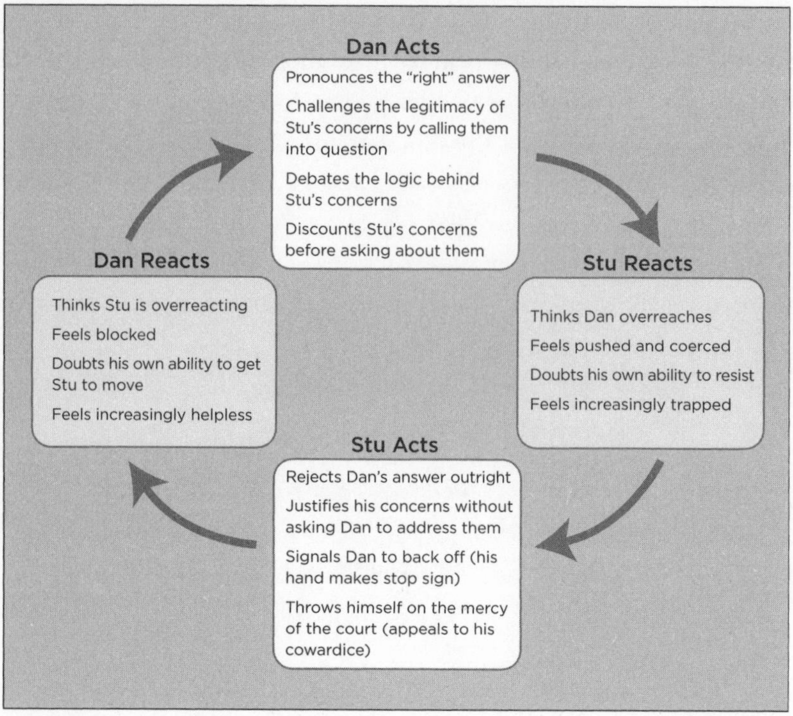

Dan Acts
Pronounces the "right" answer
Challenges the legitimacy of Stu's concerns by calling them into question
Debates the logic behind Stu's concerns
Discounts Stu's concerns before asking about them

Dan Reacts
Thinks Stu is overreacting
Feels blocked
Doubts his own ability to get Stu to move
Feels increasingly helpless

Stu Reacts
Thinks Dan overreaches
Feels pushed and coerced
Doubts his own ability to resist
Feels increasingly trapped

Stu Acts
Rejects Dan's answer outright
Justifies his concerns without asking Dan to address them
Signals Dan to back off (his hand makes stop sign)
Throws himself on the mercy of the court (appeals to his cowardice)

The next step—adding their reactions—is trickier. We don't yet know what Dan and Stu are thinking or feeling. And even if they told us, we couldn't be sure if what they said was entirely valid.[11] Only in cartoons do people have bubbles over their heads. In real life, all that thinking and feeling is going on inside people's heads, where we can't see what's happening. That's why the boxes labeled "Reacts" are shaded in gray: to remind us to hold loosely whatever we put in those boxes, because they lie in a gray zone. At the same time, we can't ignore reactions just because they're difficult to get at. Reactions are the connective tissue that holds an interaction together, tying one action to the next. That means we have to find some way to get at them.

In everyday life, we rely on three approaches to get at people's reactions: asking, speculating, or predicting what someone is feeling or thinking. While none of these approaches is totally reliable, some work better than others, especially when implemented in better or worse ways. As

Table 8 suggests, the more you move down or to the right, the more you run the risk of distorting people's reactions.[12] Conversely, the more you stay toward the top and to the left, the more you're likely to find out what people are *really* feeling and thinking.

TABLE 8: Getting at People's Reactions		
	BETTER WAYS	**WORSE WAYS**
Ask	Stop the action and ask an open-ended question like, "What's your reaction?"	Later on, ask a leading question based on how *you* would feel: "Did you feel anxious last week when Dan persisted?"
Speculate	Based on what people have said about their reactions in similar situations, hypothesize what they *might* be feeling or thinking in this one. For example, "Based on what Dan and Stu said in their assessments, Dan *may* think Stu is overreacting and slowing things down; and Stu *may* think Dan is trying to win a debate. Let me ask if that's the case here."	Based on *your* reactions to similar situations, make assumptions about what these people *must* be thinking or feeling in this one. For example, "If I were Dan, I'd think Stu was acting immaturely, and it would piss me off. Dan *must* be pissed off. If I were Stu, I'd think Dan was being unfair, making me do things I don't want to do, and that would piss me off too. Stu *must be* pissed off."
Predict	Based on a relatively developed theory about how people tend to react to different behaviors, make predictions about how these people *might* be reacting here. For example, "Under these circumstances, many people might feel blocked or pushed. Let me test to see if that's the case here."	Based on a relatively simplistic grasp of people's motivations derived exclusively from *your* experience, make predictions about how people in this situation *must* be reacting. For example, "Dan cares only about control; he *must* be livid that he can't get his way. Stu only cares about protecting himself; he *must* be scared to death by what Dan's doing."

Calibrating Your Understanding

The point of mapping isn't to nail down, once and for all, the way a relationship works. It's to map a pattern well enough for the purposes of changing it. The test of a good map, then, isn't whether it's right or wrong, but whether it's good enough to serve change. To calibrate whether that's the case, you need to discuss maps in light of data from other meetings, adding to and modifying the map until everyone thinks it's good enough to inform change.

Sometimes in calibrating a map, people will differ over how best to describe an action or a reaction. When that happens, it's tempting to get into an argument over who's right. Like the old beer commercial, one person argues, "Less filling!" while the other claims, "Tastes great!" One person sees and appreciates one aspect of what happened; the other sees and appreciates another.

For illustrative purposes, let's say that after seeing the map, Dan disagrees with the characterization of his opening move as "pronouncing the right answer." Let's say he thinks we should call it "an effort to help." Instead of getting into an argument, we're better off paying attention to what he sees that we don't.

And what might he be seeing? The word "effort" is a tip-off, as would be words like "trying," "intending," or "hoping." In calling his move an "effort to help," Dan is turning our attention to what he was *trying to do* as opposed to what he *was actually doing*. He's pointing to his *intentions* or *motives* instead of *his actions*. And at that level, chances are, he's right; he probably was trying to help. At the same time, his *actions* suggest that his way of helping is to pronounce the "right" answer. If that's the case, then both descriptions are true: the map focuses on his actions, and Dan focuses on his intentions while taking those actions. While it's true that other intentions may also be at play—he may be trying to convince Stu, or hoping to get Stu to do things his way—that doesn't mean he isn't also trying to help. People rarely have one intention or purpose in mind when acting.

By taking into account what Dan sees, we can more quickly turn his attention to what he doesn't see: the way he pursued his intentions and the results of his efforts. After all, the data are pretty compelling: Dan's actions didn't leave Stu feeling helped, and Stu certainly didn't budge. So if Dan was trying to help—and we have no data to assume otherwise—he may need to reconsider his approach. He'll be much more likely to do so if we don't argue with him over what he was or was not *trying* to do.

Besides, we'll never know for sure what was going on inside Dan's head or Stu's or anyone's for that matter. When it comes to what people feel, think, or intend, we're forever hampered by *asymmetric access*. As observers, all we have to go on are clues—what actors say or do, their tones of voice, their body language—to glean what they might be thinking, feeling, or intending.[13] Indeed, an overwhelming amount of research demonstrates that our interpretations of others' intentions are more often wrong than right.[14] Only those acting have direct access to what they're feeling and thinking, and even they can't say for sure what's going on.[15]

While this asymmetric access can never be eliminated, it can serve as a constant reminder that we should be forever humble about what's going on in the hearts and minds of those whom we observe. The best we can do is make it as easy as possible for people to tell us what they're feeling, thinking, and intending as accurately as they can.[16]

This means demonstrating—not just espousing—a genuine interest in what people have to say. Only then will they have a genuine interest in telling you. And remember: people will watch what you do closely. When you ask questions, they'll notice whether you're trying to understand them ("What's going on?") or lambaste them ("Why on earth would you do that?"). And when you listen, they'll look to see if you're capturing what they're saying accurately or simply caricaturing it. These things matter, and they'll be on the lookout for them.

Once people map the pattern underlying repetitious interactions, they can see what they're each doing to contribute to that pattern, putting them in a much better position to alter it. With the aid of that map, Dan can see that his debating contributes to Stu's "overreactions," and Stu can see how his outright rejections increase the odds of Dan debating. With one person debating and the other rejecting, it's easy to see why it's taking so long to communicate. By putting familiar problems (taking a long time to communicate) in unfamiliar light (what each person is doing to slow things down), maps produce what some writers call a "shock of recognition," engaging people's emotions as well as their intellects.

→

TAKING ACTION
How to Map Patterns of Interaction

Now that you've seen how we mapped Dan and Stu's relationship, here's what you can do to map yours.

• Identify one or two interactions that illustrate the concerns raised in your relationship assessment from Step 1.

• Capture the interaction by taping or taking close notes on what you each said and did and on what you each felt and thought at the time.

• Describe in concrete terms what you each did (and did not do); do not speculate about what you were trying to do or intending to do.

• Describe your reactions (what you were actually thinking and feeling at the time); do not justify, interpret, or explain them.

• Organize your description into a map that shows how each of your actions contributed to reactions that make the other's actions more understandable.

• Calibrate your map by modifying or adding to it based on what happens in other interactions.

• If, based on the map, you both want to invest further, proceed to Step 3. If you had trouble taking Step 2, get help first.

Step 3: Design Action Experiments

Many of us figure, "If I try harder and harder to change some pattern of interaction and it doesn't change, it must not be changeable." But this overlooks another possibility: that we're trying the wrong things. In fact, our efforts may be part of the problem. Often the problem isn't *how hard* we try; it's *what* we try.

STEPS TOWARD CHANGE	
STAGE I **Disrupt**	Assess the Relationship
	Map Patterns of Interaction
	Design Action Experiments
STAGE II **Reframe**	Freeze Frame
	Invent New Frames
	Design Frame Experiments
STAGE III **Revise**	Revisit Past Events
	Restructure Knowledge
	Return to the Future

To change patterns, you have to throw a monkey wrench into the works by thinking—and then acting—outside the pattern.[17] If you find that difficult to imagine, let alone do, you have lots of company. That's why it's best not to take this step until you've mapped the pattern that concerns you. Maps give you the understanding and distance you need to think outside the box. With map in hand, you're no longer *in* the pattern, you're *outside,* looking back at it. From this perspective, you are in a much better position to invent action experiments—experiments designed to disrupt the pattern and make it more amenable to change.[18]

The first step in any action experiment is to go back and look at the interlocking actions and reactions depicted in a map and to ask the question: *What actions can I take to make it hard for the other person to react the way he or she does?* Usually this question will require you to invent actions that are "counterintuitive"—actions that lie outside of your intuitive way of seeing and doing things. For this reason, the perspective of a skilled third party often helps, because he or she can imagine options, as I do below, that those in the pattern can't:

Diana: Stu, let me suggest something counterintuitive. When Dan says, "I think you ought to do this, this, and this," instead of rejecting him outright, put him to work. Tell him what you need to feel more comfortable and ask him to make it more concrete for you. That way you're less likely to get Dan the debater and more likely to get Dan at his best—a fine teacher. And Dan, when Stu rejects what you're saying and blocks, I'd slow down and ask him what he needs to be more comfortable, then I'd go back and help him see what leads you to be comfortable already.

In making these suggestions, I had the map in mind. That map alerted me to how trapped Stu felt and how helpless Dan felt. I predicted that these two moves—Stu putting Dan to work, and Dan helping Stu—would disrupt the pattern: If Stu can put Dan to work, perhaps he won't feel so trapped that he has to reject Dan's views outright; and if Dan is given the space to explain his views, perhaps he won't feel so helpless that he has to debate Stu's concerns before understanding them. He might even *want* to understand them, as a good teacher does.

Suggestions like these, although simple, go against the grain of people's behavioral repertoires. Indeed, if they don't, they probably won't disrupt the pattern, because *all patterns are a product of people's intersecting behavioral repertoires*. It's only reasonable, then, that people will worry about trying out a new action. That's why I wasn't surprised or offended when Dan reacted to my suggestion by saying, "I hear what you're saying, but we're in implementation mode on a number of key points here. I don't think we can postpone thinking about this one." Instead of discounting or debating his concern, I used it to encourage him to try something new:

Let me stay with this for a second. I'm sympathetic to the worry that time is running out. So my advice for you is as counterintuitive as it is for Stu. If you're in such a hurry, then the last thing you want to do is have Stu kick you out of the conversation, which is exactly what he's doing.

Right now, your speeding up isn't saving time; it's slowing things down. He'll listen more, and listen more efficiently, if you slow down, ask him about his concerns, then go back to the basics on ownership in addressing them.

It's not as obvious to him as it is to you why he won't get into trouble. In fact, he's really worried about it, so there's already static in the system. Don't add more.

This line of thinking made sense to Dan, and he agreed to give it a try. The next few weeks provided several opportunities for them to experiment with new actions. While they were a bit clumsy in execution, Dan and Stu saw that these actions allowed them to conduct their business more swiftly. No longer debating or blocking quite as much, they were able to get more done, *and* they felt better about themselves and each other.

The old pattern was disrupted. Yet even had the experiment "failed," as many initial experiments do,[19] that too would have been okay. It would have given us the information we needed to go back to the drawing board and design another experiment.

TAKING ACTION
How to Design an Action Experiment

Now that you've seen how we designed Dan and Stu's action experiment, here's what you can do to design your own.

- Use the map you created in Step 2 to move outside the pattern that concerns you, so you can look back at it and see how it works.

- Ask yourselves, *What actions can I take to make it hard for the other person to continue acting and reacting the way he or she now does?*

- Invent actions that lie outside the box defined by the pattern—actions that might put a monkey wrench in the way it works.

- Even if the new actions look like the cure that makes the illness worse, try them. Right now, you just want to shake the pattern up and make it more amenable to change.

- If, based on the experiment, you both want to invest further, proceed to Stage II. If you had difficulty with Stage I, get help first.

Stage I Results

This last step launched Dan and Stu's relationship into a state of flux, making it more amenable to change. With the old pattern disrupted, they could no longer rely on mindless routines. They had to pay closer attention to what they were each doing, leading them to notice and puzzle over things they'd previously taken for granted. What's more, once their action experiments succeeded in disrupting the pattern, they saw that their actions did make a difference, and they found themselves reacting somewhat differently to each other. As a result, by the end of Stage I, Dan and Stu were able to:

▶ Imagine a significantly better state of affairs;
▶ Demonstrate a greater ability and willingness to try new things;
▶ Feel and express more hope for the relationship.

Even so, Dan and Stu continued to struggle from time to time. When things got especially tough, they'd revert back to old behaviors, feeling neither comfortable nor confident enough to use the behaviors they were learning. And for good reason: they weren't very good at them yet. Under stress, Dan would grit his teeth and sound impatient every time he asked Stu about his concerns, while Stu would screw up his face and look pained every time he resisted the urge to block Dan.

While all this is to be expected, it creates a dilemma:

▶ On the one hand, the only way to disrupt a pattern is to try out new actions.
▶ On the other hand, these new actions will at first look clumsy, awkward, or insincere, leading people to become anything from annoyed to suspicious.

Left unaddressed, this dilemma can slow change down. But if people understand that this dilemma is a necessary by-product of this stage, they can use it to catapult them into the next stage of change. This is because the dilemma's resolution depends on people becoming so adept at taking new actions that those actions feel natural to them and genuine to others. Yet, as the next chapter shows, the only way people can do this is to alter the way they see themselves in relation to each other. That's the core task of the next stage of change, and accomplishing it allows new patterns of interaction to emerge.

6
Reframe How You See Each Other

I'm not sure what to do.
I don't want to go into the pool until it's warm,
but it won't be warm until I go in.

—My good friend Max Sossa, 8 years old at the time

All too often and much to our dismay, frustrating patterns of interaction persist despite our efforts to change them. The reason is simple: we give short shrift to the interpretations that keep them going. Left to their own devices, these interpretations have a nasty habit of getting stuck in one gear. No matter what someone does, we see him or her the same way. Soon, our emotional reactions get caught in a rut, and our interactions start spinning their wheels. From this point on, we're trapped.

As long as Dan sees Stu's blocking as irrational, and Stu sees Dan's lecturing as an effort to impose his will, they'll continue to reenact the same Push–Block pattern day in and day out. While new actions might disrupt the pattern briefly, the only way they can create a significantly new pattern is by transforming the way the two see each other. In this second stage, Dan and Stu do just that by taking three steps:

Step 1: Freeze Frame
Step 2: Invent New Frames
Step 3: Design Frame Experiments

To complete these steps successfully, Dan and Stu will have to tackle the central paradox of this second stage: *they will have to act as if they believe to be true those interpretations they "know" to be false.* As the saying goes, seeing is believing. People will shift frames only if they believe it's warranted, and they will believe it's warranted only if they see evidence to that effect. It's not enough, then, simply to imagine a different way of seeing. People must try—through their actions—to *create* experiences that make a new way of seeing come true.

That's why each step in this stage is designed to build just enough confidence for Dan and Stu to *act*—not merely think—outside the box. Only by seeing things differently will they be able to create a new pattern. Let's see how they fare.

Step 1: Freeze Frame

No matter how complex a situation gets, we're rarely at a loss for ways to interpret it (see Chapter 3). Our minds are sense-making engines, spitting out one interpretation after another so we can put to rest whatever anxiety, confusion, or puzzlement we feel. By the time that mental engine's done selecting, labeling, weigh-

STEPS TOWARD CHANGE	
STAGE I Disrupt	Assess the Relationship
	Map Patterns of Interaction
	Design Action Experiments
STAGE II Reframe	Freeze Frame
	Invent New Frames
	Design Frame Experiments
STAGE III Revise	Revisit Past Events
	Restructure Knowledge
	Return to the Future

ing, and organizing thousands of little data points into one big interpretation, we can't imagine seeing things any other way. Yet if asked, we'd be hard-pressed to say why, because all that interpretive activity takes place outside our awareness—under the hood, so to speak.

This is a big problem. While reactions tend to vary from pattern to pattern within a relationship, the interpretations embedded in those reactions tend to grow more stable with time. As Figure 9 depicts, these more stable interpretations—what I call frames—turn patterns of interaction into more enduring relationship structures *without our even realizing it.* Once these frame-based structures take hold, they determine the range and quality of patterns that a relationship has at its disposal. By shifting frames—first with effort, then automatically—you shift the structure underlying a relationship, increasing the range and quality of its patterns.

In this first step of Stage II, we use Dan and Stu's reactions to freeze frame—that is, to bring their frames into the foreground. That allows us to see how, under stress, their frames are pulling them back into old patterns and preventing new ones from emerging (see Figure 9).

Figure 9: Freeze Frame

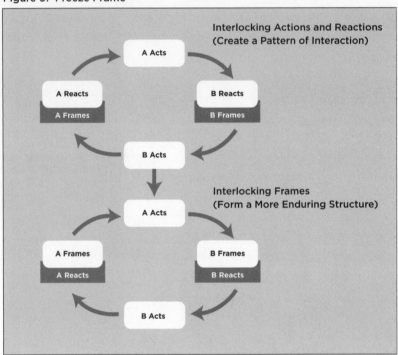

We did three things to freeze frame. First, we used emotionally charged moments to uncover their reactions; second, we named the frames embedded in those reactions; and finally, we mapped the way their frames intersected to maintain troubling patterns.

Using Emotionally Charged Moments

People's reactions are much easier to access in the heat of the moment when they're bubbling close to the surface.[1] Like all of us, Dan and Stu had a number of such moments. But an especially hot one occurred while they were discussing how Stu's business unit, Focuspoint, would interact with Merrimac's core business.

Minutes into the discussion, everyone in the room could feel the tension. Looking more and more agitated, Dan spoke faster and faster in an increasingly contemptuous tone of voice about why Stu's view was wrong, layering one reason on top of another. And while Stu said very little— only a sighing "I know, Dan"—his body language spoke volumes: he squirmed in his seat; he pushed back his chair; he grimaced; he pulled his chair forward; he grimaced again.

While I could see they were upset, I couldn't see why. To find out, I

"Oh, and your feelings have been trying
to get in touch with you."

interrupted them and asked them to describe, as best they could, what they were thinking and feeling. They replied with the following:[2]

> *Dan:* I'm thinking this is a *really* important issue, and I've got a deep conviction Stu's going in the wrong direction. I feel like I've got to get through to him, but I can't figure out a way to get him off the direction he's headed. So now I'm convinced there's going to be a train wreck, and he's gonna get killed and Focuspoint along with him. So I feel this overwhelming sense of helplessness *and* obligation, at which point I panic.
>
> *Stu:* Dan keeps pushing me to do things that make me feel exposed. Today he keeps lecturing me on things I already know, which makes me feel like he thinks I'm stupid! Last week, when I didn't get what he was saying, I figured, "Geez, I really *must* be stupid!" What he was saying wasn't at all obvious to me, even though it was sounding awfully obvious to him—at which point I don't have a clue what to do. Then I *really* feel exposed, so I just freeze.

These accounts of what was going on inside their heads helped us see how they were reacting to each other in the heat of the moment. While such accounts can never tell us the whole truth and nothing but the truth, they're far better than conjecture alone, and they gave us enough fodder with which to explore how they were framing each other when upset.[3]

Naming That Frame

With these accounts in hand, we took up three questions:

- ▶ How are they seeing (or framing) the situation? What do they think it's about?
- ▶ How are they seeing themselves in relation to each other?
- ▶ What goals or purposes are they setting for themselves as a result?

In each case, we grounded our search in what was happening in the moment, repeatedly asking: *given the way Dan and Stu are reacting and acting right now, how must they be framing things?* In searching for an answer, we paid close attention to the language they used and especially to the metaphors, because they reveal a lot about how people frame things. Stu's account, for instance, speaks of Dan *pushing* him, of *making* him feel *stupid* and *exposed*, at which point he *doesn't have a clue what to do,* leading him to *freeze*. Dan's account speaks of Stu *going in the wrong direction,* of the *train wreck* that's coming, of his *overwhelming sense of helplessness and obligation,* leading him to *panic*. In this language, we can discern the broad outlines of their interlocking frames, which I capture in the map in Figure 10.[4]

Figure 10: Mapping Interlocking Frames

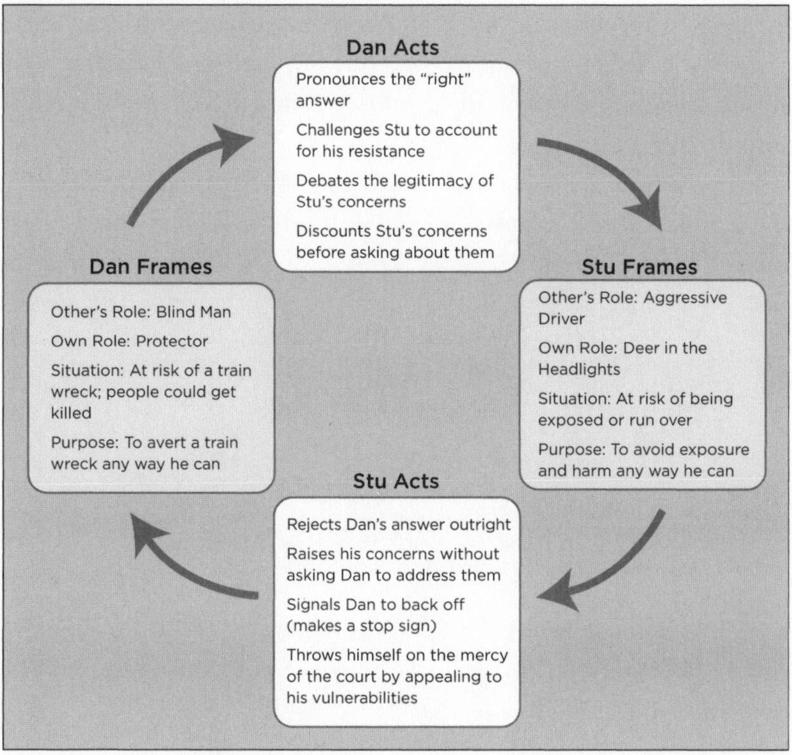

Dan Acts
- Pronounces the "right" answer
- Challenges Stu to account for his resistance
- Debates the legitimacy of Stu's concerns
- Discounts Stu's concerns before asking about them

Dan Frames
- Other's Role: Blind Man
- Own Role: Protector
- Situation: At risk of a train wreck; people could get killed
- Purpose: To avert a train wreck any way he can

Stu Frames
- Other's Role: Aggressive Driver
- Own Role: Deer in the Headlights
- Situation: At risk of being exposed or run over
- Purpose: To avoid exposure and harm any way he can

Stu Acts
- Rejects Dan's answer outright
- Raises his concerns without asking Dan to address them
- Signals Dan to back off (makes a stop sign)
- Throws himself on the mercy of the court by appealing to his vulnerabilities

Mapping Interlocking Frames

As Dan and Stu's frames came into sharper focus, I mapped how they intersected to keep the two stuck in the same repetitious pattern despite a mutual desire to break free (see Figure 10). Looking at the map, they could see that it really wasn't the other guy who was getting in the way; it was their interlocking frames.

As the map illustrates, Dan and Stu's frames fit together perfectly to keep them stuck. Convinced that Stu is blind to the dangers around him, Dan casts himself in the role of his protector, leading him to work frantically and helplessly to avert a train wreck (he pronounces the "right" answer; he challenges, debates, and discounts Stu's views). Though these actions all follow naturally from his frame, they lead Stu to see himself as the proverbial deer in the headlights—powerless, stupid, and exposed—with an aggressive driver bearing down on him. With no clue what to do, he freezes (he forms a stop sign with his hand to get Dan to back off; he appeals to his vulnerabilities). Like Dan, Stu's actions follow naturally from his framing, but they only reinforce Dan's "deep conviction" that Stu needs his protection.

The point is, as long as their interlocking frames remain intact, Dan and Stu won't be able to create a fundamentally new pattern—no matter how much they want to or how hard they try.

→

TAKING ACTION
How to Freeze Frame

Now that you've seen how Dan and Stu explored their frames, here's how you can get started on doing the same.

• Stop in the heat of the moment and capture your partner's reactions (and your own) by asking an open-ended question like "What's going on?"

- No matter how tempting, don't react to what you hear. You can't tell what your reactions—or your partner's reactions—are saying about you, him, or the relationship. Think of them as "data," and use them to uncover your frames.

- To uncover your frames, ask yourselves: *Given the way I'm reacting, how must I be seeing myself, my partner, the situation, and my purpose in it?*

- Take a few moments to write down your answers before discussing them with each other. Then go back over them to make sure they're connected to what you felt, thought, and did.

- Discuss what you've learned with each other *without justifying your reactions or your frames.* Stay focused on exploring and mapping how your frames intersect to maintain the interlocking actions you mapped in Stage I.

- If, based on your new map, you both want to invest further, proceed to Step 2. If you had trouble taking Step 1, get help before proceeding.

Step 2: Invent New Frames

With their map in hand, Dan and Stu could see that their patterns of interaction were products of their own making, even if they felt those patterns were out of their control. This new awareness opens up new possibilities: perhaps Stu's freezing and blocking is just his way of avoiding exposure, and perhaps Dan's

STEPS TOWARD CHANGE	
STAGE I **Disrupt**	Assess the Relationship
	Map Patterns of Interaction
	Design Action Experiments
STAGE II **Reframe**	Freeze Frame
	Invent New Frames
	Design Frame Experiments
STAGE III **Revise**	Revisit Past Events
	Restructure Knowledge
	Return to the Future

lecturing and debating is his way of protecting Stu. No longer convinced that the way they see things is the way things are, they could entertain new ways of seeing. But right now, they can only see things through their frames. This is where third parties come in handy, because they can see things those caught up in a pattern can't. In Dan and Stu's case, that third party was me, and so for the next few weeks, we worked together to invent new frames.

Stu: Reframing Dan

When we began our work together, Dan and Stu said they wanted to create a more reciprocal relationship. Toward that end, Stu suggested that he and Dan do a better job of "containing their reactions." That way, Dan's annoyance and Stu's fears wouldn't conspire to put Stu in a one-down position. On the face of it, his suggestion makes good sense. But containing reactions can only take people so far. Given the way Dan and Stu see each other when they're upset, their reactions are likely to get so intense that they'll flood whatever dam they build.

To set a new pattern in motion, Dan and Stu will need to do something other than contain their reactions. *They will need to reframe how they see themselves in relation to each other, so they don't have those reactions in the first place—or not so intensely.*

But just how is Stu supposed to do *that*? I suggest that before he does anything, he stop and say to himself: "Wait a second. Maybe Dan doesn't think I'm stupid. Maybe he isn't making me feel exposed. Maybe he's just feeling helpless or anxious. Maybe he needs my help." This mental reminder, informed by the map, takes Dan out of the driver's seat and puts Stu in it, where he stands a much better chance of turning their one-way pattern of interaction on its head.

After making the suggestion, I listen carefully to see whether Stu picks up on it, especially since it goes against the grain of his framing *and* more widely shared assumptions about authority relations. Much to my surprise, far from resisting my suggestion, Stu runs with it, saying, "So when I'm feeling lectured and trying to get him to stop, instead I might listen to him and try to help him." That's right, I tell him. And when he listens, I add, he's going to have to listen with a different ear. Stu suggests he understands this when he goes on to say:

So, when I hear that professorial tone of voice, and I feel criticized and exposed, that has to be a sign for me that something is happening with him, independent of me, and I have to stop and find out what's going on with Dan.

At this point, Dan joins the conversation to acknowledge his tone and to clarify what it means:

I recognize the tone you're describing. It's very censorious. It's like, "Who the hell are you kidding, you stupid idiot." But usually that's a sign that I'm feeling anxious. Unlike you, in those moments I don't freeze. I just sound critical or angry."

This acknowledgment hits Stu hard. For the first time, he can see that Dan really does need his help, and he readies himself to give it. What Dan does next makes it easier to do.

Dan: Reframing Stu

Despite Dan's formal power, he spends a lot of time feeling helpless. The idea that a CEO feels helpless always comes as a surprise to people lower down in organizations. Most people fantasize that CEOs have endless levers at their disposal with which to make things happen—especially if they, not their CEO, were pulling them. Most people can't see or imagine the constraints under which CEOs operate, and those who do often underestimate their effect. What's more, conventional wisdom is adamant about the role CEOs must play: Never show your vulnerabilities. Exude confidence and power. Absorb the anxieties of your subordinates. Never let 'em see you sweat. If you want a friend, get a dog.

In Dan's relationship with Stu, he has an unprecedented opportunity to reframe his role related to subordinates. Right now he's convinced that his subordinates' success depends heavily on his constantly "protecting" them by motivating, pushing, lecturing, inspiring, or cajoling them. Within the confines of this role, he believes it's inappropriate to share his burdens or to ask for emotional support.

When I make this observation, Dan agrees, then offers his own more understated observation in a subdued, almost cynical tone of voice: "I'd say I'm rather conservative when assessing the probability that I'd ever get [emotional support]."

This puts Dan in a terrible position. Convinced that his followers will get hurt without his protection, he must continuously scan his surroundings for signs of danger. Equally convinced that he can't rely on anyone for support, he ends up feeling isolated and burdened. When I suggest as much to Dan, he exclaims, "Exactly! This job's fairly solitary. There are any number of things I can get agitated about and very few people I can talk to about them."

When I suggest that he might talk to Stu and ask for his help, he takes to the idea, at first haltingly, then with more conviction. "You know, you're right," he says, sounding somewhat surprised. "Stu *can* help. I think I can talk about what I'm feeling fairly freely with Stu, and I know I'd find it helpful." Though a modest idea on the surface, it reflects a new way of seeing: maybe Dan can get help, even from those he's felt compelled to protect.

Dan's ready to take the next step.

TAKING ACTION
How to Invent New Frames

Now that you've seen how Dan and Stu invented new frames, here's what you can do to reframe yourself in relation to others.

- Look at the map created in Step 1, depicting how your frames interlock to keep old patterns in place.

- Consider the self-reinforcing nature of your frames—that is, how your frames lead you to act in ways that reinforce the other's frame of you, and so on.

- Help each other invent frames that will create a new pattern. The best frames are those that make it easier for both of you to be at your best.

- Come up with things that you can say to yourself in the heat of the moment to bring the new frame to mind.

- If, based on what you invent, you both want to invest further, proceed to Step 3. If you had any trouble taking Step 2, get help first.

Step 3: Design Frame Experiments

Thinking outside the box—or, better yet, *acting* outside the box—is critical to relationships. Things change, people grow. As a result, opportunities come and go; demands go up and down. In the case of Dan and Stu, the firm's new strategy gives them an opportunity to work more closely together—an opportunity that

STEPS TOWARD CHANGE	
STAGE I **Disrupt**	Assess the Relationship
	Map Patterns of Interaction
	Design Action Experiments
STAGE II **Reframe**	Freeze Frame
	Invent New Frames
	Design Frame Experiments
STAGE III **Revise**	Revisit Past Events
	Restructure Knowledge
	Return to the Future

demands greater interdependence. To take advantage of this opportunity and meet its demands, Dan and Stu want to create a more reciprocal relationship. Toward that end Dan and Stu have already taken two steps: mapping the interlocking frames that put reciprocity out of reach, and inventing frames that promise more give and take. These two steps give them enough conviction to try out new actions. In the third step, they use this conviction to devise *frame experiments*—experiments designed to create experiences that alter their frames, allowing new patterns to emerge.

Taking Small Steps to Make a Big Difference

People often assume that big changes require big moves, but nothing could be farther from the truth. Most people are so fearful of making big moves they do nothing. When it comes to making big changes, all people really need to do is take a series of small steps, each one generating the data and the confidence they need to keep going until bigger changes result.

In Dan and Stu's case, all Dan needs to do—at least at this point—is protect Stu less by censoring himself less; all Stu needs to do is ask Dan what's going on. These two moves will initiate subtle shifts in the informal distribution of burdens and power that defines their relationship. These shifts, while small at first, will invite further moves, eventually creating a pattern with a new look (comrades-in-arms instead of aggressive boss lecturing submissive subordinate), a new feel (less anxious, more connected), and a new function (mutual support instead of unilateral protection).

Though easier to imagine, even the smallest moves can be hard to take, especially if they go against the grain of people's behavioral repertoires or the larger culture. Dan's tendency to lecture and debate in a denigrating tone of voice is deeply ingrained in him *and* shared by many a CEO in our culture. Similarly, Stu's tendency to block anything that might expose his vulnerabilities is also deeply ingrained in him *and* shared by many a subordinate in our culture.

To see if we can alter tendencies that are both deeply ingrained and highly shared, we design a frame experiment for Dan and Stu each to try in the hopes of creating a new pattern.

Designing Stu's Experiment

By the time we reach this third step, Dan and Stu are ready to try something different. But they're having difficulty imagining what that something might look like, because they're so used to seeing each other in a particular light. This dilemma prompts a perplexed Stu to ask me if there's "some routine" he can use to create a new pattern, something that tells him what to do when Dan raises his voice. He then adds, "I'll figure out how to deal with the emotions once I've got the behavior down, but it would help to have some kind of routine to try."

This comment suggests that Stu intuitively grasps the paradox of this stage. *He's going to have to act his way into feeling differently, not feel his way into acting differently.*[5] When I go on to suggest two routines, we have a short but telling exchange:

Diana: One routine is to tell yourself, "Oops, Dan is in trouble." But you'll have to say that to yourself whether you believe it or not [chuckling].

Stu: [Also chuckling] That's the point. I don't have to believe it. I'm not looking for something I have to believe yet.

Diana: The next thing is to say out loud, "Dan, what's going on?" That's all. Nothing else.

Stu: Okay, I'll give it a try.

Stu is one step ahead of me here. He understands that he doesn't have to believe Dan's in trouble. He simply has to act *as if* he believes it. While Stu's ready to give it a try, I suspect he's more apt to succeed if he can connect the new move to the pattern we're trying to change. With this in mind, I go on to observe:

When you freeze and say, "Dan, I'm stuck," or "Dan, stop!" you keep the pattern the way it's always been: Dan helping you get unstuck and you responding to all that "help." You completely change that pattern by saying "Dan, what's going on?" and then listening to him. With that one move, you'll learn a lot about how he ticks, and he'll be much more able to recoup.

Like all frame experiments, this one is designed to create experiences that his old framing can't. Up until now, it hadn't occurred to Stu to ask Dan how he's feeling. This made it impossible for him to see Dan's vulnerabilities or to help him. By asking Dan what's going on, Stu will act *as if* Dan needs help, leading him to discover that Dan often feels as anxious as he does, and to see that he (Stu) has the power to help Dan handle his anxieties more effectively. *Once Stu sees and experiences these things for himself, his old frame will shift, leading him to feel and do things differently—without having to think about it. It will just come naturally.*

Designing Dan's Experiment

Dan would be the first to argue that people need an appropriate amount of autonomy and control to succeed. But when pressures mount, he has trouble figuring out how much (or what kind) of control and autonomy is appropriate. Like many CEOs, he often finds himself erring between two extremes: Sometimes he exerts too much control, other times too little. Sometimes he gives people too much autonomy, other times too little. Sometimes these differences reflect a conscious choice; other times—too many times—he feels compelled to do one or the other, because like many CEOs, he feels trapped in a dilemma that goes something like this:

▶ If I give people more autonomy and exert less control, they're more likely to fail, get hurt, harm others or the business, and ultimately blame me.

▶ Yet if I give people less autonomy and exert more control, they're more likely to *feel* like failures, get hurt, harm others or the business, and ultimately blame me.

Caught between two equally troubling options, Dan often finds himself in a no-win situation. The best he can do is bounce back and forth between the two, dissatisfied with the results each option produces. Going forward, any experiment we design will have to address this dilemma and address it better than his current oscillating approach does.

We have our first chance to design such an experiment during a business meeting in which Stu presents some ideas for Focuspoint's new Web site. Excited by the new technology, Dan jumps in to build on Stu's ideas. Stu, who rebuffs Dan, says his suggestions are too complicated to implement. When Dan asks why, Stu cites imperfections in Merrimac's current accounting system, saying they make Dan's suggestions impractical. Upset that Stu would accept such imperfections, Dan challenges and debates Stu's argument in the same way he has in the past.

Only this time things turn out differently. Before the argument can spin out of control, we stop the action and design a frame experiment for Dan to try. The exchange that follows begins after I ask Dan how he's hearing Stu, so I can see how he's framing things:

Dan: I hear him putting forth what are to me two equally absurd possibilities. One possibility is that we're going to be *completely* incompetent for the rest of our lives and *never* learn how to keep track of time. I think the financial accounting system *is completely* unacceptable. But it's not going to stay that way, full stop! So if someone can't keep track of time, fire 'em!

Diana: Tell me the second thing you hear that's "absurd."

Dan: He thinks I'm suggesting that we keep track of every 30 minutes we spend [explains why he's not saying that]. I don't think what I'm suggesting is an enormously complex system. But what Stu's proposing *is* complicated. It will *never* be understood by *anybody* and, since they won't understand it, *they won't buy it.*

Diana: Let me ask you a question—

Dan: [Interrupting] I don't understand what the BIG problem is—

Diana: [Interrupting] And you'll never understand as long as you ask it that way!

Dan: [Laughing] Probably. But I thought you were going to say, "as long as I live."

Stu: [Also laughing] I'll tape your mouth shut; maybe then you'll understand!

Dan's hyperbolic statements alone indicate he's *very* upset: "We're going to be *completely* incompetent for the rest of our lives," "It will *never* be understood by *anybody*," "If someone can't keep track of time, fire 'em!" It's easy to see from these cascading exclamations, each one delivered in a contemptuous tone, that Dan's button is pushed. But we can't yet see what that button is or how Stu pushed it.

That's why, when he disdainfully concludes, "I don't understand what the BIG problem is," I counter with "And you'll never understand as long as you ask it that way!" This unexpected response stops Dan in his tracks, and he laughs at himself: "I thought you were going to say, 'as long as I live.' " The tension broken, Stu can now poke fun at Dan ("I'll tape your mouth shut"), while I can use the moment to ask him what he's feeling, prompting him to reflect:

Dan: At first, I felt excited about what Stu was doing and the ideas I had about how he might go about it. Then there was a very short period of genuine mystification, because I didn't understand what the big problem was with what I was suggesting. Then there was a period of, "Oh my God, maybe he's really saying"—and this is the real nightmare scenario—"'I, Stu, designed this system around a structural failure of the company,'" which will only preserve the structural failure of the company. So I'm thinking, "That's not an option." That's a real hot button for me.

Stu: Yeah, you clearly got mad about something, and I couldn't figure out what it was.

Dan: It was all the stuff about, "I don't trust us to be competent. Maybe in the year 2020, but not now."

Stu: I understand. But I don't get mad about stuff like that. So I didn't quite know what you were reacting to or what to react to myself, so it just spiraled until all of a sudden, I felt, "I can't even talk about this now." That's when I shut down. Still, there was a little voice saying, "Why am I shutting down?" Now I can see: it's because of the anger!

From this exchange we learn two things. First, we learn that Stu's comment inadvertently activated Dan's nightmare scenario: the firm's imperfections will persist because people like Stu will design around them, forever dooming the firm to mediocrity. Within the confines of this framing, Dan sees Stu putting the firm at risk, which obligates him to grab the wheel from Stu so he can put himself in the driver's seat, as he's done in the past. Second, we learn that while Stu can see that Dan's upset, he can't fathom why. All he knows is that Dan is bearing down on him, talking faster and louder with each passing second. And so Stu freezes, as he has in the past.

Only, this time Stu's got this "little voice"—this more reflective voice—asking him why he's shutting down, as if it might not be the only response possible. And this time, Dan turns on a dime, switching from a highly agitated state of mind to a highly reflective one.

In a matter of seconds, we're able to convert a bad moment into an opportunity to deepen our understanding of the relationship. Dan, who can now talk more freely, can recount with much greater clarity how his feelings went from excitement to mystification to anxiety and anger. He can also name the button Stu pushed—his "nightmare scenario"—and he can put his finger on what pushed it: Stu's comment about the accounting system.

This gives Stu a much better understanding of Dan. He can now see that Dan's reactions say something not just about Stu but about Dan— what triggers him and how he reacts. What's more, Stu can see why he shuts down in those moments: "It's because of the anger!" That anger— and the uncertainty about its source—is just too much for him.

With these insights under our belts, we begin to design Dan's frame experiment. No longer caught up in his reactions, Stu steps in to help, offering a suggestion that Dan then builds on:

Stu: If you said something like, "People say that all the time around here, and it drives me crazy," I would have said, "Huh. It kind of drives me crazy too, although I don't get that mad about it."

Dan: I was actually trying to do that in the moment, but I couldn't because it took me a while to figure out what I was mad about. Sometimes I know what I'm mad about but not today.

Stu: Yes, I've seen that.

Dan: Maybe it would change the pattern if I just said, "Let me think out loud for a moment," or "Stu, are you saying we have to keep these bad systems until 2020? If you are, what you're saying is making me nervous, because in my mind, you're speaking to something very fundamental."

By helping Dan design his frame experiment, Stu conducts his own. Throughout this exchange, he's helping Dan, not blocking him, which allows him to find out more about what makes Dan tick. He discovers that Dan gets mad about things that don't trouble Stu that much, making it easier for Stu to help Dan in those moments. In the end they come up with something new for Dan to try: *say what's going on with you, not what's wrong with others,* and *ask for help if you don't know what's going on with you.*

If Dan makes these moves, he will see for himself that people like Stu can be of help, at least some of the time, and that he doesn't need to protect them, at least not all of the time. And once Dan sees that, his frame will shift, leading him to relax more and worry less.

The men's ability to recoup in this meeting is encouraging, as is their ability to learn from what happened. It indicates that they're ready to recast the way they see themselves in relation to each other and equally ready to conduct experiments to see if they can make that recasting come true. Over the next few months, Stu made a point of asking Dan what was going on when he seemed irritated or impatient, and Dan responded by telling him directly what he was feeling and reflecting with Stu on what those feelings said about the two of them and their relationship. These experiments gradually gave rise to a more reciprocal pattern—one with less protection and more give and take. As a result, they no longer felt as constrained as they had in the past, allowing them to pick up the pace with which Focuspoint got up and running.

TAKING ACTION
How to Design a Frame Experiment

Now that you've seen how we designed Dan and Stu's frame experiments, here's what you can do to design a few of your own.

- Look at the frames you invented at the beginning of this stage and ask, *If I thought this frame was true, what would I say and do?*

- Let your partner know when you're experimenting and ask for his or her help in interpreting the results.

- When interpreting the results, don't look to confirm old frames; look for even subtle shifts—either in what happened or in your experience.

- If you can't find any, look at the actions you took and see if they really do follow from the new frame.

- If they do, reconsider the frame you invented to see if it is really new or just a slight variation on an old theme.

- Depending on what you learn, either stay the course, or go back and redesign the experiment.

- If, based on the experiment, you both want to invest further, proceed to Stage III. If you had difficulty with Stage II, get help before proceeding.

Stage II Results

By the end of this stage, Dan and Stu's frame experiments have led them to reframe how they see themselves in relation to each other. Stu now sees that when Dan starts debating and lecturing, he's usually feeling helpless and anxious, prompting him to help Dan rather than freeze or block. This leads Dan to revise his view that Stu needs a lot of protection, and it opens up the possibility of getting emotional support from Stu. This relaxes Dan and makes it easier for him to talk about his anxieties directly, which makes them less mystifying and troubling for Stu.

These experiences—experiences they couldn't create within the confines of their old frames—give rise to new ways of seeing and set in motion a more virtuous cycle of interaction.

By the end of this stage, Dan and Stu are able to do several things they couldn't do before:

▶ Use upsetting moments to learn, so they can change themselves and their interactions more quickly and effectively;
▶ Make progress on controversial tasks more quickly and effectively;
▶ Operate more freely within the relationship (less walking on eggshells) *and* with a greater sense of connection (more camaraderie, less adversity).

As a result, when Dan and Stu differ on substantive matters, they're less likely to get bogged down, and if they do, they're more able to recoup. At the same time, they continue to get into trouble when they're under intense pressure, because this second stage of change poses a dilemma:

▸ On the one hand, the only way people can reframe one another is to say how they see and feel about each other when they're upset.
▸ On the other hand, saying how they see and feel about each other when they're upset runs the risk of pushing the other person's buttons and resurrecting old patterns.

Left unresolved, this dilemma can slow down the pace of change or bring it to a halt. Efforts to resolve it, however, catapult people into the next stage of change. During that stage, people explore what their reactions say about them and how they view the world *independently* of the other person. As we'll see with Dan and Stu, this exploration prompts them to reexamine and restructure the experiential knowledge they use to frame each other, strengthening their relationship and enhancing their leadership.

7
Revise What You "Know" to Be True

If it's hysterical, it's probably historical.

—**Michelle Conlin**[1]

Dan and Stu came by their quirks honestly: they learned them. Over the years—as they grew up at home, went off to school, and took up careers at work—they converted one experience after another into knowledge about how to handle different people and situations. When they first met, they drew on this *experiential knowledge* to set the structural foundation of their relationship. Now it is only by restructuring that knowledge that they can reset it. This brings us to the third and last paradox of change: *to move forward, they must go back and revisit the knowledge they bring to their relationship.* This chapter shows how Dan and Stu did this by taking three steps:

> **Step 1:** Revisit Past Events
> **Step 2:** Restructure Outdated Knowledge
> **Step 3:** Return to the Future

By revisiting historical events in the context of their relationship, Dan and Stu are able to create new knowledge out of current events. By the end of this stage, they're able to use this knowledge to accelerate their growth and the growth of the firm.

Step 1: Revisit Past Events

Dan and Stu have already traveled a long distance. By the time they reach this last stage of change, they've not only suc-ceeded in disrupting a highly entrenched pattern, they've set a more flexible one in motion. Still, when pressure mounts and time dwindles, they continue to get caught in the old pattern, and they will

STEPS TOWARD CHANGE	
STAGE I Disrupt	Assess the Relationship
	Map Patterns of Interaction
	Design Action Experiments
STAGE II Reframe	Freeze Frame
	Invent New Frames
	Design Frame Experiments
STAGE III Revise	Revisit Past Events
	Restructure Knowledge
	Return to the Future

continue to do so until the newer, more flexible pattern takes hold—that is, when it becomes a more enduring structure. To convert an unstable pattern into a more stable structure, we explore the events[2] and capture the knowledge that prevent new patterns from taking hold.[3] For continuity's sake, I start with Stu, then turn to Dan.

Stu: Avoiding the Limelight

Like all of us, Stu has a large stock of experiential knowledge at his dis-posal, only a fraction of which comes into play with Dan. Our attention, then, is focused only on that knowledge he used first to form, then to build the structure underlying his relationship with Dan. Within this structure, you might recall, Stu is prone to viewing Dan as an aggressive driver relentlessly bearing down on him, while viewing himself as the proverbial deer in the headlights with no means of defending himself. Seeing things this way, Stu feels his only options are to freeze and block or to duck and cover whenever Dan begins to debate or lecture.

To alter this structure, we have to understand what leads Stu to see things this way and not another. After all, while many senior leaders at Merrimac find it difficult to deal with Dan in his worst moments, not everyone views him the way Stu does, nor do they interact with him in the same way. To get at Stu's part in the structure, we need to figure out what Stu brings to the relationship independently of Dan. What he brings, we discover, is his own history.

We got our first glimmer of this history when Dan made what he assumed was a benign suggestion—namely, that Stu hire a "chief of staff" to help him manage his expanding responsibilities. Much to our surprise, the idea horrified Stu, who saw in it everything he dreads about advancing as a leader. In the course of exploring his reactions, we discovered the source of Stu's dread, and along with it, the historical origins of his reactions to Dan and other leaders at Merrimac. We launched our exploration right after Stu made fun of his trepidation:

> *Diana:* I know you're joking, but what's the trepidation?
>
> *Stu:* It makes me feel overexposed, more important than I am—all the things I don't like: being onstage, being noticed, and being different. I can't just stand up and do what Dan did the other day: give a terrific speech off the top of his head. That stuff just doesn't come naturally to me. I don't know what to do, I know I'm going to look silly, and I know it shows. All my emotions are perfectly visible, and I feel as if everyone's looking at me and laughing at me and I get very nervous.
>
> *Diana:* I think *you* start looking at you.
>
> *Stu:* I do!

Stu's account told us a lot about what he does and doesn't "know" when he's onstage, either figuratively or literally: he *knows* he's going to look silly, he *knows* it's going to show, and he doesn't have a clue what to do about it. In his mind every one of his emotions, which he now feels acutely, is there for everyone to see and ridicule. Stu's anxieties start to mount, he starts to fumble, and his worst fears are realized.

A few minutes later, Stu connected his fears to a voice mail he sent Dan earlier in the week, giving us an opportunity to trace their origins.

> As I reflect on this fear of being laughed at, something else just popped up, which is that incredibly intemperate voice mail I sent to you, Dan, about my work on [New Product]. That voice mail is connected to this. You took something that I had a suspicion wasn't going to be very good, and you exposed it to three people who can devastate me.

I just made a connection to why I went through the roof. So what led me to go off like that? It's obviously tapping into something that's very close to the surface.

Stu's language is revealing: he feels *exposed* when his *not very good work* is given to people who can *devastate* him, sending him *through the roof*. This way of capturing his experience reveals two things: the theme implicated in his reactions—exposure—and how close to the surface the events are that gave rise to that theme, as his answer to my next question confirms:

Diana: So what do you imagine is going to happen when they look at your work?

Stu: I'll get laughed at. Get rejected. I spent a lot of time having that happen as a kid. Up until I was about thirteen years old, I lived in a neighborhood where everybody had been in the same neighborhood for a long time, and we all went to the same elementary school together. I was a pretty oddball kid, and I wasn't particularly good at athletics, so the other kids would laugh at me and run away. And then there was the classic joke, "Invite Stu over and then not be there." [After a pause] You know, it's funny. I haven't thought about this for years. When you asked why I had a really hard time, my first reaction was, "I don't know why. It just is." But then it came to me: I'm afraid somebody's going to laugh at me just like they did when I was a kid.

Many of us underestimate the residual effects of childhood events like these. But these kinds of events—no matter what they are or why they matter—live on well into adulthood, shaping how we see ourselves and the people around us. While the events themselves may fade into the fog of memory, the feelings they generate often remain as sharp as the moment they occurred, as Stu suggested when he went on to say:

I don't remember everything that happened exactly, but I do remember the humiliation and the anger, and I have a very keen sense of the

degree to which children are, for the most part, immensely cruel creatures. I hated childhood. I was always an outcast.

You can see in these two remarks what Stu took from his childhood:
that he's an oddball, an outcast, while his peers are immensely cruel creatures. This conception of himself in relation to others lives on into the
present despite his becoming a highly respected and well-liked head of a
successful business unit. Had Stu not eventually learned how to navigate
his childhood circumstances successfully, he wouldn't have made it that
far. But he did. In fact, by the time he was seventeen, he'd managed to
transform himself from an outcast into a popular success, working on the
school paper, getting good grades, and winning wrestling matches. "All
of a sudden, I was worth talking to," he says with a note of disdain before
adding:

> That whole experience, combined with staying out of trouble with my
> father, led me to think, "Don't get noticed. If you get noticed, some-
> body's going to laugh at you, especially if you make a mistake or you
> look weird." I still have this intense dislike of being laughed at, and I
> still have a huge amount of contempt for these people.

Stu's intense dislike of being laughed at is matched only by his equally
intense conviction that it's inevitable, and that some people—those who
resemble his peers at school or his father at home—have the power to
devastate him. That conviction is directly connected to his relationship
with Dan and to his current model of success as a leader:

> My model for success is, "Never let anyone see you coming." When I
> ended up at the top of my class in college, people were literally saying,
> "Where did *he* come from?" That's just fine with me. I like coming up
> from behind. It feels safer. I work hard, I keep my head down, I don't
> bother people, and I show up at the top. I hate being out front. I hate
> it viscerally.

You can see in Stu's account how the theme of exposure emerged.
You can also see how this theme, once it had taken hold, activated intense

emotions—fear, anger, contempt—all of which acted like Velcro, both attracting and attaching to it:

▶ *Stories:* When I was a kid, other kids invited me over, then wouldn't be there.
▶ *Propositions:* If you get noticed, somebody will laugh at you. If you work hard, keep your head down, and don't bother people, you will show up at the top.
▶ *Moral Values:* Looking more important than you are is bad. Coming up from behind is good. Mistakes are bad. Success is good.
▶ *Action Strategies:* Stay out of trouble and don't get noticed.

This stock of knowledge may have served Stu well in the past, but it was interfering with his relationships and with his development as a leader now. Understanding this, Stu was eager to see if he could restructure this knowledge. But before illustrating how he did so, let's first look at the events that shaped Dan's life, what he made of those events, and their effect on his relationship with Stu.

Dan: Protecting Against Catastrophic Loss

In turning to Dan, we set out to understand where his debating and lecturing behavior came from. We could see that Stu's freezing and blocking triggered these behaviors, but we couldn't see what led Dan to respond this way and not another. And while we now understood that Dan's anger was rooted in anxiety, we didn't understand where that anxiety came from. We knew Dan worried about people getting hurt and perhaps blaming him, but what led him to worry about that and not something else? And what led him to convert his worry into those contemptuous lectures tailor-made to push Stu's buttons?

Until we understood this, Dan was apt to revert to old patterns under stress. We got our first chance to explore these questions during a meeting in which I broached my puzzlement:

This sensitivity to people getting hurt—and this feeling compelled to do something about it—you have to ask yourself the question: what did you learn such that you're left with this idea that people will get hurt and that only you can do something about it?

In turning to this question, Dan recounted not a single event but two streams of events, each one raising the specter of loss and the need to rely on himself, unprotected by others. The first set of events took place when he was a child living with his family in a Third World country:

> When I was a little kid, I mostly worried—not that something bad would happen *from* my parents—but that something bad would happen *to* my parents. If I got a "D" on my report card, yes, I was worried on that day about their reaction. But my big fear was that my parents would get killed and I'd be left without them. My first memory of life—any memory I have—is of dead bodies. I can date it almost to the day. I was two years old.

Dan went on to recount how his family had traveled that day from the country's capital to a summer resort, accompanied by a military convoy due to recent fighting between the government and communist guerrillas. A few hours into the drive, the convoy came to a halt:

> Everyone was sitting there in these clanking jeeps armed with machine guns. It was horribly hot. Finally, a guy came down the line, tapping on the windows, telling us, "We'll be here for a while. You can get out." As we got out, on the ground were six to nine people lying there, stretched out in Vietnam-style pictures, all of them dead, one of them with a bullet in his head. We all looked at them for a while, then drove away. That's the first memory I have.

After saying "the whole thing was much more interesting than scary," he explained:

> The searing memories—the ones that are terrifying—aren't actually of dead people, because they're already dead. It's these horribly deformed people—the people with flies all over their suppurating stumps. I remember walking on these sidewalks. You'd know it's coming.

They're on the sidewalk, and they're begging. You're going to have to walk right by them, and you're going to be two feet away, although when you're a kid, you're even closer. Half the time the adults are in some chitchat, and you're not sure they even notice. Even now, I get the willies a little bit when I think about it, although not really. Now there are the shades that come down over my eyes.

But before those shades descended, I ask, what did he make of this, and how did he feel about it?

You worried. You're in a part of the world where you see dead bodies, and you aren't really sure what your parents are doing. They'd simply go out, and you'd stay home. I spent a lot of time worrying about whether my parents would come home, whether something might happen to them. I was always very glad they got home.

After months of making his way around suppurating stumps and the occasional dead body, Dan concluded that the world is a pretty dangerous place. This conclusion—coupled with the specter of losing his parents—left Dan worried. He couldn't help but imagine the worst. He may even have believed that by imagining the worst, he could stop the worst from happening. After all, whenever he worried, his parents came home.

Small wonder that Dan entered adulthood with a nonstop engine of anxiety. But where and how did he learn to convert that anxiety into contempt? Later on in the same meeting, we got the beginnings of an answer when Dan recounted a second stream of events:

I always felt loved by my parents. But as far back as I can remember my father could be very caustic and emotional in his criticism. I don't know whether I ever consciously worried I would lose his love, but I sure as hell wanted his respect, and I *knew* I could lose that, especially when he'd say that bewildered "How could you think *that*?!"

The tone with which Dan mimicked his father was uncanny, almost eerie: it's the very tone he uses when *he's* anxious. When I pointed this out, Dan stopped in his tracks. "I guess I *am* my father at times," he told me. "While I hate and fear the idea, I also feel a great sense of relief. It's like, 'Oh, is that what it is?' At least now I can think about it." In thinking about it, we went on to explore what led Dan to adopt his father's voice as his own, piecing together this paraphrased account:

Early on, like most sons, Dan cherished his relationship with his father and felt secure in his affections. He spoke with tenderness about how his dad, a warm and emotional man, would hold his hand as they walked down the street, giving each other a quick squeeze—their secret way of saying "I love you." When it came to his dad's respect, however, things felt more tenuous. Throughout Dan's childhood, his dad held him to exacting standards, expected exceptional performance at school, and demanded compliance through example and critique.

His dad, who treated people graciously no matter their social status, elicited admiration and respect everywhere he went. As a parent, he expected no less of his kids, and he let them know it whenever they fell short. Dan, ever anxious to secure his dad's respect, worked hard to live up to his expectations and dreaded his admonishments, especially when they were delivered in that slightly bewildered, contemptuous tone of voice he used when disappointed.

As Dan grew older, he grew tired of his dad's caustic comments, and like many teenagers, felt they were unfair and unreasonable. No longer willing to take it, Dan started to fight back. Figuring the best defense was a good offense, he started to lash out at his dad with the same caustic, contemptuous tone his dad used with him. Much to Dan's surprise, his father backed down. Soon Dan found himself winning arguments he used to lose, making it harder and harder for his dad to assert his authority.

During this same time, his father got increasingly caught up in his own midlife troubles. More interested in his own happiness than in his children's welfare—at least in Dan's eyes—Dan felt abandoned and let down. Outraged by his dad's apparent selfishness, Dan stopped seeing his father as the loving dad with whom he'd held hands. Now all he saw was an unreliable, self-indulgent kid masquerading as an adult. At this point, as far as Dan was concerned, his dad was gone; he could no longer rely on him.

The specter of loss in a dangerous land, combined with the loss of his father, had a profound effect on Dan, eventually giving rise to the twin themes of loss and reliability. Now anytime circumstances activate these themes, Dan experiences intense anxiety, which he instantly converts into the anger and contempt he first saw in his father, then adopted as his own to protect himself. As was the case with Stu, these emotions act like Velcro, simultaneously attracting and attaching to his themes a rich stock of knowledge, including:

▶ *Stories:* When I was a kid, I lived amid suffering and violence, where my parents were at risk of getting killed any time they went out.
▶ *Propositions:* If you want to win an argument or protect your esteem, discount and denigrate others before they discount and denigrate you. If you constantly imagine the worst, you can prevent it from happening. And, if you want someone to rely on, get a dog; people will just let you down.
▶ *Moral Values:* People in power who act like self-sufficient adults are good; those who act like self-indulgent kids are bad. Depending on oneself is good; depending on others is bad. Taking care of others is good; taking care of yourself is selfish.
▶ *Action Strategies:* Never rely on anyone if you can avoid it, especially men. Take care of unreliable others as you wish they'd take care of you. Anticipate how others will let you down and inoculate yourself against any disappointment.

This stock of knowledge may have served Dan well in the past, but as Merrimac grew—and along with it, Dan's need to rely on others—it was breaking down. It was time to see if he could restructure this knowledge in the context of his relationship with Stu and others at Merrimac.

TAKING ACTION
How to Revisit Past Events

Now that you've seen what Dan and Stu did to revisit past events and to capture their experiential knowledge, here's how you can take this step:

- Figure out what kind of help you need to make the most of this step and be sure to get it.

- With that help, identify the historical events that most remind you of this relationship.

- Write down what happened in those earlier moments and what you took or learned from them. Put aside what you wrote for 24 hours.

- Go back and read what you wrote; then extract from your account any stories, propositions, values, and practical strategies you see, as I did here.

- Explore how the knowledge you've built out of past experience is affecting your development and your relationships, including this one.

- If you think your past is jeopardizing your success or the success of key relationships, proceed to Step 2—but only after lining up the help you'll need to make the most of it.

Step 2: Restructure Outdated Knowledge

Now that we had a better window into the knowledge Dan and Stu used to form their relationship, we were ready to take the next step: resetting the basis of their relationship by restructuring the experiential knowledge they bring to it. To help Dan and Stu take this step, I created several documents based on what you've

STEPS TOWARD CHANGE	
STAGE I **Disrupt**	Assess the Relationship
	Map Patterns of Interaction
	Design Action Experiments
STAGE II **Reframe**	Freeze Frame
	Invent New Frames
	Design Frame Experiments
STAGE III **Revise**	Revisit Past Events
	Restructure Knowledge
	Return to the Future

just read. With these documents in hand, we were able to consider two questions: where is their experiential knowledge breaking down, and how can we restructure it so that it better fits their current circumstances and abilities? The following pages recount where these questions led us.

Stu: Turning the Light on Others

We started out by asking how Stu's knowledge was holding up. Not so well, we quickly discovered. Indeed, this became glaringly obvious as soon as Stu connected what he'd learned so far to his longstanding difficulties with George Quipsalot, another leader at Merrimac.

> This is why I have so much trouble with George: he can make fun of me in a way that makes me feel defenseless. I don't think he intends to be cruel, and I don't think he has a clue that he makes my skin crawl. But when he gets really sarcastic, he's my worst nightmare from high school: popular, always has something to say, never at a loss. Completely my opposite.

In Stu's nightmarish way of seeing things, he and George *are* complete opposites: George is popular, Stu's an outcast; George is never at a loss, Stu's always at a loss; George always has something to say, Stu never has anything to say. So even though you'd be hard-pressed to find a more popular leader at Merrimac, or one who had more to say, Stu still sees himself as that oddball kid surrounded by people all too ready to make fun of him.

This example, fresh in Stu's mind, gave us our first opportunity to entertain three possibilities that had never occurred to Stu. First, Stu's "come from behind" theory, while serving him well in the past, was now breaking down under the pressures of a role that required him to go on-stage and to look important—in short, to be exposed. Second, the be-havior Stu saw as evidence of George's cruelty might just as easily be viewed as evidence of his vulnerabilities. Third, although Stu may have been defenseless as a kid, he was far from defenseless now. In point of fact, he was a man of many talents with a remarkable intellect and a good deal of social and political capital.

Stu readily accepted the first two ideas: that his "come from behind" theory wouldn't work in his new role and that sarcasm could indicate vulnerability as much as cruelty. But he had trouble accepting the notion that he (Stu) wasn't defenseless. "The only way I know how to defend myself," he told us, "is to put up an impenetrable shield."

Dan disagreed. "I wouldn't underestimate the degree to which people see you as a pretty formidable debater," he told him. "When you're in your comfort zone, the other person has to watch out, or he may lose." He then drove the point home by returning to George:

> Dan: Sometimes when George gets sarcastic, it's like one of those classic tricks: he's losing the game, and so he knocks the table over. In an argument with you, it's, "Say something sarcastic about Stu, so he'll dissolve and leave me alone." I'm not saying he does it consciously, but I think he's got great antennae, and he'll do the "Hey, look at that bird!" as a way of distracting you while he regroups and tries to figure out what to do next.
>
> Stu: [After a brief pause] What you just said clicked seriously.

By placing George in a one-down position relative to Stu, Dan not only gave Stu another way of seeing George, he gave him another way of seeing himself relative to George: it was Stu, not George, who was win-ning the game! What's more, Stu's arguments were so powerful that the other guy—in this case, George—had to resort to card tricks to regain the upper hand. The implication was clear. It was no longer, "If you want to win the game, keep your head down and stay out of trouble." It was more like, "If you want to win the game, don't fall for the card trick." This time, the recasting worked: what Dan said "clicked seriously."

Stu now saw that his success as a leader would, in part, depend on his putting the past where it belonged: in the past. This made his relationship with Dan critical, because that relationship was slowly but surely helping him restructure how he saw himself in relation to people in power, as he illustrated a few weeks later with the following story:

> Last week I got into a tough discussion with Jack Gregory, a very smart CEO who's very much a debater. We'd been debating whether he should buy another company, and for a whole host of reasons, I thought it was a bad idea and told him so, at which point, he turned to me and said: "If the answer isn't buying another company to get bigger, what are we supposed to do? You haven't proved that what you suggest will work or is feasible." At first, I broke out in a sweat. But then I said to myself, "No, this guy's struggling with something. He doesn't know he's putting me in a box by asking me to prove something that can't be proved. Maybe if I find out what he's worried about, we can start to get out of the box."

What's notable about this vignette isn't so much that Stu found a way out of an adversarial dynamic, although he did. It's that he was able to shift his attention away from his vulnerabilities and onto the other guy's struggles. From this new vantage point, he could see a way out of the box: he didn't have to erect an impenetrable shield; he could ask what was worrying the CEO.

Out of this experience and others like it, Stu gradually restructured his concept of himself in relationship to others. In each case, he revised outdated knowledge and built new knowledge about how to conduct himself as a leader in relationship to others. No longer seeing either his peers or his superiors as the cruel or all-powerful bullies from his childhood, he understood that people like Dan, George, and Jack have their own vulnerabilities. More important, he came to see that he was neither defenseless nor at a loss for words, but someone capable of talking his way out of boxes and even helping others when *they're* at a loss.

As this suggests, Stu was able to generalize from his relationship with Dan to other relationships like those with Jack and George. In the next step, this process of generalization accelerates and deepens. But before seeing how, let's take a look at what Dan did to restructure the knowledge he'd built around the theme of reliability.

Dan: Learning to Rely on Others

For twenty years Merrimac had been growing quickly in size and complexity, putting more and more pressure on Dan's role at the center of the firm. From a structural perspective the problem was as simple as it was hard to solve: too many people were looking to him for too much, while he was looking to too few people for too little. The balance of trade—that delicate exchange of give-and-take—was out of whack, and it was putting a ceiling on the growth of the firm and its leaders, including Dan. Like most problems of this kind, it has many causes. But one of the most important ones is the implicit premise that *it's dangerous to rely on people* and the associated strategy to *always be on guard to make sure really bad things don't happen.* As Dan said early on:

> You have to be suspicious of the people you rely on. It's dangerous not to be, because people have weaknesses. Even strong people have weaknesses. . . . If I were to hold forth on whether you should be intimate as a leader, I'd say, "Look, one of the things you can't do is be unilaterally intimate with people. As a leader, that's not going to work, because you're either going to put stuff on them they can't deal with, and, despite their best efforts, they will become unproductive, or they will take what you have given them and abuse someone with it. On average, they'll not be able to handle it. You have to be selective."

Most people would agree that you have to be selective. The trouble is that, when assessing someone's reliability, many people make two mistakes. The first is to compare the other person's weaknesses to their strengths, making the person *look* a lot less reliable. The second and less-detectable mistake is to act in ways that bring out the worst in the other person, as Dan did with Stu, making him *act* less reliably.

Having observed Dan make both errors, I might have suggested, as I initially did, that he discuss his doubts and concerns more openly with people to sort through any biases he might have and to put some of his worries to rest. But given the state of his relationships—and his concept of his role relative to others—such advice wasn't very practical, as Dan demonstrated when he said:

> I *know* what's going to happen. They'll probably cave in and collapse. They'll say, "Dan thinks so little of me," or, "I'm so hapless," or "I can't get this. I'm going to give up." "I'm going to go somewhere else." "I'm going to go off in a corner and die."

Notice his line of thinking here. If he tells people what he really thinks, he *knows* what's going to happen. Either they'll "die," as he worried his parents might, or they'll "cave in and collapse," as his father did. Either way, he can't rely on them. This makes talking openly about doubts, concerns, and criticisms a very weighty matter, as Dan himself went on to explain:

> Deciding whether to proceed is a very heavy decision. It's like the judge who's thinking about whether to sign a death sentence: do I really want to do that? A lot of these people will leave, and for some of them, it's absolutely the wrong thing to do. They're better off here. What you want is for them to accept something as real that they don't want to face. What you don't want is for them to blow their brains out. But you can make them do that pretty easily. I've seen it happen frequently.

Dan talked here as if he has the power, as judge, to determine whether someone lives or dies. If he tells people the truth, they'll leave, which is the equivalent of blowing their brains out. Since he's seen it "happen frequently," he's trapped. And since he can "make them do it pretty easily," he can't get out of that trap without killing someone.

To free himself, Dan was going to have to see that the problem, which he located exclusively outside of himself, also resided inside his head—that is, in the knowledge he'd built out of experience. This knowledge primed him to see himself (as a leader), his followers, and stressful situations in a particularly lethal and anxiety-producing light *and* to act accordingly, signaling to people that they could rely on him while telling himself he couldn't rely on them. Given the lopsided nature of this implicit contract, Dan found exactly what he expected to find: people looking to him for reassurance or motivation, people getting upset when he didn't provide it, and people blaming him for the upset. No surprise that by the time we began our work together, Dan couldn't count on most of the people around him.

This reality, which is partly of Dan's making, poses a dilemma. If I simply tell him to rely more on others, I'll be doing to Dan what everyone else is doing: relying on him to bear a disproportionate share of the burden for solving the problem.

This is why the work with Stu is so important, and why it's so important that Stu take the lead even though he's the nominal follower. Here's someone who's ready to challenge Dan's way of thinking while remaining open to challenge himself. The fact that Stu can still get anxious and upset from time to time is all for the better, because—despite his imperfections—he doesn't leave and he doesn't collapse, nor does he die or kill anyone else. He simply hangs in there, earning Dan's respect and the right to challenge the way Dan thinks:

Stu: I think you expect certain things of leaders and you get particularly mad when people don't act that way.

Dan: That's probably true, but I'm trying to figure out who you've got in mind versus who I have in mind when you say that.

Stu: [Lists the names of people] Including me, on occasion, although not much until recently, given I was coming up from behind [laughing].

Dan: [Also laughing] That's helpful. That's a very important group of people.

Stu: The interesting thing for me is that you start out cutting these people a lot of slack, but then it tips, and you don't cut them *any* slack *at all*. Oftentimes it's unclear where your tipping point is [goes on to give an example].

Observations like these, coming from Stu, are much more powerful than any I can make, because they communicate two messages simultaneously. First, they tell Dan that he can count on Stu to tell him the truth without complaining or blaming him. Thus the medium is the message: Stu's matter-of-fact but warm tone, neither condemning nor softening what he sees and says, commands Dan's attention and respect. Second, the observations themselves focus on Dan's "expectations" and on Dan's "tipping point"—putting a spotlight on Dan's internal workings for the first time. This combination of messages—*you can rely on me* and *let's take a look at you*—turns Dan's attention to what goes on inside his head.

In shifting to what goes on inside Dan's head, we discussed three documents, in which I reconstructed the experiential knowledge Dan had built around the theme of reliability. The first document, based on the data you see in this chapter, captured Dan's personal narrative around reliability. According to this narrative, the only way Dan can ensure a happy ending is to do all he can to protect people whose character flaws blind them to the dangers around them. In reality, things don't turn out so well. Once enacted, all this narrative does is leave Dan feeling burdened, resentful, and trapped at the center of the Merrimac universe.

Still, as soon as someone's reliability is called into question, Dan fills in the blanks of this skeletal narrative with specific names and circumstances, making old sense of current events. No matter how problematic the consequences—and they are quite problematic—Dan will resist change until he sees that it isn't the situation alone that dictates his choices and his actions; it's his personal narrative. *That narrative, and the knowledge he's built on it, governs what he can and cannot see in situations and what he can and cannot make out of them as a result.*

Seeing the narrative on paper, Dan paused to reconsider his experience as a leader: perhaps the results he gets aren't inevitable; perhaps they're partly of his making. This possibility provided Dan the impetus to explore the same questions we asked of Stu:

▶ In what ways, if any, is this narrative breaking down and under what circumstances?
▶ What results would other narratives create if he acted upon them as if they were true?

To answer the first question, we didn't need to look very far. Dan's mounting sense of frustration was enough to tell him that, under the pressure of growth, his character in the narrative was struggling. At the same time, our work with Stu and other senior leaders provided compelling evidence that he could in fact rely not on everyone for everything but on a select number of people for different things and that the deathly consequences he imagines were highly unlikely.

Dan had no difficulty seeing all of this. But the second question—the question of alternatives—is far trickier, because here we run into Dan's *implicit theory of learning*. For years Dan had gone beyond the call of duty in his efforts to develop people, investing more in people's learning than any CEO I've ever met. These efforts, partly driven by the firm's need for more leaders, were informed by a widely shared and highly problematic cultural belief that learners are empty vessels in need of filling. According to this belief, all you have to do when developing someone—figuratively speaking, anyway—is pry open their heads and pour in what you know. This makes endless lectures not only reasonable but downright necessary.[4]

"Sir, the following paradigm shifts occurred while you were out."

Upon this cultural belief Dan built his own unique theory of learning, using his narrative about reliability to give that belief its own peculiar twist. As a result, when people fail to act like empty vessels—say, by raising doubts or by differing with him—he views them through the lens of his narrative, imagining them to be self-indulgent kids, too blind or too full of hubris to learn quickly. If you want to speed up learning, says his implicit theory, you have to work harder and harder—and faster and faster—to *get* people to see this or that, lecturing them here, debating them there. Before you know it, learning becomes a life-or-death struggle in which Dan feels compelled to cajole or subtly coerce people into adopting his view. Once in the grip of this theory, Dan doesn't realize that far from speeding up development, he is slowing it down.

The second document, which drove home the downside of his theory, made Dan eager to try an alternative. But he was so trapped in his informal role—and in the self-fulfilling prophecies it created—he was at a loss. What could he actually *do* differently, he asked, to work his way out of his current role as a leader? A third document addressed this question by suggesting how Dan might transform the narratives and theories that were undermining his leadership and his relationships (see Table 9). On the left side is his current way of operating when his reliability button is pushed. On the right is an alternative based on a different narrative and theory. By giving Dan practical suggestions for what he might do when his button is pushed, the document helped Dan revisit and revise what he "knew" to be true in those moments.

By focusing on Dan and Stu's relationship, and not on Dan alone, Dan learned that he could in fact rely on Stu, whose own changes made that reliance tenable.[5] With each person's progress now accelerating the other's, Dan came to see Stu and other members of his team in a new light. Eighteen months later, Dan told me in a somewhat surprised tone of voice that he no longer felt anxious or mad about other people's shortcomings or limits. "I just don't have the same emotional agita," he said. "Even when people make mistakes, I'm not annoyed. In fact, I'm sitting here asking myself, 'Why aren't I mad about this?' Well, I'm just not." His next set of reflections suggest why:

TABLE 9: Action Sequences	
CURRENT ACTION SEQUENCE	**ALTERNATIVE ACTION SEQUENCE**
You get a snippet of data that some-one may not be learning fast or well enough, getting himself, you, or the firm into trouble as a result.	You get a snippet of data that some-one may not be learning fast or well enough, getting himself, you, or the firm into trouble as a result.
• You start interpreting these data, using your narrative about reliability to fill in the gaps and to imagine a disastrous ending.	• You discuss what you're seeing—and any worries it creates—with people who will neither collude with your view nor dismiss it outright.
• Your hypervigilant radar now turned on, you start looking for evidence that suggests the ending you fear most will come to pass.	• You ask people for evidence that might moderate your concerns, not just confirm them, helping you develop a more nuanced view of the person.
• The more evidence you see and the less counterevidence you notice, the more your anxiety mounts.	• The more nuanced your view, the more able you are to discuss your concerns productively with that person.
• The more your anxiety mounts, the more people look like the two-dimensional characters in your narrative: self-indulgent kids incapable of taking care of themselves or anyone else.	• The more productively you discuss your concerns, the more clearly you each see what those concerns are saying about you and what they're saying about the other person.
• To save the day, as your character in the narrative dictates, you work behind the scenes to protect the firm, others, and yourself from harm.	• No longer seeing the other person as a problem you must solve, you're able to work together to address any concerns you have about each other.
• When others continue grimly on in blind oblivion, you feel less respect for them and the need to speak the truth mounts.	• As you work together to address your respective concerns, you take increasing responsibility for helping each other address them.
• Finally compelled to speak, you let weeks or months of pent-up anxiety and frustration leak or blurt out.	• No longer feeling compelled to speak or not speak, you're free to address things as they arise.
• Caught unaware, the "problem" person gets very upset, confirming your view that he can't take the "truth" and resigning you to the inevitability of a deadly crash.	• More aware and less constrained, you feel more connected to each other and more confident that you can create a good outcome together.

My relationship with these guys has moved from a source of worry to a source of satisfaction, partly because I talk with them more and understand them better, but partly because objectively, they're in a better place. I used to feel in the classic lifeguard situation where you're trying to save people who are trying to pull you under. That feeling just no longer exists. I no longer feel that they have to be saved or that I have to save them.

By focusing on Dan's relationship and not on Dan alone, we get this felicitous mixture of others getting better and his understanding of them getting better—all of it freeing up Dan to restructure the knowledge that's been telling him for years *You've got to save these guys*. No longer compelled to save people—and no longer mad or anxious that he can't— he can reset his relationships on a more flexible basis. Freer to respond to them in any number of ways, he's able to derive satisfaction from his relationships and the greater mutuality they afford.

TAKING ACTION

How to Restructure Experiential Knowledge

Now that you've seen what Dan and Stu did to restructure their experiential knowledge, here's how you can do the same:

- Figure out what kind of help you need to make the most of these steps, and be sure to get it.

- Ask yourself: in what ways are my circumstances and relationships different now from what I experienced earlier in life?

- Ask yourself: in what ways am I different today than I was earlier in life (aside from my waistline)?

- Review the stories, propositions, values, and strategies you wrote down in Step 1.

- Ask yourself: how would I revise my stories, propositions, values, and strategies so they better fit my relationships and circumstances today?

- Write down what you would like to do differently in your most important relationships as a result of what you've learned.

- Proceed to the next and last step to consolidate the changes you've made so far and to redefine your relationship on a new basis.

Step 3: Return to the Future

To sustain progress without my help, Dan must continue to rely on others, and Stu must continue to brave the limelight, *even when events press long and hard on old experiential knowledge.* This third step addresses the question of sustainability under pressure by turning our attention back to the future. Here we consolidate the gains we've made, define new objectives, anticipate new challenges, and set the terms of a new relationship.

STEPS TOWARD CHANGE	
STAGE I **Disrupt**	Assess the Relationship
	Map Patterns of Interaction
	Design Action Experiments
STAGE II **Reframe**	Freeze Frame
	Invent New Frames
	Design Frame Experiments
STAGE III **Revise**	Revisit Past Events
	Restructure Knowledge
	Return to the Future

Consolidating Gains

Eighteen months into our work together, I put together a notebook that showed how far Stu and Dan had come. On the business front, it catalogued their various accomplishments: Stu successfully launching his own business; Dan making real headway on the group strategy; the two of them demonstrating to others how they could launch a new business quickly and well. On the relationship front, it used transcripts to illustrate the greater reciprocity characterizing their relationship: Stu seeking to help Dan while challenging him more productively; Dan seeking to understand Stu's concerns while offering counsel Stu could use.

All these data suggested to us that their investment was paying off. The pattern of interaction that occasionally derailed them—Dan lecturing and debating, Stu blocking and hiding—was no longer wielding the same power. Both Dan and Stu were now able to see, interrupt, and alter the pattern before it wreaked havoc. More important, they were able to help each other put a more satisfying pattern in motion. At this point, their relationship would never be the same. No longer built on a foundation of unilateral protection but on a mutual commitment to learning, it could only grow stronger with time.

Defining New Objectives and Anticipating Future Challenges

Despite these gains—perhaps because of them—Dan and Stu still had their work cut out for them. Even the best relationships confront setbacks, upsets, and failures. Besides, nothing stays the same. As long as Merrimac continued to grow and change, they'd have to as well.

That's why, far from bringing things to a close, this last step launched the work yet to be done. In taking this step, Dan and Stu defined new objectives and identified the challenges they'd face as they tried to achieve them. Dan went first, saying he wanted to gradually extricate himself from the center of the firm and transfer more leadership to others. Stu said he wanted to play a more central role in the firm, taking on leadership within the group, not just his unit.

Both objectives are developmentally appropriate. At this point in Dan's life and in the life of the firm, Dan *should* be looking to extricate himself from the center of Merrimac's universe. Similarly, Stu *should* be looking to step up and take more leadership. What's more, the two objectives go hand in hand: Stu's stepping up making it easier for Dan to extricate himself, and Dan's extricating himself making it easier for Stu to step up.

But nothing in real life is ever as easy as it looks on paper. Getting from here to there would undoubtedly pose challenges. It was best to anticipate what those were, we reckoned, so we could figure out ahead of time how Dan and Stu might handle them. In thinking together, we anticipated that Dan would face some version of the following challenges:

▶ Given that Dan had operated at the center of the Merrimac universe since its inception, most people would continue to expect him to deliver the goods—whether those goods took the form of a pep talk, a prized resource, much-needed protection, or special mentoring. As frustrated as people might have been with the bottlenecks caused by Dan's centrality, they would be even more frustrated when they could no longer count on it.

▶ If people reacted poorly to the changes Dan was making in his role—and some inevitably would—they could easily resurrect his implicit premise *(It's dangerous to rely on people)*, and his implicit strategy *(Always be on guard to make sure really bad things don't happen)*, luring him back into the center where he would feel trapped once again.

▶ If Dan started to feel trapped, his natural affection and respect for people would come under threat, and he'd find it harder to build the kind of collegial relationships that he wanted and that a growing professional firm needed to succeed.

In turning to Stu, we thought he'd have to master some version of the following challenges:

▶ As Focuspoint became more important to the group, Stu would face substantive business challenges and a related set of relationship challenges. On the business front, he'd need to figure out where the most promising synergies lay within the group and how best to exploit them; on the relationship front, he'd need to keep key relationships on a synergistic track, even when feeling exposed or ridiculed.

▶ For Stu, this would be tricky at best. As "the poster child" for building new entities within the group, Stu now had a great deal of visibility with key people in the company, putting him right smack in the middle of powerful, fast-talking people. If these people ridiculed

Stu out of their own insecurities, it could easily resurrect Stu's implicit premise that he should avoid the limelight because there lies nothing but ridicule and sorrow.

▶ If Stu started to feel caught in other people's headlights, his desire and ability to take leadership at a group level would plummet, as would his partnership with Dan.

Setting the Terms of a New Relationship

Far from discouraging them, these challenges strengthened Dan and Stu's resolve to continue working on their relationship. To give ballast to that resolve, they made a series of commitments that defined how they wanted their informal relationship to look going forward. Among these commitments were the following:

▶ Instead of a one-way relationship in which Dan pronounced and Stu denounced, they would take mutual responsibility for creating a two-way dynamic.

▶ To create that two-way dynamic, they would join together to find solutions that work for both of them (instead of Dan's pushing and Stu's blocking).

▶ To move forward together, they would challenge each other to grow *while* providing each other the support they would need to sustain that growth under pressure.

▶ To challenge and support each other, they would acknowledge and reflect on their reactions while helping each other handle them more constructively.

Undoubtedly, they would need help from time to time. But by this point, they would be able to find that help in each other.

TAKING ACTION
How to Return to the Future

Now that you've seen how Dan and Stu turned to consider the future, here's how you can do the same.

- Capture the progress you've made to date—both on the business front and on the relationship front.

- Take stock of what you've accomplished and figure out a way to celebrate together.

- Identify the objectives you would each like to achieve in the future and anticipate the challenges those objectives will pose for your relationship.

- Set the terms of your new relationship by making explicit commitments to each other.

- Make sure the commitments specify what you will actually do to sustain the changes you've made and to master future challenges.

- Make sure the commitments specify how you will help each other when you need it.

- Going forward, look to each other for help when either of you falls short of your commitments or finds them hard to meet.

Stage III Results

By any of our original measures, Dan and Stu are now in a very different place (see Chapter 5: Table 6). Far from going stale, their relationship now serves as a model for others. Their old one-way structure—with Dan pushing and Stu blocking—has been replaced by a reciprocal structure that allows for greater mutuality and flexibility. Within this new structure, Dan is gradually learning how to rely on others, while Stu is learning how to brave the limelight. As a result, they're able to keep growing while tackling controversial issues—each time with a little less anxiety, a little more confidence. By the time we end our work together:

▶ They respond more flexibly to each other and more effectively to the demands around them. No longer trapped by their knee-jerk reactions to each other, they are able to make decisions more quickly and effectively together.

▶ They treat their relationship as a context for growth. No longer so intent on protecting themselves or each other, they are able to explore their anxieties, beliefs, and interests openly so they don't unknowingly affect what they decide or how they decide it.

▶ They recoup quickly when they get into trouble. Even their hottest conflicts strengthen rather than damage their relationship, because they are able to cool down together and use what happened to learn.

In short, Dan and Stu have developed enough resilience to continue building even more resilience in the future (see Chapter 4). With our initial mission accomplished—by their metrics and my own—we might simply declare victory and go home. But just as the first two stages end with a dilemma, so does this one. That dilemma goes something like this:

▶ In order to secure whatever changes you've made, you need to solidify them—internalizing what you've learned and perhaps institutionalizing it.

▶ But the more you internalize and institutionalize change, the harder it can be to make new changes, reducing flexibility and making adaptation more difficult.

Engaging this dilemma head-on catapults people right back to the beginning of Stage I, where they start all over again, only this time on their own. From here on, Dan and Stu must stand ready to disrupt any patterns that start limiting their growth or the growth of the firm. Looking back now, five years after the fact, I can tell you this: that's exactly what they did.

PART III

Making Change Practical

Purpose: To show you how to master the practical challenges you'll face while strengthening relationships within your team.

Synopsis: Many change efforts stall because even the best-laid plans are disconnected from reality. To make relationship change practical, you must master three challenges: figuring out where to invest limited resources; balancing the demands of change with the demands of running a business; and sustaining motivation for change over time. This part of the book offers you some tools with which to master these three challenges.

8
Focus the Change Effort

That's pretty much how I feel about relationships. They're totally irrational, crazy, and absurd. But I guess we keep going through it, because most of us need the eggs.

—Woody Allen, *Annie Hall*

A t the end of *Annie Hall*, the classic 1977 film about relationships, Woody Allen tells an old joke about this guy who goes to a psychiatrist and says, "Doc, my brother's crazy. He thinks he's a chicken." Horrified, the doctor asks why he hasn't already committed him. "I would," the guy answers, "but I need the eggs." The point is, as difficult as relationships sometimes are, we need what they give us, even if it's all in our heads. And there's no getting around it. While relationships give us many things, from a much-needed sense of connection to much-needed political support, they also take effort. Sometimes lots of effort.

But not all relationships within teams require or deserve the same *amount* of effort, or the same *kind*. Dan and Stu decided to invest a lot of time and energy in transforming their relationship, and they did so for one reason: the success of their leadership and their firm turned on the success of their relationship. Not everyone will make the same choice—or need to. To help you decide *which* relationships to invest in and *when*, this chapter provides two tools: an Investment Matrix that tells you where to focus your investments, and a Sequencing Matrix that tells you when to invest in which ones. Together these two tools give you a way to think strategically and practically about developing greater resilience at the top of your organization.

The Investment Matrix

In any business, people make a basic distinction between two types of costs: operating costs and investments. Where the former keeps a business going today, the latter keeps it going tomorrow. The same basic distinction can be made about relationships.

All relationships entail relatively fixed operating costs. If you want a relationship to go well, you have to raise sensitive topics with care; you have to deal with your own or other's emotional reactions; you have to repair any ruptures. All of these activities maintain relationships, and all of them take time, energy, and money.

In business, investments represent a different kind of cost. On the one hand, they're more flexible than operating costs. You can ramp them up and down more easily. On the other hand, if you don't invest enough, or if you don't invest strategically, you can't keep up with your competitors. New products or services don't get introduced fast enough, causing revenues to fall. Or increasingly inefficient systems don't get updated fast enough, causing costs to rise.

Again, the same basic logic holds for relationships. All relationships require investment to keep up with the shifting demands of any organization. Otherwise, they tend to get in the way: an organizational redesign calling for greater cooperation doesn't work as intended or a new strategy falls flat because people don't get the right information to the right people at the right time.[1] Just as you can reduce the costs associated with outdated formal systems by upgrading them, so can you reduce the costs of relationships by transforming the informal structures underlying them.

In each case, you replace an outdated, inefficient system with a more effective and efficient one. Only, in the case of relationships, you seek to redesign a relationship's informal structure so it's better able to handle even the most difficult of relationship tasks well—whether it's recouping when things go wrong, or reviving a relationship that's dying.

Making investments is inherently difficult. Whether you're thinking about a business or a relationship, today's pressing demands will always clamor for more attention, and those demands will make a compelling case: if they don't get what they need, there'll be no tomorrow to invest in. So whenever you invest, you have to make choices—sometimes hard choices.

In making those choices, many people's first instinct is to focus on "problem" relationships. But that focus is far too broad to be practical: most firms would have a very long list of candidates, and no firm can afford to invest in all of them. Besides, by focusing only on problems, you set your sights too low.

At the same time, if you take a more ambitious tack—aspiring to turn every good relationship into a high-performing one—you'll still have far more change on your hands than you can handle, and not all relationships require the same level of excellence.

To make change practical, people need a framework that can help them focus their investments. The matrix in Figure 11 groups relationships in terms of their relative importance and interdependence, identifying four segments, each one calling for a different approach.

The basic idea behind the matrix is simple: *Invest in transforming only those relationships that are both highly important and highly interdependent.* All other relationships can be handled through more conventional approaches.

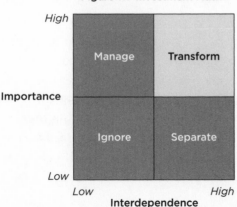

Figure 11: Investment Matrix

Importance

Perhaps it goes without saying, but I'll say it anyway: all relationships are intrinsically important. They make or break our sense of well-being, our effectiveness, our self-esteem, our sense of ourselves, our connection to others, even our purpose in life. So when I speak of importance here, I do so only relative to a firm's limited investment resources. In this narrow sense, you can assess the importance of a relationship along three dimensions—*strategic, symbolic,* and *developmental*—each dimension posing a question and imposing a constraint:

▶ **Strategic:** To what extent are the people in the relationship uniquely qualified to fulfill a strategically critical role? The more vital people's talents, knowledge, or experience are to a strategically critical role, the harder it is to replace them or to redefine the role.

▶ **Symbolic:** To what extent do the people in the organization look to the people in the relationship, or to the relationship itself, for meaning, guidance, or a sense of purpose? The more symbolically important a relationship is, the faster events related to that relationship will travel throughout the organization, shaping the way people interpret things, including the future, the firm's strategy, and leadership's commitment to it.[2]

▶ **Developmental:** To what extent does a relationship either reveal a leader's liabilities or showcase her strengths? The more a relationship has the potential to bring out the best or the worst in a leader, the more impact it will have on her development as a leader as well as on others and the firm.[3]

Interdependence

Any expert on the formal design of organizations will tell you the same thing: the more interdependent people are, the more they rely on their relationships—not on formal mechanisms—to get things done and to resolve conflicts along the way.[4] What they don't tell you is that the more people rely on their relationships, the more demands they put on the informal structures underlying them. It is in the context of these informal structures that people will resolve their differences, make decisions, learn, and so on. In assessing interdependence, and thus the demands a relationship will have to meet, three dimensions are critical: *information, coordination,* and *decision making.* Each one poses a question and implies a demand:

▸ **Information:** To what extent do people in a relationship need to share information quickly and fully to accomplish key tasks?[5] The more that people depend on one another for information, the more their relationship must facilitate the flow of reliable information, including sensitive information or "undiscussables."

▸ **Coordination:** To what extent do people in a relationship need to coordinate key activities to get things done? The more that people need to coordinate, the more a relationship must be able to navigate situations where the need to cooperate (to achieve joint goals) collides with the need to compete for limited resources.

▸ **Decision Making:** To what extent do people in a relationship need to be involved in the same decisions? The more that people need to be involved, the more their relationships must facilitate timely and wise negotiation of differences, even fundamental ones.

Segment-Specific Approaches

The matrix identifies four different ways of approaching relationships, depending on their degree of importance and interdependence: *ignoring, separating, managing, or transforming.*

Which approach is the most effective (does the job best) and the most efficient (at the lowest cost) depends on the circumstances.

▸ **Ignoring:** If two or more people don't depend much on each other and their relationships aren't strategically important, you can ignore these relationships and any negative effects they create, at least until circumstances suggest otherwise. The costs created by these relationships will be less than the cost of investing in them, so don't bother.[6]

▶ **Separating:** If people's roles are highly interdependent but the people aren't uniquely qualified to fulfill those roles, structural separation is often the best way to handle relationship problems that resist resolution. Here leaders might transfer or promote one of the people into a new role, create a new structure that reduces interdependence, or even fire one or the other person. Any of these options will likely work better and be less costly than spending the time and money needed to transform the relationship.[7]

▶ **Managing:** If people are vital to their roles but the roles themselves aren't that interdependent, you should be able to effectively manage any negative effects a relationship creates, because they should be infrequent. When applied appropriately, this approach reduces the impact of occasional relationship snafus by avoiding them, insulating people from them, or protecting one or the other person in the relationship. If the people involved aren't interdependent and the snafus are infrequent, this option is the least costly.[8]

▶ **Transforming:** This approach makes sense when people are vital to strategic roles *and* when their success cannot be achieved without their depending on each other. Under these circumstances, it's much harder to ignore relationships, to manage their ill effects, or to separate people structurally. These relationships destroy so much value—and it's so costly to replace the people in them— that it's usually more efficient and effective to transform these relationships than to manage or ignore them or to separate the people involved.[9]

Relationships that are highly important and highly interdependent are those that operate along organizational fault lines—interfaces where coordination is as essential as it is difficult. It's on these critical few relationships that a firm's leadership should focus its limited resources.

Sequencing Matrix

Once you've identified those relationships most in need of investment, you can use the matrix in Figure 12 to sequence those investments over time. As the Sequencing Matrix implies, it's best to start with high-impact relationships that stand the best chance of succeeding. That's why Merrimac focused first on Dan and Stu. Not only did they have a great chance of succeeding, but the impact of that success was likely to be high.

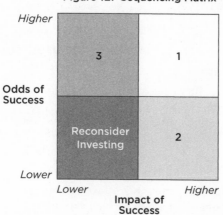

Figure 12: Sequencing Matrix

In terms of impact, you can assess any relationship along two dimensions:

▶ **Impact on People:** To what extent will changes in the relationship free people to do their jobs more easily and effectively? The more the relationship prevents people from doing key jobs well, the sooner changes should be made. To what extent will the people in the relationship be more effective and fulfilled? The more people's relationships are undercutting their effectiveness or their well being, the sooner changes should be made.

▶ **Impact on the Business:** To what extent will changes in the relationship make it easier for people to make decisions and take actions

*"O.K., if you can't see your way to giving me a pay raise,
how about giving Parkerson a pay cut?"*

together more quickly and wisely? The more people's differences
are harming critical decisions or the pace with which they get made,
the sooner changes should be made.

In terms of success, you can assess a relationship along three dimensions:

▸ **Motivation:** To what extent do the people in the relationship see
important benefits for themselves and the firm? The more benefits
they see, the more willing they'll be to change.
▸ **Readiness:** To what extent are the people in the relationship willing
and able to invest their time and energy *relative to other things*? The

less hampered they are by business crises, whether self-imposed or created by circumstance, the more able and willing people will be to invest their time and energy.

▶ **Difficulty:** To what extent do the people in the relationship think it's possible that they played some role in creating circumstances they don't like? The more aware people are of themselves and their impact, the more willing they will be to change.

Keep in mind that odds can and should be changed. So while you're focusing on relationships in the first cell of the matrix, you might turn your attention to increasing the odds of success for those in the second cell— for example, by pointing out the changes people in the first cell are making. Soon after, you might launch some type of programmatic intervention for people in the third cell. Although less customized, well-designed programs can prepare people for more significant investments later by increasing their awareness of themselves and their role in relationships.

The fourth and last cell is a bit odd. By definition, this matrix focuses only on those relationships you consider worthy of investment. So, in theory, no one should show up in this cell. But chances are, when pressed to choose among the chosen, some will show up here. If so, you might reconsider whether these relationships really are worth the investment.

Key Points

All relationships require effort to work, but not all relationships within teams require the same amount or kind of effort. When it comes to relationships that operate along organizational fault lines, people should invest in making them strong enough to handle the tensions that will build up and the conflicts that will erupt at each of those interfaces.

9
Choose the
Right Strategy

When a company runs into trouble, we have no difficulty talking about its performance. We may not always agree, but we have a wide range of tools and techniques to help us analyze the market and figure out what went wrong.

Not so with relationships. Relationships are so much a part of the woof and warp of everyday life they're hard to see and even harder to talk about.

That's why most of us focus on individual people rather than patterns of interactions when our relationships run into trouble. But this is like focusing on one or another competitor or customer instead of looking at the dynamics of the marketplace. It skews our perspective and prevents us from seeing the larger forces at play or from spotting potentially powerful leverage points for change. Even worse, by focusing on only one or another piece of the puzzle, we're apt to create damaging self-fulfilling prophecies—sparking in relationships the equivalent of price wars among competitors.

The tools so far in this book have been designed to help you see and talk about your most important relationships. This chapter takes a further step by introducing a model that will show you how to strengthen your relationships while making progress on business issues.

The FREE Model

Any team charged with making decisions or getting things done will struggle from time to time. Disagreements—especially those that touch on clashing interests and beliefs—always prove harder to resolve than anyone would like. And the more time that passes, the more frustrated and impatient people become, triggering relationship conflicts that jeopardize not only progress on the business front, but the team's future functioning as well.

"I've tried the stick, and I've tried the carrot.
Now I'm going to try the .357 magnum."

Yet even in a team's worst moments, it's rarely the case that everyone is squabbling. More typically, some team members will be in the thick of it while others remain on the sidelines, watching a heated discussion turn into an increasingly acrimonious debate. When that happens, those caught up in the debate often don't know how to get out, while those on the periphery don't know how to help. If anything, those watching feel compelled either to take sides or to withdraw altogether to avoid getting caught in the middle. But as the diagram in Figure 13 shows, there is a third option: intervening to help those in a conflict use their differences well.

Figure 13: The Third Option

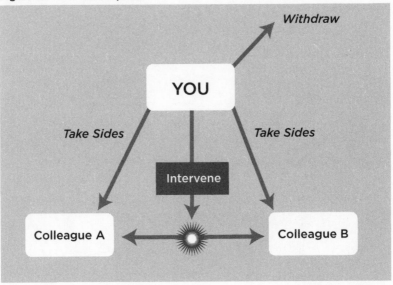

The FREE model, shown in Figure 14, describes a set of three strategies you can use to intervene when two or more people on your team get caught in a conflict that's jeopardizing the quality of substantive discussions *and* the fate of key relationships. While all three strategies keep one eye on the business and the other on relationships, each one serves a different purpose:

Figure 14: The FREE Model

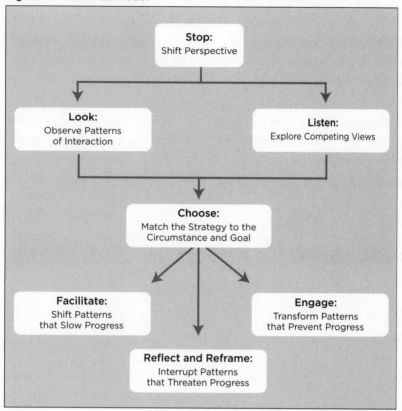

▶ **Facilitate:** Shift patterns that slow progress without stopping to discuss them.

▶ **Reflect and Reframe:** See and interrupt patterns that continue to stall progress.

▶ **Engage:** Transform patterns that repeatedly prevent progress.

All three strategies work together to free teams up when they're getting stuck, which is why I call it the FREE model. Each strategy is designed to strengthen relationships *while* making headway on the business, but each one makes more or less sense depending on the circumstances. That's why, before choosing a strategy, it's wise to take three steps:

▶ **Stop:** Gain enough perspective to make sound assessments.
▶ **Look:** Map patterns in your head so you can assess their impact on progress.
▶ **Listen:** Explore what lies behind views so you can assess how hot a topic is.

As you'll soon see, no one strategy can do everything. Each strategy involves trade-offs. In fact, if you rely too much on any one strategy, you'll just make matters worse, either failing to address business issues fast enough or failing to dislodge dysfunctions that repeatedly get in the way. You're better off thinking of the strategies as an ensemble that works together, not alone, to strengthen relationships while getting things done. What's most important is the ability to choose and shift among the three strategies. Let's start there, then turn to each strategy.

How to Choose the Best Strategy for the Job

Whenever you face a complex situation, you have to make complex judgments about what's going on, what goals to shoot for, and what to do. To make these judgments well, you need to first stop, look, and listen— each step freeing you from your automatic reactions, so you can make better choices in the heat of the moment. Here's how:

Step 1: STOP

When a conflict leads people to say things that challenge—or worse, be-little—*our* beliefs, motives, or values, we can't help but get "hooked." Before we know it, we feel *compelled* to take sides or to withdraw for fear of losing control. That's why, when a conflict heats up, the first thing *you* need to do is cool down, so you don't make matters worse.

The best way to cool down is to take a moment—not to count to ten, but to jot down the thoughts and feelings that are going through your mind. This immediately puts your reactions "out there" on paper, where you can see them and start to loosen their grip.

Next, reflect on your reactions by using Table 10 to identify the assumptions behind them. Are you blaming either yourself or others for what's happening? Are you thinking one person is entirely right, the other obviously wrong? Are you attributing nasty motives or stupidity to those who think differently than you do? If so, you're going to need to shift perspective, because you're seeing things in *either/or* terms, which will only suck you into the conflict and render you helpless (see Chapter 4).

To shift perspective, try entertaining the assumptions on the right side of the table. These assumptions, which look at conflict from a more relational perspective, put you in a much better position to see the things each side misses and to invent options neither side alone can imagine.

If you find it hard to shift perspective when you're hooked, you're not alone. In fact, if you're like most people, you'll find all sorts of ways to convince yourself that the assumptions on the left really do apply in this

TABLE 10: Shifting Perspective		
ASSUMPTIONS	**EITHER/OR PERSPECTIVE**	**RELATIONAL PERSPECTIVE**
About Substantive Disagreements	Assume only one person can be right, and so the other must be wrong.	Assume each person sees things the other misses and misses things the other sees.
	Assume the rightness of one view is a matter of obvious fact, not opinion or interpretation.	Assume people's different beliefs and interests lead them to see the same things differently.
About Relationship Troubles	Assume one or the other person is causing the difficulty: "He is making the other feel this or do that"; "She gave the other no choice."	Assume each person is contributing to the difficulties: "They're each making it hard for the other to be at his best."
	Assume that one or the other is mad or bad—that is, crazy, stupid, incompetent, or immoral.	Assume they're each doing the best they can and could use your help.

case. If that happens, remind yourself that you're better off starting on the right, so you don't create self-fulfilling prophecies that prevent you (or others) from being at your best. After all, you can always shift back to the assumptions on the left if the evidence is incontrovertible. But even then, make sure you or others aren't helping to create that "incontrovertible" evidence. And keep in mind, that you don't have to be convinced that the assumptions on the right apply. You just have to hold them as possibilities while you look and listen, so you can see and imagine things that the assumptions on the left rule out from the start.

Step 2: LOOK

To choose among strategies and to use them well, don't look at who's doing what to whom but at how each person is contributing to a pattern that's getting in the way of progress. Any pattern that's affecting the *breadth* or *depth* of deliberations deserves special attention, because it will quickly undermine the quality and speed of resolution.

Patterns that narrow a conversation usually take the form of adversarial, repetitious debates among a very small number of people, while patterns that create superficial discussions usually take the form of abstract assertions and counterassertions about the right values or ends to pursue—disconnected from data, dismissive of all other ends or values, and with no regard for how anyone might get from here to there.

When a conversation starts to narrow a discussion or to skim the surface of an issue, you can use the Act-React Template in Figure 15 to map in your head how each person's actions are contributing to the pattern that's creating these results (for more, see Chapters 3 and 5).

Once you see a pattern, you can assess its potential impact. Let's say your map shows people caricaturing each other's views, belittling each other's concerns, and locking into positions. Odds are, you're going to need to intervene to help those people out. Keep an eye on the pattern and its impact on the discussion's breadth and depth, and listen closely to what people are saying so you can assess how hot the topic is and what's at stake for those involved.

Figure 15: The Act-React Template

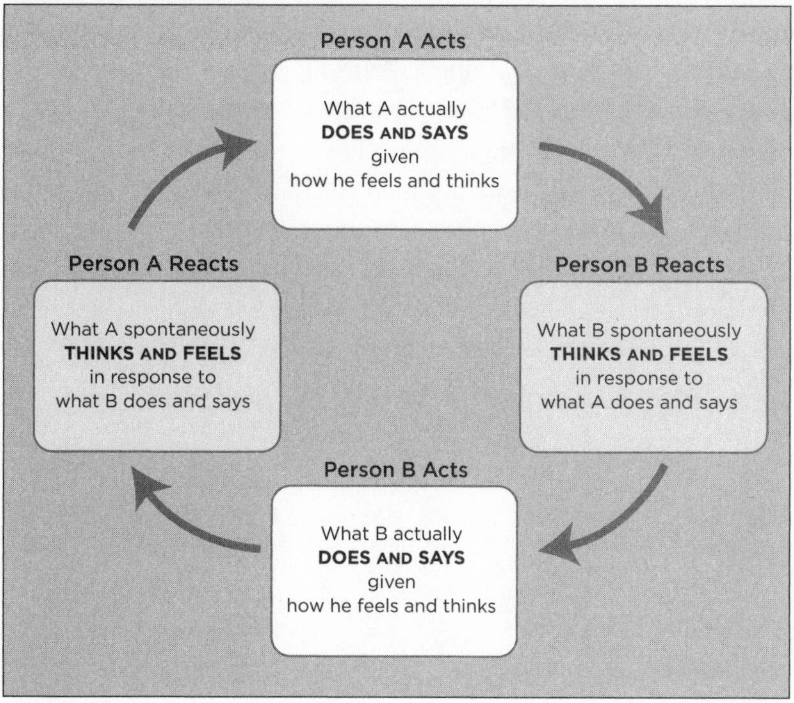

Step 3: LISTEN

You know your team is dealing with a hot topic as soon as subjective considerations come into play: political interests, emotional needs, cultural beliefs, personal values. If you then add to that volatile mix a high degree of uncertainty—facts are in dispute or hard to get; goals aren't shared or clear—then you have the makings of a *really* hot topic.[2]

As soon as people start discussing a hot topic, you need to listen for two types of logic (see Table 11). Most obvious to the ear is *analytic logic:* "Recent trends suggest that the market for our core business is growing more competitive, and our returns suggest that we're not keeping up. I think we should either come up with a new strategy for that business—one that goes after the lower end of the market—or exit it altogether."

Less obvious to the ear, but equally important, is *emotional logic:* "I feel like we're missing the boat on the real issue here! What kind of company do we really want to be? Just last week I heard people wondering if we'd lost our way on that. I don't want to get into a slugfest with competitors at the low end of the market, and I don't believe anyone else does either."

TABLE 11: Two Trains of Thought		
	ANALYTIC	**EMOTIONAL**
Thought Process	The relatively conscious, analytic thought people use to move from data to conclusions, given their theories (whether implicit or explicit).	The less conscious, more emotional thought people use to move from subjective considerations (needs, values, interests) to their views and positions.
Language System	The language of data and analysis: "I think. . . ," "The facts suggest . . ."	The language of feeling and story: "I feel . . . ," "I'm upset."
Access	Relatively easy to retrieve and to put into words.	Harder to retrieve or put into words; "leaks out" through tones of voice and body language.
Discussability	Relatively discussable.	Relatively undiscussable.
Implications	Resist the temptation to focus all of your attention here.	Signal in word and deed that emotional needs, cultural beliefs, and political interests are discussable.

In real life, of course, these two trains of thought are linked—two cable cars moving down the same track. But because analytic logic is so much easier to retrieve and discuss, people tend to focus all their attention there. As a result, so much goes undiscussed that people go around in circles, unable to come up with solutions, or any that last. Later on in this chapter, you'll see how to intervene in ways that take both trains of thought into account.

Step 4: CHOOSE

When choosing which strategy to use, try to think of all three strategies along a continuum (see Figure 16). On one end of that continuum is *facilitating*. This strategy, the least obtrusive of the three, keeps people's attention squarely focused on the substance while subtly shifting patterns of interaction that are slowing progress. On the other end of the continuum is *engaging*. This strategy, which is the most obtrusive, shifts the group's attention away from business issues and onto patterns of interaction that continually prevent progress on critical business issues. Between these two is *reflecting and reframing*, a midway strategy that touches on patterns just long enough to disrupt them while returning quickly to the substantive issues at hand.

Figure 16: A Strategic Continuum

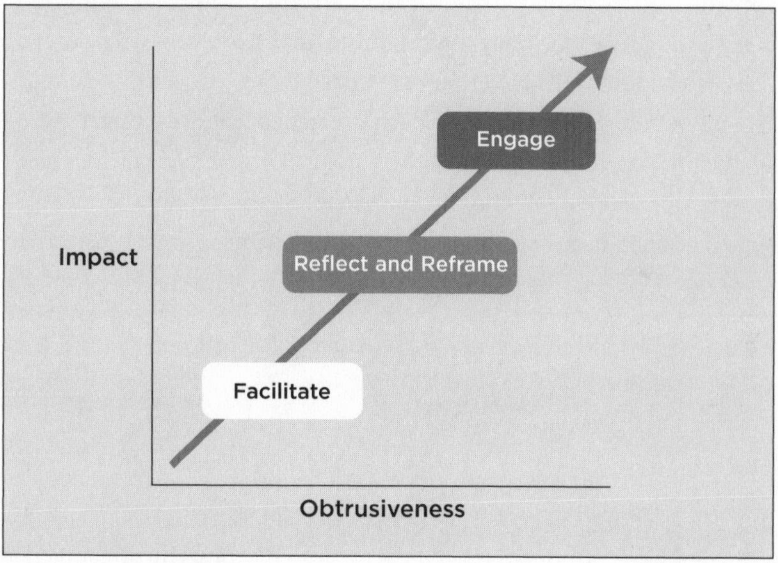

As the diagram suggests, the higher up the continuum you go, the more impact you'll have on a team's functioning but the less business you'll get done. Conversely, the lower you go, the more business you'll get done but the less impact you'll have. Teams do best when they are free to move up and down the continuum, shifting back and forth among all three strategies depending on the circumstances at hand.

How to Intervene Effectively

When you stop, look, and listen before acting, you increase the odds of selecting the best strategy for the job—and, having selected it, of helping the whole system, not just one or another person in it. This section goes a step further by showing you how to implement each strategy and by describing in greater detail the circumstances under which each one makes more or less sense.

Facilitating

Of all the strategies, this one focuses the team's attention most squarely on the business. It does so by shifting patterns that turn discussions into superficial, repetitive debates without drawing attention to them. It includes moves that broaden and deepen a group's understanding of both the analytic and emotional logic behind different views so people can make better judgments together (see Table 12).[3]

It makes the most sense to facilitate when progress must be made quickly and interactions aren't so dysfunctional that their impact can't be managed. Under these conditions, people won't feel the need—and won't have the heart—to look at their relationships, so don't bother.

	TABLE 12: Facilitating Moves	
	EXPLORING ANALYTIC LOGIC	**EXPLORING EMOTIONAL LOGIC**
To Broaden Deliberations	• How do others see it? • What are others' thoughts? • Does anyone have a different view or different data? • What other data might we need to better understand this? • What do others think we should do?	• What concerns do others have? • What are others hoping to see? • What are others worried about? • What do others want to see happen? • What would others find motivating?

	EXPLORING ANALYTIC LOGIC	EXPLORING EMOTIONAL LOGIC
To Broaden Deliberations	• Are there other options we haven't yet considered?	• What would give others confidence that we're doing the right thing? • What do others feel is at stake here?
To Deepen Deliberations	• What leads you to think that is the case? What data do you see? • What data might alter your view? • What do you think that option will get us? What results will it produce? • How come you don't like this other option? What do you think will happen if we pursue it? • What leads you to think so?	• What leads you to be concerned about X? • What about Y is important to you? • Why is it so important to you? • What, if anything, might lead you to feel differently? • What do your reactions have to teach us? What are they saying about this group, about this firm, and about you? • What possibilities might you entertain, if you weren't so upset?

Reflecting and Reframing

Like facilitation, this strategy gives precedence to business topics. But unlike facilitation, it draws people's attention to patterns of interaction that are getting in their way (see Table 13). The objective is to make conflicts more discussable by legitimizing differences and to stop people from blaming each other by interpreting behavior from a relational standpoint (see Table 10).

This strategy is best used when progress must be made quickly but interactions are becoming so repetitive and superficial that facilitation alone can't shift things. Under these conditions, you're best off naming the patterns that are getting in the way. This way people can work together to alter them while paving the way for engaging the patterns, if needed.[4]

TABLE 13: Reflecting and Reframing Moves		
	SUBSTANTIVE DISAGREEMENTS	**BEHAVIORAL DYNAMICS**
Reflect and Reframe	• These are complicated issues where reasonable people can disagree. What data might we generate to move us closer to agreement? • These are controversial issues that go beyond facts to touch on people's values, preferences, and interests. Let's see if we can understand those better and generate options that address them. What are people concerned about or hoping for here?	• You two are starting to make the same assertions and counterassertions. Can you say what data you have that led you to be so convinced and what data might modify or change your views? • For some time now, two or three people have been dominating the discussion while others have stayed pretty quiet. Those of you who haven't yet weighed in, what are your thoughts on the topic?

Engaging

This strategy, which has the greatest impact on relationships, is by far the most obtrusive and usually requires the help of a highly skilled third party. Unlike the first two strategies, this one takes attention completely away from the business and focuses it squarely on what people are doing with each other.[5] This strategy can be used both "online" while you're addressing business issues or "offline," where you can suspend the pressures of business to address dynamics that repeatedly get in people's way. The aim of the online strategy is to ready people to do the work they need to do offline to transform their relationships (see Table 14).

This strategy is best used when patterns of interaction continually prevent people from making the kind of progress they want or need to make despite the use of less obtrusive interventions. Under these circumstances, you're better off putting the time aside and getting the help you need from a third party to transform those patterns.

TABLE 14: Engaging Moves		
	ONLINE	**OFFLINE**

Engaging	• Right now, everything you're doing seems to be tailor-made to bring out the worst in the other (illustrate). I'd like to suggest that we slow down and take a look at what you're each doing to produce results neither of you like.
	
	• Let's see if we can understand what's leading each of you (or all of you) to perpetuate dynamics you'd like to change.
	
	• By your own definition, everything you're each doing is backfiring: nothing is getting done, time is awasting, and others are getting impatient. Yet you each persist. How come?
		• Stage I: Disrupt Patterns (see Chapter 5):
		
		  ▸ Assess the relationship
		  ▸ Map Patterns of Interaction
		  ▸ Design Action Experiments
		
		• Stage II: Reframe Each Other (see Chapter 6)
		
		  ▸ Freeze Frame
		  ▸ Invent New Frames
		  ▸ Design Frame Experiments
		
		• Stage III: Revise What You "Know" (see Chapter 7):
		
		  ▸ Revisit Past Events
		  ▸ Restructure Outdated Knowledge
		  ▸ Return to the Future

Key Points

By drawing on three strategies—*facilitating, reflecting and reframing,* and *engaging*—people can make changes in their relationships while attending to business. Each strategy varies in terms of its obtrusiveness and impact. To figure out which strategy to use when, you must first *stop* (to gain perspective), then *look* (to map patterns in your head), and *listen* (to explore competing views). Only then can you choose wisely and, having chosen wisely, implement well.

10
Motivate Change

> There are no safe paths in this part of the world. Remember you are over the Edge of the Wild now, and in for all sorts of fun wherever you go. . . . Stick to the forest-track, keep your spirits up, hope for the best, and with a tremendous slice of luck you *may* come out one day.
>
> **—the wizard Gandalf in J. R. R. Tolkien's** *The Hobbit*

Everyone likes what change promises, but few relish what it demands: the time and effort it takes; the sacrifices we have to make; not knowing whether we'll succeed (or, if we succeed, whether we'll like what we get). Change is hard—so hard that many people give up before they even start. Yet as hard as change is, three common mistakes make it even harder:[1]

▶ **We set unrealistic expectations.** We cling to the mistaken belief that it's possible to make even significant changes quickly and with little effort, then despair and give up as soon as reality sets in.

▶ **We don't anticipate barriers or see the need to help each other overcome them.** We assume that if people want to change, they will change relatively quickly. We fail to understand that ingrained ways of seeing and doing things—what some call habits—lie largely outside our awareness. Instead of helping each other see what we can't see on our own, we grow cynical and give up.

▶ **We micromanage the pace and direction of change.** Whenever plans meet reality, slippage happens. Instead of putting that slippage to work to see what it has to teach us, most of us try to stamp it out. Exhausted from the effort, we abandon hope for change.

These three mistakes dampen our natural enthusiasm for change. Soon our motivation wanes. Where we used to go that extra mile, we now cut corners. We tell ourselves it's too hard or it's taking too long. Besides, while things aren't perfect, they're better than they were, so why work so hard? Before you know it, you've given up.

To stay motivated over time, you need a way to withstand the demands of change and to keep going in the face of setbacks. This chapter offers three principles for keeping your spirits up in the face of a challenging and risky venture:

- **Principle 1:** Use dual vision to set your sights.
- **Principle 2:** Build resilience while taking stock.
- **Principle 3:** Put the fun back in the dysfunctional.

These principles, each with its own set of practices, will help you create the motivation you need to sustain even the toughest changes.[2]

Principle 1:
Use Dual Vision to Set Your Sights

Many change efforts, whether designed for people or for organizations, swing back and forth between two poles. Some promise more change than they can deliver in a short time: personal transformation in a few days or cultural transformation in a few months. Others aspire to too little: a handful of insights after months of analysis. Similarly, some change efforts rivet on practical results to the exclusion of all else—"We'll cut costs! Beat the competition! Save time and money!"—while others focus only on more existential aspirations: "You'll have a sense of purpose! You'll be fulfilled! You'll feel more connected!"

To be motivated enough to invest in a risky and demanding change effort—and to keep investing over time—people need to set goals that are ambitious and realistic on the one hand and practically important and personally meaningful on the other.

Be Ambitious *and* Realistic

Most people won't invest much in an endeavor that doesn't promise much or that promises a lot but can't say how it will deliver. For change to be worth trying, people need a model of change that shows them how a series of smaller, more modest goals will eventually add up to bigger and bolder ones.[3] The three-stage model used in the Dan and Stu case study is one example (see Chapters 5 through 7). That model helped Dan and Stu see how relatively modest goals at Stage I, once met, would pave the way to more ambitious goals at Stage II—which, once met, would pave the way to even more ambitious goals at Stage III. At the same time, the model shed light on the steps they would need to take to move from one set of goals to another.

By staging change, you make fundamental change more feasible, and you keep people motivated long enough to pursue them. And because the model anticipates the dilemmas and paradoxes that arise at each stage, people are no longer shocked or dismayed by them. They can set them to work, using them to achieve ever more ambitious goals.[4]

Set Goals That Are Practically Important
and Personally Meaningful

Most people have a simultaneous interest in practical outcomes (making decisions, increasing revenues, keeping their jobs) and in existential outcomes (a sense of efficacy, connection, meaning, or self-respect). Although we rarely think about these two needs together, they coexist in our consciousness more or less peacefully. When that peace breaks down, as it's wont to do, people tend to declare war on one or the other, either making existential concerns submit to practical matters or vice versa. Although this war, once declared, is waged more or less consciously and intensely within each of us, most people conduct it with others as well—

one person pointing to the bottom line, the other to existential angst; one person saying, "Get over yourself!" and the other, "Get a life!"

This polarizing tendency leads people to set goals that speak to either practical matters or existential concerns—but not to both. But since even the most pragmatic among us have existential concerns, and even the most touchy-feely among us worry about practical matters, it becomes increasingly unacceptable if one or the other need goes unmet over the course of change. People end up either feeling great but not accomplishing much, or accomplishing a lot without it meaning much. To sustain people's commitment to change over time, then, change efforts must articulate goals that are *both* practically important *and* personally meaningful.

Principle 2:
Build Resilience While Taking Stock

Most people don't expect change efforts to be perfect, but they do expect observable, meaningful progress as a result of their efforts. If they can't see that progress, get confused over whether it's real, or get unduly thrown by setbacks, they'll grow discouraged and stop trying. To keep people motivated, you need to take stock of progress and use any setbacks to build resilience over time. You can accomplish this by assessing your progress in ways that build confidence and by putting setbacks, mistakes, and failures to work.

Build Confidence by Assessing Progress

In assessing progress, people tend to make one of two mistakes: either they look at how far they still have to go and ignore how far they've come, or they look at how far they've come and overlook how far they still have to go. It's the proverbial tendency to see the glass as half empty or half full. Whereas the former immediately discourages people, the latter leads them to underestimate what's left to do. Either way, sooner or later people end up too disappointed to sustain change.

To avoid making either mistake, it helps to have relatively clear metrics—ones that help you see how far you've come and how far you have to go. When it comes to relationship change, the most useful metrics tell you what you would need to feel, think, and see to be confident that you're making good headway at each stage. This means going beyond the tendency to make global evaluations—"We're doing great!" or "We're doing horribly!"—and looking at what people are actually thinking, feeling, and doing. This is why, in the case of Dan and Stu, we looked at transcripts and asked what they were thinking and feeling at different points in time. With these data in hand, we could see the ways in which their relationship was changing and the ways in which it needed to change further. This gave them confidence that changes were indeed being made and that these changes would accrue over time, keeping their spirits high enough to weather the occasional blow or upset.

Put Setbacks, Mistakes, and Failures to Work

Nothing kills motivation more than lambasting people for the inevitable setbacks, mistakes, or failures that accompany change in any relationship. That's why reflecting and reframing are so important (see Chapter 4). Anytime something goes wrong or someone gets upset, great! That's grist for the change mill: take a look at what it has to teach you.

Most people espouse this sentiment, especially in the wake of books on organizational learning. But very few people are able to hold onto that view in the face of their own or others' mistakes, setbacks, or failures. They feel too embarrassed, or they get too angry, or their worst fears get confirmed.

This gap between what people espouse and what they do is to be expected. The last thing people need is to feel embarrassed about being embarrassed, or angry about being angry, or fearful about being afraid. Rather than ask people to suppress their reactions to mistakes, it's best to use their reactions just as you would use the mistakes themselves. After all, reacting poorly to mistakes is simply another mistake, right? So why not use it for what it has to teach us? Once you lower the bar on what's acceptable to explore, you can use it all—no matter what it is—for purposes of change. That alone will speed up the pace of change and keep people motivated to continue.

"Why can't you be more like Hutchinson?
You don't hear him complaining."

Principle 3:
Put the Fun Back in the Dysfunctional

You can't change a relationship without exploring delicate issues or taking some emotional risks. At times the endeavor will feel so weighty you'll want to take a pass. To make the costs of change easier to bear, it helps to lighten things up by laughing at the unlaughable and manufacturing hope where none lies.

Laugh at the Unlaughable

Relationship change is challenging enough without making it too earnest or grim. To withstand the tumultuous feelings that accompany any change effort, you have to have fun; you have to laugh; you have to enjoy yourself. If it's all drudgery, you won't stick with it. Besides, if you look long enough, you can usually find comic relief in any circumstance, and if you can't, then create it. I've been known to stoop so low as to sing a verse of the song "Feelings" before asking a couple of analytic types to tell me how they were feeling. I'm convinced they told me just to get me to stop singing. But it worked: they laughed and said how they felt, confident in the knowledge that anything they said couldn't be more humiliating than what I'd just done. So have fun. As long as it's not at someone else's expense, it can leaven even the heaviest moment.[5]

Manufacture Hope

Hope is the single most important emotion to cultivate when you're trying to change a relationship. It makes people far more resilient in the face of setbacks and far more likely to invest in turning things around.[6] But how do you go about cultivating hope where none exists? You don't. You have to manufacture it. The trouble is that most people do just the opposite. They manufacture despair. They guard against disappointment by expecting little and hoping for less, and they end up with just that: little and less.

Since a relationship's prospects are inherently ambiguous, why not cast them in a hopeful light, at least provisionally? Even when that stretches your imagination beyond the breaking point, you're still better off *acting* as if you're hopeful. As Dan and Stu's case shows, you're much more likely to create a positive self-fulfilling prophecy by acting hopeful. Acting as if good things might follow increases the odds of creating circumstances that justify that hope. And remember, you can always stop hoping, but it's awfully hard to jump-start hope once pessimism sets in.

Key Points

There's no getting around it: change is difficult, and the more significant the change is, the more difficult it will be. Yet many of us render it even more difficult by making three common mistakes: setting unrealistic expectations, failing to anticipate and to help each other overcome predictable barriers, and micromanaging the pace and direction of change. You can counter these mistakes by following the three principles introduced in this chapter:

▸ **Setting your sights using dual vision.** Be ambitious and realistic, and set goals that are practically important and personally meaningful.

▸ **Building resilience while taking stock.** Build confidence by continually assessing progress, and put setbacks, mistakes, and failures to work.

▸ **Putting the fun back in the dysfunctional.** Laugh at the unlaughable and manufacture hope when there's none to be found.

When you put these principles into practice, you generate the motivation and energy needed to sustain change over time.

CODA

Relational
Sensibilities

Purpose: To identify the sensibilities that enable great leaders to navigate even the most complex relationships, and to explore ways to cultivate those sensibilities in all of us.

Synopsis: One hallmark of great leadership—especially in today's interdependent world—is the ability to discern with subtlety and navigate with deftness even the most turbulent emotional, moral, and political crosscurrents in relationships. More often than not, such leaders are able to pursue hardheaded political and economic goals through what we think of as softer *relational sensibilities.* These sensibilities cannot be taught through theory and technique alone. But they can be cultivated by helping people create new meaning out of difficult experiences in the context of strong relationships.

11
Sensibilities
for a Change

Am I not destroying my enemies when I make friends of them?

—Abraham Lincoln

No leader operates alone. Not Jack Welch, the much celebrated former CEO of General Electric, as he himself points out. Not the iconic leaders of great movements, as the many friends of Dr. Martin Luther King Jr. have testified. Not even the president of the United States, as historian Doris Kearns Goodwin's account of Abraham Lincoln's wartime cabinet reveals.[1]

Every leader, no matter how powerful, leads through relationships. Those leaders who are especially adept at doing so demonstrate a set of highly developed *relational sensibilities,* among them curiosity and courage, humility and hope, appreciation and acknowledgment, nuance and novelty, generosity and generativity, and empathy combined with a sense of accountability.[2] Within these pairs, each sensibility tempers or bolsters the other, serving leaders in much the same way aesthetic sensibilities serve the artist—by significantly enhancing the way they perceive, experience, and respond to the world around them.[3]

We can see these sensibilities at work and witness their power in a speech that comes from a very different time and context: Abraham Lincoln's second inaugural address. In this address, delivered as the American Civil War came to a close, Lincoln sought to win the peace by tending to the shattered relationship between North and South. Considered by many to be his finest speech, this seven-minute address illustrates well what Doris Kearns Goodwin observed: "In the hands of a truly great politician the qualities we generally associate with decency and morality . . . can also be impressive political resources."[4]

From Abraham Lincoln's address, we can learn about the sensibilities that defined his greatness. From his life, we can learn how to cultivate those sensibilities in mere mortal leaders.

Imagine the Time and the Context

After four years of fighting, the Civil War was finally drawing to a close, but not before it had destroyed more American lives than any war before or since. On the day of the president's inauguration, all those gathering in the nation's capital were anxious to hear news of the war's end. The late winter weather did not cooperate. A cold, torrential rain began early and, like the war, refused to stop. Even so, an unprecedented number of people made their way along muddy streets to hear what Lincoln had to say. With 623,000 lives gone—one out of every eleven men of service age[5]—most wanted to hear only one thing: claims of victory and promises of vengeance. To them, justice meant retribution, and peace without justice meant no victory at all.

Never has a leader said more with fewer words. In a 703-word address, 505 of them no more than one syllable,[6] Lincoln asked the nation "to think with him about the cause and the meaning of the war."[7] No finer example exists of a leader pursuing a hardheaded political goal through what we think of as softer sensibilities.[8]

In the few minutes he spoke, Lincoln took up three questions: Who caused the war? Why did we have to lose so much? And how can we possibly move forward together? Lincoln's answers to each question risked disappointing his audience. Instead of appealing to people's yearning for victory and craving for vengeance, he called for healing and spoke of the North's complicity in slavery and ultimately the war.[9] How Lincoln reached across the divide that stood between him and his audience, so that they might reach across the divide that stood between North and South, is a testament to his genius.

Behind this genius are the same set of sensibilities I've observed in other great leaders who lead through the relationships they form with their followers.[10] Lincoln shows that it's what you *see and bring out in followers* that makes a truly great leader. As you read what Lincoln said over 150 years ago (see box), pay attention to what he brings out in you today.

Lincoln's Second Inaugural Address[11]

Fellow Countrymen:

At this second appearing, to take the oath of the presidential office, there is less occasion for an extended address than there was at the first. Then a statement, somewhat in detail, of a course to be pursued, seemed fitting and proper. Now, at the expiration of four years, during which public declarations have been constantly called forth on every point and phase of the great contest which still absorbs the attention, and engrosses the energies of the nation, little that is new could be presented. The progress of our arms, upon which all else chiefly depends, is as well known to the public as to myself; and it is, I trust, reasonably satisfactory and encouraging to all. With high hope for the future, no prediction in regard to it is ventured.

On the occasion corresponding to this four years ago, all thoughts were anxiously directed to an impending civil war. All dreaded it—all sought to avert it. While the inaugural address was being delivered from this place, devoted altogether to *saving* the Union without war—insurgent agents were in the city seeking to *destroy* it without war—seeking to dissolve the Union, and divide effects, by negotiation. Both parties deprecated war; but one of them would make war rather than let the nation survive; and the other would accept war rather than let it perish. And the war came.

One eighth of the whole population were colored slaves, not distributed generally over the Union, but localized in the Southern part of it. These slaves constituted a peculiar and powerful interest. All knew that this interest was, somehow, the cause of the war. To strengthen, perpetuate, and extend this interest was the object for which the insurgents would rend the Union, even by war; while the government claimed no right to do more than to restrict the territorial enlargement of it. Neither party expected for the war, the magnitude, or the duration, which it has already attained. Neither anticipated that the cause of the conflict might cease with, or even before, the conflict itself should cease. Each looked for an easier triumph, and a result less fundamental and astounding. Both read the same Bible, and pray to the same God; and each invokes His aid against the other. It may seem strange that any men should dare to ask a just God's assistance in wringing their bread from the sweat of other men's faces; but let us judge not that we be not judged. The prayers of both could not be answered; that of neither has been answered fully. The Almighty has his own purposes. "Woe unto the world because of offences! For it must needs the offences come; but woe to that man by whom the offence cometh!" If we shall suppose that American Slavery is one of those offences which, in the providence of God, must needs come, but which, having continued through His appointed time, He now wills to remove, and that He gives to both North and South, this terrible war, as the woe due to those by whom the offence came, shall we discern therein any departure from those divine attributes which the believers in a Living God always ascribe to Him? Fondly do we hope—fervently do we pray—that this mighty scourge of war may speedily pass away. Yet, if God wills that it continue, until all the wealth piled by the bondsman's two hundred and fifty years of unrequited toil shall be sunk, and until every drop of blood drawn with the lash, shall be paid by another drawn with the sword, as was said three thousand years ago, so still it must be said "the judgments of the Lord, are true and righteous altogether."

With malice toward none; with charity for all; with firmness in the right, as God gives us to see the right, let us strive on to finish the work we are in; to bind up the nation's wounds; to care for him who shall have borne the battle, and for his widow, and his orphan—to do all which may achieve and cherish a just, and a lasting peace, among ourselves, and with all nations.

Relational Sensibilities

In four paragraphs, Lincoln sets out to recast the war and, in recasting it, set the stage for peace. Far more than rhetorical technique is at work here—far more than a masterful politician attuned to his audience's needs and preferences.[12] Behind Lincoln's mastery is a finely honed set of sensibilities. These sensibilities informed the way he put his rhetorical skill to use and determined the political ends toward which he deployed his mastery. Let's look at each pair of sensibilities, then explore how we might cultivate them in all leaders. [13]

Curiosity and Courage

The curiosity Lincoln brought to the problem of slavery was anything but idle. It was the curiosity of a restless mind able to keep tough questions alive and to pursue them with courage wherever they led. *How did this war come to be?* For four years Lincoln had struggled with this question, trying to understand what "great good" could come of this "mighty convulsion."[14]

And for more years still, he'd grappled with the moral implications of slavery, struggling to understand how a country founded on democratic principles could defend the existence—let alone promote the expansion—of slavery. In the end, he came to see that slavery was not just evil at its "core" but in its "circumference." [15] As Ronald White Jr. recounts in *Lincoln's Greatest Speech:*

> Whereas for a long time he had been willing to contain slavery politi-
> cally and geographically, he had come to the conclusion in the midst
> of the Civil War that its moral implications could not be contained.
> Slavery made a lie to democratic principles. [16]

Having arrived at this conclusion, Lincoln might have decided to play to his political base in the North, blaming the South for slavery and for the war. But he made a different choice. When he speaks of slavery, he doesn't call it Southern slavery but "American Slavery," and when he speaks of the war, he doesn't point a finger only at the South but speaks of God giving to "*both* North and South, this terrible war, as the woe due to those by whom the offence came. . . ." [17]

In choosing these words, Lincoln decided to confront the ethical behavior of an entire nation.[18] "Instead of self-congratulation, he asked his fellow citizens for self-analysis," White observes. "No president, before or since, has so courageously pointed to a malady that resides at the very center of the American national family."[19]

With enough curiosity to ask tough questions and enough courage to face tough answers, Lincoln distinguished himself from all other politicians—in his day and in our own.

Hope and Humility

These two sensibilities—*hope* and *humility*[20]—make for mighty strange bedfellows. While one rests on an abiding belief in our ability to create a better future, the other leans on an equally abiding belief in the limitations of human actors. Yet the two show up together in Lincoln's address, two bookends buttressing the ideas within. In his opening, Lincoln provides no grand plans, offers no comforting reassurances—only a bit of hope coupled with a good deal of humility. Dispensing with the war's progress in a single phrase—"it is, I trust, reasonably satisfactory and encouraging to all"—he goes on to speak of its prospects, saying only, "With high hope for the future, no prediction in regard to it is ventured."

This understated account springs from years of reflection on the limited role of human actors, even those with the power of the presidency. "If I had my way," Lincoln wrote Eliza Gurney three years earlier, "this war would never have commenced. If I had been allowed my way this war would have ended before this, but we find it still continues."[21]

As unable to stop the war from starting as he was to bring it to an early close, Lincoln makes no boasts or promises. Instead, he puts the future course of the war in the hands of God, while putting in the hands of an embattled nation the only hope for peace:

. . . if God wills that [the war] continue, until all the wealth piled by the bondsman's two hundred and fifty years of unrequited toil shall be sunk, and until every drop of blood drawn with the lash, shall be paid by another drawn with the sword, as was said three thousand years ago, so still it must be said "the judgments of the Lord, are true and righteous altogether."

Then, moving from what God might will to what the nation must do,[22] he adds:

With malice toward none; with charity for all; with firmness in the right, as God gives us to see the right, let us strive on to finish the work we are in; to bind up the nation's wounds; to care for him who shall have borne the battle, and for his widow, and his orphan—to do all which may achieve and cherish a just, and a lasting peace, among ourselves, and with all nations.

In this final passage, Lincoln defines the work his fellow countrymen have yet to finish. What makes the passage so remarkable is not just what it says, but what it doesn't say. Nowhere in the passage can you find absolute certainty about who's right—for only God knows what's right. And nowhere can you find absolute certainty about whose might will prevail—for only God is Almighty and he may will that the war continue.

Instead what you find is a list of tasks to be completed: binding up the nation's wounds, caring for all those who have borne the battle, and caring for their widows and orphans. Only through these humble tasks—tasks of nurturance, not of war—can the nation hope to achieve and cherish a just and lasting peace.

When you juxtapose Lincoln's final passage against the certainty with which so many claims are made today—about God's intentions, about wars being won before they're begun, about evil empires versus God-loving peoples—it's startling.

Appreciation and Acknowledgment

These two words mean very different things to different people.[23] I bring them together here to convey a special meaning: that you can *understand people's internal experiences and external circumstances with so much acuity* (appreciation) *that you make it easier for them to accept the role they played in creating those experiences and circumstances* (acknowledgment).

You can see these companion sensibilities at work in how Lincoln lays the groundwork for the entreaties with which he ends his address. Acutely aware that people are worn out, anxious, and impatient,[24] Lincoln knows that the charity he asks for in the end "might be too much to expect of those who encountered such great losses."[25] Even so, he doesn't seek to reassure or comfort. Rather, he invites his audience to come along with him as he recounts events, explains causes, and contemplates the war's deeper meaning. As he takes each of these three steps, he demonstrates an understanding of people's experiences and circumstances, earning him the right to point to the role they've played in creating them. Let's look at how he takes each step.

Recounting events. In this first step, Lincoln goes back in time to recount what both sides were thinking, feeling, and intending as the war approached:

> On the occasion corresponding to this four years ago, all thoughts were anxiously directed to an impending civil war. All dreaded it—all sought to avert it. While the inaugural address was being delivered from this place, devoted altogether to *saving* the Union without war—insurgent agents were in the city seeking to *destroy* it without war—seeking to dissolve the Union, and divide effects, by negotiation. Both parties deprecated war; but one of them would make war rather than let the nation survive; and the other would accept war rather than let it perish. And the war came.

In this opening account, Lincoln focuses not only on what was happening four years earlier but on what was going on in the hearts and minds of people in the North and South:

▸ *What both sides were thinking and feeling:* "On the occasion corresponding to this four years ago, all thoughts were anxiously directed to an impending civil war. All dreaded it . . . ."
▸ *What both sides intended:* ". . . all sought to avert it."
▸ *What both sides were willing to do:* ". . . one [side] would make war rather than let the nation survive; and the other would accept war rather than let it perish."
▸ *What both sides felt they couldn't control:* "And the war came."

In this public rendering of people's private mental states, Lincoln puts to good use his ability not just to *read* but to *appreciate* the experience of *all* the people, not just *some* of the people. In so doing, he invites his audience to see beyond their caricatures of each other to the complex feelings, thoughts, and intentions that both sides experienced. It's as if he's saying there are no good guys or bad guys—just anxious people with good intentions and limited abilities, unable to avert a war they dreaded. And so the war came.

Explaining causes. In taking this second step, Lincoln shifts attention away from people's internal experiences and onto their external circumstances, pointing to the war's cause:

One eighth of the whole population were colored slaves, not distributed generally over the Union, but localized in the Southern part of it. These slaves constituted a peculiar and powerful interest. All knew that this interest was, somehow, the cause of the war. To strengthen, perpetuate, and extend this interest was the object for which the insurgents would rend the Union, even by war; while the government claimed no right to do more than to restrict the territorial enlargement of it.

In this passage, Lincoln implies that circumstance, not malevolence, spawned the South's interest in slavery and in its perpetuation: the region's political economy depended on it. Here he seems to be saying there but for the grace of God goes the North; had its economy been similarly dependent, the North might have been similarly interested. In taking this tack, Lincoln helps his audience appreciate, as he does, the different circumstances the two regions faced, so that it might better understand the war's causes and more easily forgive its consequences.

Contemplating deeper meanings. With these two steps behind him, Lincoln is ready to take up the war's deeper meaning. To do so, he turns to the Bible, knowing that those listening had done so as well, and he draws on their shared belief system to examine God's hand in the war.[26]

"The Almighty has his own purposes," he starts; then, quoting from the Bible, he adds, "'Woe unto the world because of offences! For it must needs the offences come; but woe to that man by whom the offence cometh!'" This passage—one his audience had probably read many times—becomes a set piece for his reflections:

> If we shall suppose that American Slavery is one of those offences which, in the providence of God, must needs come, but which, having continued through His appointed time, He now wills to remove, and that He gives to both North and South, this terrible war, as the woe due to those by whom the offence came, shall we discern therein any departure from those divine attributes which the believers in a Living God always ascribe to Him?

This passage is by far the most controversial. By supposing that God has given the war to both North and South as the woe resulting from the offense of American slavery, he's in effect asking the North to acknowledge its own hand in slavery and in the war. It's not by chance that he makes this request only after demonstrating an appreciation for the internal experiences and external circumstances of both sides.

Yet even now, he knows he runs a big risk—that of offending his audience's less developed sensibilities. And so he places these potentially divisive meanings in the context of a common Bible, appealing to his audience's shared belief in a Living God. Thus, by the time Lincoln poses the question—"shall we discern therein any departure from those divine attributes which the believers in a Living God always ascribe to Him?"— nary a head could say no. [27] It was Lincoln's extraordinary ability to appreciate what both sides were up against that earned him the right to look at their collective role in slavery and in the war.

Nuance and Novelty

Nuance (the ability to pick up on subtleties, not just patterns) and *novelty* (the ability to construe things in a fundamentally new light, not simply rehash old positions) make it possible for leaders to resolve even the most intractable conflicts.

For decades before the war came, politicians in both the North and the South had been turning each other into cardboard villains with evil intentions lurking behind every action and morally bankrupt values lying behind every hint of self-interest. Ultimately this—not clashing interests alone—is what made civil war inevitable.

Lincoln understood this. In fact, by the time he delivered his address, he'd come to believe that most Americans "battled in confusion," not truly understanding "the causes and consequences of the war."[28] What troubled him most was that each side was convinced that they alone were defending some God-given right and that the other side was intent on destroying that right.[29] Worried that a "nation divided in war would remain divided in peace,"[30] he strove throughout his address to help people see the war and each other in a new light by drawing attention to aspects of the situation his audience's caricatures of one another failed to grasp: *what both sides had in common.* As Lincoln saw it (italics are mine):

▶ "*Both* parties deprecated war."
▶ "*All* dreaded it—*all* sought to avert it."
▶ "*Neither* anticipated that the cause of the conflict might cease with, or even before, the conflict itself should cease."
▶ "*Each* looked for an easier triumph, and a result less fundamental and astounding."
▶ "*Both* read the same Bible, and pray to the same God; and *each* invokes His aid against the other."

To prevent his audience from rejecting this more nuanced view of the South before even considering it, Lincoln builds a rhetorical bridge. On one side of this bridge, he anticipates his audience's skepticism: "It may seem strange that any men should dare to ask a just God's assistance in wringing their bread from the sweat of other men's faces"; [31] while on the other side, he strives to put that skepticism to rest by alluding to a frequently quoted passage from the Bible: "but let us judge not that we be not judged."

It is on this rhetorical bridge—connecting an unfamiliar idea to a familiar belief system—that Lincoln frames the war as the righteous result of a moral offense committed by *both* North and South. In proposing this novel notion, Ronald White argues, Lincoln wasn't just setting the historical record straight:

> Lincoln understood, as many in his own party did not, that the Southern people would never be able to take their full places in the Union if they felt that they alone were saddled with the guilt for what was the national offense of slavery. [32]

Lincoln's exceptional ability to see things others did not is what allowed him to win the peace, not just the war. By proposing a more nuanced view of the war and its contestants, he gave the nation a new way of seeing the war and each other—a way of seeing that both sides would need to create a lasting peace.

Generosity and Generativity

"I don't like that man," Lincoln once said, then added, "I must get to know him better." In this comment, Lincoln exemplifies two other sensibilities that informed the way he conducted himself in relationships *and* the way he conducted the war: *generosity* (the ability to *see* the best in others) and *generativity* (the ability develop and to *bring out* the best in others).

Lincoln brought both these sensibilities to the way he conducted the war. Though he executed the war with great determination, he never once approached it with malevolence. "I shall do nothing in malice," he wrote in 1862. "What I deal with is too vast for malicious dealing." [33] As Lincoln saw it, neither side intended what the war had brought: "Neither party expected for the war, the magnitude, or the duration, which it has already attained. . . . Each looked for an easier triumph, and a result less fundamental and astounding."

Unlike many others on the day of the inaugural speech, Lincoln had no trouble forgiving the South. He never saw evil intent in their actions. All he saw were the same efforts to avert war that he saw in the North. Nor did he see any calculated intention to destroy hundreds of thousands of lives. All he saw was the same astonishment at the war's consequences.

That's why, when his address comes to a close with the phrase "With malice toward none; with charity for all" it rings true. His entire speech had been an extended entreaty to both sides to see and bring out the best in each other—to be charitable, not malicious. Says White:

> Other words of his, from the Gettysburg Address—"of the people, by the people, for the people"—endure because they define America. *"With malice toward none; with charity for all"* defined Lincoln's vision for a post–Civil War America.[34]

This vision, which defined Lincoln's legacy long after his assassination, looked beyond people's immediate desire for vengeance to see and bring out their more lasting desire for peace.

Empathy Combined With Accountability

In most cultures, empathy and accountability are a null set: where you find one, you can't find the other. Either you empathize with how people feel and the circumstances they're up against, *or* you hold them accountable for their actions and the consequences they create.

In Lincoln's address, empathy and accountability work hand in hand. One moment, he's empathizing with what everyone's up against or with what they're feeling, thinking, and intending. The next, he's confronting everyone with the moral and practical consequences of their collective actions. Had Lincoln's empathy been untempered by accountability, he could not have looked at what both sides did to create consequences they later regretted. Yet had his sense of accountability gone untempered by empathy, he could not have asked an embittered nation to offer only charity to the other side. By bringing the two together, Lincoln asked both sides to rise to the occasion, and he made it more likely that they would.

To work together well, empathy and accountability depend on all the other sensibilities. Lincoln's ability to empathize with his fellow countrymen springs from his own struggle to fathom the war's meaning (curiosity); from recognizing the limited control people can exert over events (humility); from understanding people's experiences and circumstances (appreciation); from grasping subtleties that go beyond conventional wisdom (nuance); and from seeing the best in both sides (generosity). Far from a rhetorical gambit, then, Lincoln's empathy is a deeply authentic expression of how he feels, and it comes across that way.

Similarly, when Lincoln holds the nation accountable for the offense of slavery, he doesn't simply round up the usual suspects and hold them to account. He confronts the ethical behavior of an entire nation (courage); he asks the North to accept its role in slavery and the war (acknowledgment); he holds out hope that the nation can bind up its wounds and create a just and lasting peace (hope); he offers a new way of understanding the war to make that hope more realistic (novelty); and he speaks to and cultivates the best in people throughout the address (generativity). Instead of punishing either side for creating a result more fundamental and astounding than either expected, he inspired both sides to do better.

Implications: The Softer Side of Power

Had Lincoln vilified the South or relished in the North's triumph, he still would have won the war but he could not have set the stage for peace. The power to create a lasting peace in part resides in the softer sensibilities that Lincoln brought to his leadership. With these sensibilities, Lincoln was able to reach across the divide that separated him from his followers, so they could reach across the divide that separated them from each other. In an age when neither geography nor borders can stop the spread of violence, it may be an idea whose time has come.

While the full impact of Lincoln's address can never be assessed, three days after the speech twenty-nine-year-old Charles Francis Adams Jr. wrote to his father, "This inaugural strikes me in its grand simplicity and directness as being for all time the historical keynote of this war." Adams should know. Recently promoted to colonel, he'd fought at Antietam and Gettysburg; he'd served the previous summer with the fifth Massachusetts Cavalry, an African American regiment; and his family claimed among them two presidents: John Adams and John Quincy Adams.[35]

Cultivating Sensibilities

By studying how these sensibilities developed naturally in Lincoln, we can learn a lot about how to cultivate them in today's leaders. Goodwin's account of Lincoln's life and relationships suggest that these sensibilities spring from a combination of three factors, all of which need to be in place: challenging experiences, new meaning, and strong relationships. Let's look at how each of these factors shaped Lincoln's sensibilities and explore the implications of each for how we might improve the way we develop leaders.

Challenging Experiences

By the time Lincoln was twenty-six years old, he'd lost his mother, his older sister, an infant brother, and his first love. Though his stepmother lived on, the only person left standing from his biological family was his father, who deprived Abe of his last chance for schooling by hiring him out to neighbors to pay off a family debt.[36] Far from defeating Lincoln, these losses and disappointments only served to strengthen his character, as Goodwin shows by contrasting Lincoln with his two main rivals for the 1860 Republican nomination, William Seward and Salmon Chase:

> . . . his familiarity with pain and personal disappointment imbued him with a strength and understanding of human frailty unavailable to a man of Seward's buoyant disposition. Moreover, Lincoln, unlike the

brooding Chase, possessed a life-affirming humor and a profound resilience that lightened his despair and fortified his will.[37]

You can see this "profound resilience" at work in the summer of 1855
when "disappointment piled upon disappointment." As Goodwin tells it,
a distinguished lawyer from Philadelphia by the name of George Harding
asked Lincoln to help out on a celebrated patent case being tried in Chicago.[38] Though Harding was only looking for a lawyer who "understood
the judge and had his confidence," Lincoln was "thrilled," devoting all
his energies and talents to developing materials for the case.

A month later, however, the case was moved to Cincinnati, and, unbeknownst to Lincoln, Harding hired in his place the renowned lawyer
Edwin Stanton. Unaware he'd been replaced, Lincoln showed up in Cincinnati ready to impress Harding, only to learn that Harding had no need
of him. Worse, after introducing himself, Lincoln overheard Stanton as
he pulled Harding aside to whisper, "Why did you bring that damned
long-armed ape here? He does not know any thing and can do you no
good."

Despite his humiliation, Lincoln stayed on to hear the case, only to
discover that Stanton's arguments far surpassed his own. According to
one observer, an undeterred Lincoln stood "in rapt attention . . . drink-
ing in his words." After the case ended, Lincoln told the observer he was
going home "to study law," explaining:

> For any rough-and-tumble case (and a pretty good one, too), I am
> enough for any man we have out in that country; but these college-
> trained men are coming West. They have had all the advantages of a
> life-long training in the law, plenty of time to study and everything,
> perhaps, to fit them. Soon they will be in Illinois . . . and when they
> appear I will be ready.

So what can this 150-year-old account teach us about developing leaders today? According to theoretical economist Paul Ormerod, in his recent
book *Why Most Things Fail*, for companies to succeed, they must expect
and react flexibly to failure, as Coca-Cola did after New Coke bombed.

"Coke reacted rapidly and flexibly to the disaster," he points out, even though it meant "abandoning its meticulously crafted strategy."[39]

This advice is hardly new. But it still goes largely unheeded, because most leaders today don't know how to put failure to good use as Lincoln did.

Why is this? One reason is that most leaders make it to the top because they rarely fail, leaving them at a loss when they do. But another reason—one we can influence—goes to the heart of most leadership programs. The vast majority of them emphasize practice over experimentation, giving participants little opportunity to fail—or to learn how to put failure to good use. If anything, today's programs protect participants from the pain of failure by giving instructions so precise that little can go wrong, by focusing mostly on people's strengths, and by calling their weaknesses not weaknesses but "areas needing development." The implicit motto of such programs seems to be: practice, practice, practice, because practice makes perfect.

No program should set out to create failure or humiliate participants. But developmental efforts would serve leaders better if they created opportunities for participants not just to practice but to experiment, then taught them not just how to fail but how to succeed at failing. After all, it's not failure alone but the ability to put failure to good use that creates flexibility and resilience. That ability depends on the next two factors: the meaning we make out of disappointing experience, and the strength of the relationships that shape, even transform, that experience. These two factors allow us to convert pain and failure into resolve, so we're ready for whatever our competition throws at us when they come to town.

New Meaning

Lincoln was able to make good things out of bad experiences because of the meaning he saw in them and took from them. From the time he was a young boy, he read voraciously, he listened sympathetically, and he created captivating stories. All three activities allowed him to transcend or recast painful experiences—or at the very least, endure them with good humor.

Early in his life Lincoln first broke free of the confines of a backwoods existence by reading books.[40] Finding those books, however, wasn't easy. Unlike his cohorts later in life, no one gave him books or the opportunity to read them at his leisure. He had to create that opportunity for himself by borrowing books he didn't have, or rereading those he did. Once, he even worked two days to pay for a book he'd accidentally damaged. Perhaps that's why, when he finally got his hands on a book, he scoured it for interesting new thoughts and ideas. Notes Goodwin:

"When he came across a passage that struck him," his stepmother recalled, "he would write it down on boards if he had no paper," and "when the board would get too black he would shave it off with a drawing knife and go on again."[41]

Later on Lincoln came to read people just as closely as he read books. He studied everyone he met, asking them probing questions and listening to what lay in their hearts when they answered. By taking the time to read people this closely, Lincoln could make sense of their positions— even when he vehemently disagreed with them, as he did in 1854 when the South sought to expand slavery into the new territories through the Kansas-Nebraska Act. Though he brought all his rhetorical skill to repudiating the act, he never repudiated the people advocating it. You can see in the line of argument Lincoln put forth then the same line of argument he used ten years later in his Second Inaugural Address:

[The Southerners] are just what we would be in their situation. If slavery did not now exist amongst them, they would not introduce it. If it did now exist amongst us, we should not instantly give it up. . . . When it is said that the institution exists; and that it is very difficult to get rid of it, in any satisfactory way, I can understand and appreciate the saying. I surely will not blame them for not doing what I should not know how to do myself.[42]

"Rather than upbraid slaveowners," Goodwin points out, "Lincoln sought to comprehend their position through empathy." And then, having comprehended their position, he confronted them "with the contradictions . . . that existed in their own laws and social practices."[43] Where under the same circumstances William Seward would appeal to a higher law and Salmon Chase to natural rights derived from heaven, Lincoln was more inclined to speak to people's hearts. This ability to first read and then speak to people's hearts allowed Lincoln to make sense of slavery in ways that others could not, ultimately allowing him to recast the meaning of the Civil War.

Throughout his life, Lincoln relied on stories to make lighter sense of painful experience. An old friend from Springfield, Illinois, once said that when Lincoln told funny stories, ". . . he emerged from his cave of gloom and came back, like one awakened from sleep, to the world in which he lived again."[44] And *New York Tribune* correspondent Henry Villard noticed that when Lincoln told these stories, he not only sought to ease his own pain but "to heal wounded feelings and mitigate [the] disappointments" of others.[45]

These three activities—reading books for ideas, reading people for understanding, and telling stories for levity—served Lincoln well. They cultivated in him a way of perceiving people and situations that was so fresh, so acute, so finely tuned that he was able to make of difficult experiences things others could not—things he could use to find common ground, to withstand adversity, to persevere in the face of failure, and to help others do the same.

Despite their importance, these activities are unlikely to be found in great supply in today's leadership programs. Ideas are too impractical, especially if they're complicated; reading people closely takes too much time and has nothing to do with taking action; and funny stories are for entertainment, not for deeper meaning. What you *will* find in great supply, though, are techniques for everything from active listening to straight talk to negotiation. These techniques—taught as they are in a perceptual vacuum—not only fail to cultivate relational sensibilities, they frequently fall flat. Without a good reading of people to guide them, these techniques often come across as gimmicks, or worse, as manipulative tricks.

To develop new sensibilities, leaders need more than techniques. They need to see and do things in new ways. To help, developmental efforts should do three things: expose participants to ideas that challenge their current ways of seeing; develop their ability to read people and situations with greater acuity; and help them reframe how they see difficult experiences.

Take the Anatomy Framework as an example (see Chapter 3). This framework challenges conventional wisdom, which holds that other people *make* us feel things.[46] In contrast, it proposes that our feelings are a joint venture—a product of our *interactions* and the way we *frame* them, given our *repertoires.* While this idea questions our current way of seeing things, it also frees us to work together to map and alter the pattern. No more waiting for the other person to change before we can feel better.

Another example is the Ladder of Reflection (see Appendix B). When used in tandem with the Anatomy Framework, it develops our ability to read people more closely. By asking us to pay attention to what's actually happening, the ladder requires us to look more closely at people. And by offering a framework rather than categories as a lens through which to look, the Anatomy Framework turns our attention away from labeling people and toward what they're doing, how they feel, and how they interact. Together the two ideas make it much harder to turn people into caricatures and much easier to make new sense of those old situations in which you feel caught (see Chapter 4 for an example).

A third example is the design of frame experiments, each one aimed at helping people transform how they see things. As Chapter 6 illustrates, when people tether new actions to new ways of seeing, they integrate new behaviors more quickly, so those behaviors feel more natural to them and less artificial to others. By giving people guidance on how to design such experiments, we help them take actions that make new ways of seeing more practical and realistic.

Lincoln devoured new ideas and studied people closely throughout his life, continually reframing how he saw everything from himself to slavery to the role of North and South to the Civil War. By doing the same things, leaders today can cultivate in themselves the same set of sensibilities we see in Lincoln.

Strong Relationships

Lincoln's earliest and most important relationships allowed him to transform painful experiences into an enduring resilience. Says Goodwin:

> If Lincoln's developing self-confidence was fostered initially by his mother's love and approval, it was later sustained by his stepmother, who came to love him as if he were her own child. . . . Sarah Bush Lincoln recognized that Abraham was "a Boy of uncommon natural Talents." Though uneducated herself, she did all she could to encourage him to read, learn, and grow.[47]

These early relationships gave Lincoln a gift for forging strong relationships. That gift sustained and buoyed him as he and his fellow lawyers eked out a living trying cases throughout Illinois. Sharing rooms, sometimes beds, they spent "long evenings gathered together around a blazing fire. . . . Everywhere [Lincoln] went, he won devoted followers, friendships that later emboldened his quest for office."[48]

This gift for forming strong relationships also served Lincoln well when he became president. Only hours after winning the election, Lincoln set out to assemble support:

> . . . keenly aware of the fractious nature of the youthful Republican Party and the ominous threats from the South, [Lincoln] understood that his country was entering a most perilous time. . . . "I began at once to feel that I needed support," he noted later; "others to share with me the burden." As the exhausted townsfolk shuffled back to their homes, . . . Lincoln began to compose his official family—the core of his administration. "This was on Wednesday morning," he revealed, "and before the sun went down, I had made up my cabinet. . . ."[49]

In assembling his support Lincoln didn't seek people who would offer him blind loyalty. Quite the contrary: he chose his most powerful and most talented rivals. Over the next four years, each of these competitors—all of whom had disparaged him at one time or another—"became colleagues who helped him steer the country through its darkest days."[50]

Seward was the first to appreciate Lincoln's remarkable talent, quickly realizing the futility of his plan to relegate the president to a figure-head role. In the months that followed Seward would become Lincoln's friend and advisor in the administration. Though Bates initially viewed Lincoln as a well-meaning but incompetent administrator, he eventually concluded that the president was an unmatched leader, "very near being a perfect man." Edwin Stanton, who had treated Lincoln with contempt at their initial acquaintance, developed a great respect for the commander in chief and was unable to control his tears for weeks after the president's death. Even Chase, whose restless ambition for the presidency was never realized, at last acknowledged that Lincoln had outmaneuvered him.[51]

These men supported Lincoln by loving and challenging him during his darkest days as commander in chief. It was Lincoln's cabinet that saw the nation through war—not any one man alone, not even Lincoln. Had he not succeeded in making friends of his political enemies, things might have turned out very differently—for Lincoln, for his team, and for the nation. As it was, Lincoln and his team were able to weather the single worst moment in American history and to create out of that moment a lasting peace.

Implications for Cultivating Relational Sensibilities

Anytime you set out to cultivate sensibilities, you face a chicken-and-egg problem. People can't develop new sensibilities without engaging in certain activities—like reading people or reframing how they see them—yet they can't undertake these activities skillfully unless they already have highly developed sensibilities.

Developmental efforts have to start somewhere. Since you can't start with sensibilities that participants don't have, you have to start with the activities that will develop them, even if those activities—absent the sensibilities—make participants uncomfortable at first. Such activities include: exposing participants to ideas that challenge their current way of seeing things, giving them tools with which to observe and read people more closely, and offering them guidance on how to conduct frame experiments. Over time, each of these activities enhances the way people perceive, experience, and respond to the world around them.

How much time it takes depends on the context in which these activities take place. The ideal context emphasizes reflection and experimentation (not just action and practice), creates opportunities to fail (not just to succeed), and builds psychologically safe relationships (not purely competitive ones). This type of context allows relational sensibilities to take root quickly, while the activities just described accelerate their development.

"With High Hope for the Future, No Prediction in Regard to It Is Ventured"

Since Lincoln's time, the world has shrunk, boundaries have collapsed, technologies have advanced, and science has solved many a mystery. Yet people keep struggling to get along and keep fighting when they don't. Despite our best efforts, we haven't made as much progress on the social front. Even today, we keep trying to change everyone else by getting them to do this or that differently. But the problem is more fundamental: it speaks to our relationships and how they both shape and are shaped by what goes on in our hearts and minds.

Lincoln was ahead of his time—and ahead of ours. We still have a lot to learn from his example, especially if we look at the sensibilities that defined his greatness and focus on cultivating them in ourselves and in each other.

My recent efforts to cultivate those sensibilities—in a seminar called "Leading through Relationships"—give me hope.[52]

One of Merrimac's many efforts to invest in relationships (see Chapters 4 through 7), the seminar began five years ago, and it included six up-and-coming young leaders, all of them men, all of them skeptical. "What is this seminar, anyway?" they asked the firm's leadership after being nominated to participate. Then, discovering it was about relationships, they secretly dubbed it "The Brotherhood of Love," convinced they were in for a long touchy-feely ride.

The first day of the seminar only confirmed their worst fears. After hearing words like "sensibilities" and learning that they would be reading books like Maya Angelou's autobiography, *I Know Why the Caged Bird Sings*, and Joseph Conrad's *The Heart of Darkness*, they knew they were in trouble. Worse, they saw from the syllabus that they had to write up three case stories, describing three relationships in detail: one with a superior, one with a peer, and one with a subordinate. And if that wasn't bad enough, they saw that they had to discuss them publicly with one another. No, this wasn't their father's Oldsmobile.

Yet by the end of the first year, the group enthusiastically elected to continue, and now, five years later, we still meet monthly. Along the way, the group grew into their tongue-in-cheek "Brotherhood of Love" appellation. The first sign came when, early on, one of the participants noticed that Maya Angelou was coming to town to spend an evening at Boston's Symphony Hall. Deciding to go, the group bought tickets, and on the night of her appearance, we all piled into our cars, scrunched down into our crowded balcony seats, and soon found ourselves carried away by a voice that rose and fell on the same sensibilities you see in this chapter. The group went in thinking it was a chick evening; they came out inspired.

The next sign came when the group confronted its first conflicts. In the course of mapping their interactions and exploring their differences— some of them quite emotional—they came to see that they'd been turning each other into caricatures, that they were inadvertently encouraging behaviors they didn't like, that what they saw was often what they got, that there was always more going on than met the eye, and that there were better or worse ways to uncover what lay there. In the course of learning these things, through both their interactions and their case stories, they came to see each other and themselves in a fundamentally new light.

Over the years, this new perspective made it easier for them to see and bring out the best in each other, to get curious and then courageous enough to satisfy that curiosity, to appreciate what they were each up against and to acknowledge their own shortcomings, to offer hope from a more humble point of view, and to empathize with others' experience while also holding them accountable for their part in creating it.

While I venture no predictions for the future of such work, I do have high hopes. This seminar suggests that it is indeed possible to cultivate sensibilities for a change. I find that encouraging because, as Yogi Berra said, "The future ain't what it used to be." Now more than ever we need to cultivate in ourselves and in our leaders the sensibilities we saw in such abundance in Lincoln.

A Thinking Person's Guide to Behavioral Repertoires

Experience is a great teacher, except when it isn't. What we make of experience—and whether it serves us or harms us—depends on the knowledge we build out of it. And make no mistake: we're all master knowledge builders, able to turn the most random events into meaningful knowledge about the world and how to operate in it. Much of this knowledge—what I call *experiential knowledge*—lies outside our awareness, where it's difficult to see or assess. Worse, the *interpretive strategies* we use to build that knowledge also lie outside our awareness, dooming us to make the same mistakes again and again without even realizing it.

This guide offers a brief overview of the experiential knowledge and interpretive strategies that define our *behavioral repertoires:* the characteristic ways we respond to people.[1] I used this guide to map the experiential knowledge that Chris and Peter brought to their relationship (Chapter 3) and that Dan and Stu brought to theirs (Chapter 7).

Experiential Knowledge

For decades, social scientists have studied the knowledge people use to make sense of the world and to take action in it. Some focus on the culturally shared knowledge we acquire as we're socialized into some group; others focus on the more variable, personal knowledge we fashion out of the unique experiences that shape our lives (see Table 15, far left column).[2]

TABLE 15: Different Types of Experiential Knowledge			
	NARRATIVE	ANALYTIC	MORAL	PRACTICAL
Personal (Highly Variable)	• Stories, personae, characters	• Implicit theories, explanations, constructs	• Principles, moral logic	• Personal action strategies
Cultural (Highly Shared)	• Scenes, roles, and stereotypes	• Implicit theories, beliefs, or assumptions	• Norms and values	• Cultural routines and scripts[3]

Whether focusing on personal or cultural knowledge, some social scientists look at the narratives we weave out of events; some study the theories and beliefs we use to explain and predict them; others explore the value systems we evolve over time, while still others catalogue the practical strategies, scripts, and routines we follow (see Table 15, top row). Let's take a brief look at each type of knowledge—at how it's built and deployed—then consider how each one works with the others to form the more or less coherent whole that governs how we interact with others.

Narrative Knowledge

As children, we're forever turning events into narratives, then storing those narratives in our more or less conscious minds. Once we're adults, we draw on those narratives to interpret people and situations, to assume and assign roles, to imagine how events might unfold, and to envision what a more or less happy ending might look like.[4]

Some narratives are culturally shared; others vary from person to person. At a cultural level, narratives include *scenes, roles,* and *stereotypes.* These are especially handy in culturally familiar situations: going to a restaurant, attending a funeral, talking with colleagues at a cocktail party, buying a rug at a bazaar. Although each situation is different, none requires much thought. We're able to recognize them immediately, because we have a large stock of *scenes* in our heads that correspond to them. We can also recognize the people in each scene: the rude patron at the restaurant, the bereaved widow at the funeral, the bon vivant at the cocktail party, the haggler at the bazaar. They're all cultural *stereotypes.* All of this makes it easy for us to assume an appropriate *role* in relation to others: the patient patron at the restaurant, the sympathetic friend at the funeral, and so on.

These energy-saving cultural narratives work terrifically well as long as people or circumstances don't go beyond what any one-dimensional stereotype, bare-boned scene, or socially conscripted role can handle. But what if that rude patron at the restaurant turns around and you discover, much to your horror, that it's not a stranger but your Uncle Harry! Then, even more stunning, you notice he's wearing a rumpled suit and launching into an agitated recitation of the Bill of Rights! Search as you might, you can't find a cultural scene, stereotype, or role that corresponds well enough to this turn of events to lend it enough meaning to respond.

To handle moments like this, you have to rely on your own private stock of *personal narratives,* picking up where cultural narratives leave off. Fortunately, all of us have plenty of such narratives at our disposal, whether they be cautionary tales, psychological thrillers, or melodramas. Built out of unsettling events, these narratives help us understand and put to rest—without much, if any, conscious thought—whatever disquiet some inchoate event evokes.

Once you find a narrative that fits well enough—one that allows you to turn Uncle Harry into a more or less sympathetic *character* and to assume a *persona* that will allow you to redeem the situation, if not for Uncle Harry, at least for yourself—some responses will seem obvious while others will never occur to you. Either way, once wrapped in this narrative blanket, whatever disquiet you feel will start to abate.

Analytic Knowledge

Out of our narratives we build thousands of generalizations about what causes what. This type of knowledge, which in its purest form says, "if this, then that," helps us explain and predict everyday events and behavior.

At a cultural level, people acquire through experience and socialization a large number of *implicit theories, beliefs,* and *assumptions*—relatively rudimentary propositions that allow some group or society to understand the social world similarly enough to take collective action. The common belief that people's behavior is caused by their disposition rather than situational pressures is one well-researched example.[5] That's why most people seeing Uncle Harry would assume he's simply nuts and not consider the possibility that he may be responding to a set of situational factors that we as observers don't see.

At a more personal level, analytic knowledge also comes in the form of implicit theories, beliefs, and assumptions, but these vary much more widely among people. They include our own *personal explanations,* complete with associated *constructs,* all of it built out of our own unique experience.[6] This knowledge allows us—in ways that are more personally meaningful—to identify and sort events, things, and people and to explain and predict their occurrence.

Take Uncle Harry. As soon as you see him reciting the Bill of Rights, you recognize his behavior as crazy, because you have instantaneously sorted it into a *construct* or *category*—a kind of mental file folder—called "crazy behavior." But to predict what Uncle Harry might do next, you still have to find an *explanation* for the crazy behavior, one that fits with past experience. All of a sudden, it "comes" to you: given your family history and what you know about mental illness, your uncle must be suffering from bipolar disorder, just like your grandfather did. This personally meaningful explanation is tailor-made to explain what your Uncle Harry is doing. It fits. Now you can be relatively confident that he won't turn around next and act completely normal. In fact, you may have to do something about your Uncle Harry.

Moral Knowledge

Out of our narrative and analytic knowledge, we build knowledge that tells us what's good and bad, and what's right and wrong. When people act differently than our theories predict or our stories anticipate, it not only surprises us, it offends our sensibilities: they've violated our sense of what's supposed to happen, of what's right.

Some moral knowledge is culturally shared. As we grow up, we internalize *cultural values* that inform the way people behave and a related set of *cultural norms* that set people's expectations for behavior. Both values and norms are reflected in and reinforced by our cultural beliefs and assumptions. For example, the belief that dispositions, not situations, cause behavior reflects and reinforces a cultural value of individual responsibility and a cultural norm of holding people accountable. Such values and beliefs are so deeply held and highly shared that when someone violates them, it can threaten our collective identity, motivating us to punish or ostracize the "offending" party to ensure our sense of well-being.

At a more personal level, we select from a cultural menu of values and norms those we want to incorporate into our own personal value system, developing that system to a greater or lesser degree. This more or less complex system provides the *moral logic* we need to reason our way through difficult moral dilemmas. Although this logic may be more or less developed,[7] its *content* consists of *principles* that reflect and reinforce our narratives and theories. So while I might condemn Uncle Harry as an irresponsible ne'er-do-well who's never worked a day in his morally bankrupt life, you might defend him, calling him a victim of circumstance who's never hurt a soul in his life and persevered despite a string of bad luck.

Practical Knowledge

As the term implies, this knowledge offers practical strategies for coping with different situations, telling us, "Do this, don't do that." Only by doing what this knowledge tells us to do can we act on what we see and understand. Some practical knowledge—politeness scripts and face-saving routines—is highly shared. All you have to do is violate one to see just how shared.[8]

Out of these scripts and routines people fashion *personal action strategies* through an ongoing process of selection, improvisation, and elaboration. We rely on these more variable strategies to improvise our way through the situations we confront given our unique life circumstances. These action strategies allow us to negotiate even the most complicated situations, as our narrative, analytic, and moral knowledge lead us to see them.

Going back to our example of Uncle Harry, let's say that in your role as a sympathetic niece (or nephew) you become quite anxious about your uncle's welfare and your own; after all, it's an awkward situation and you're not quite sure what Harry might do next. To address both anxieties, you need to find a strategy that will allow you to protect Harry *and* yourself while staying true to your role as the sympathetic family member. Again, without having to give it much conscious thought, it just "comes" to you: call for help without intervening yourself. Someone else—someone who saw Harry differently—might just as automatically enact a different strategy, either taking Uncle Harry by the hand or abandoning him altogether.

When our personal strategies backfire, we must reboot. If, after you step outside to call for help, Harry grabs your arm and hollers, "And where do you think you're going?!" like it or not, you will have to find a new way to respond. And if no response currently exists in your repertoire, well, then you'll have to cobble together a new response out of existing ones, expanding your repertoire over time.

The Pluses and Minuses of Cultural and Personal Knowledge

Both cultural and personal knowledge have their advantages and disadvantages. Cultural knowledge makes it possible for people to act in concert. The risk is that we apply old cultural knowledge when new knowledge or more personal knowledge might do better. The problem is that cultural knowledge is so highly shared that it takes on a sense of validity it rarely warrants, making it difficult to explore or discover its limits.[9]

Unlike cultural knowledge, personal knowledge gives us especially meaningful ways of understanding novel or upsetting situations. At the same time, because this knowledge is built out of unsettling events, we tend to call on it when we're under similar stress, whether or not it applies. This can lead us to repeat history again and again instead of creating a better future.

We now come to the *interpretive strategies* we use to build and deploy knowledge. How well we draw on—and how quickly we revise or develop—our stock of experiential knowledge depends on the depth and breadth of these interpretive strategies (see Table 16).

TABLE 16: Interpretive Strategies				
STRATEGY	VIEWS KNOWLEDGE	CONNECTS KNOWLEDGE	DEFENDS KNOWLEDGE	RENEWS KNOWLEDGE
Test	As a hypothesis	To what you see (the observable "facts" of the situation)	By debating: make a case based on what you see	By exploring: examine hypotheses in light of data/ what others see
Sense	As an intuition	To your feelings about the situation	By pleading: appeal to your feelings; claim a right to them	By sharing: share your feelings, and ask others to do the same
Negotiate	As a perspective	To how others see, think, and feel about a situation relative to you	By bargaining: grant the other this, if they grant you that. By agreeing to disagree	By creating: invent new insights out of each other's perspectives

Interpretive Strategies

When we differ with others, we reveal through our behavior the interpretive strategies we use to deploy, defend, and renew our experiential knowledge. In my clinical research, I've identified three distinct strategies. Each has its own way of viewing knowledge, connecting knowledge to events, defending knowledge, and renewing knowledge.

The broader and deeper your repertoire of interpretive strategies, the greater your interpretive freedom will be, allowing you to revise old knowledge and develop new knowledge more quickly. The question in terms of depth is whether you can explore what you know with people who rely on different strategies. The question in terms of breadth is whether you can *connect, defend,* and *renew* what you know. Let's consider each in turn.

Strategic Depth

The more shallow your repertoire, the more problematic differences become. People get so hung up on *how* they discuss their differences that they can't resolve them. One person talks feelings, another talks facts, yet another endlessly compares and contrasts different points of view. By dismissing a strategy outright, all you do is limit what you can learn.

Each strategy offers something the others lack. Take people who rely on their sense of things to read situations. They will focus primarily on people's feelings. Since feelings play such a pivotal role in relationships, this strategy provides an important window onto how a relationship is going and where it's getting into trouble. Those who prefer to test their views in light of observable facts help us see dynamics we might otherwise miss—namely, the external circumstances people are up against and what people are actually doing or saying. Finally, those who take multiple perspectives into account will ensure that we look at things from different points of view.

Each strategy, deployed well, has an important role to play, whether we play it ourselves or rely on others to play it for us. People who are able to take advantage of the full range of strategies fare better in relationships than those who don't.

Strategic Breadth

How well a strategy is deployed is another matter. That depends on the breadth of a repertoire—that is, on how well you connect, defend, and renew what you know. Some people have trouble *connecting* what they know to anything: people who prefer testing can't say what data would refute their view; people who prefer sensing can't say what led them to feel a certain way; and people who prefer negotiating can't say what their perspective is or how it relates to others or connects to a specific situation.

Others are so quick to *defend* what they know that they don't explore whether the knowledge they're applying fits a particular case, making them slow to revise old knowledge and even slower to create new knowledge. Still others—although a minority—tend to *renew* their knowledge so quickly that they don't ever defend it, making it difficult for them to articulate a clear and consistent point of view or to develop a reliable moral compass.

When it comes to developing enough flexibility to handle a wide range of relationships, renewal is by far the most important interpretive strategy. All of us experience *slippage* from time to time—a gap between what we see and what we know that creates a zone of uncertainty or dissonance. Some people view this slippage as a portal of discovery, offering an opportunity to renew their knowledge by revising or adding to it. For those people, the discomfort caused by uncertainty is minimal and their sense of urgency about closing the gap manageable. In contrast, others view even the slightest slippage as a gaping hole, intensifying their discomfort and amplifying their sense of urgency about closing the gap.

Those people who are able to connect, defend, and renew what they know fare better in relationships than those who don't.

The Three Rs

Knowledge building goes best when people follow the three Rs: *reflecting* and *reframing* in the context of *relationships*. Continually reflecting with others on what we "know" reduces the odds of fooling ourselves and increases the odds that we'll discover interesting, new things—that we can reframe. This is especially true when the quality of reflection is high—that is, when it's conducted not in the abstract (where it's divorced from action) but in light of specific situations and what you and others are actually feeling, thinking, and doing in them. By grounding reflection in the world of action, you're much more likely to create knowledge that's useful in action. More important, you're much more likely to stay alive mentally and emotionally and to grow alongside those who matter the most to you. Appendix B offers a tool that will help you ground your reflections so you can use them to learn and change with others.

Appendix B

The Ladder of Reflection

Ever since organizational learning pioneers Chris Argyris and Donald Schön introduced a tool called the Ladder of Inference, countless people have appropriated it for their own purposes, calling it everything from the Ladder of Influence (a Freudian slip, perhaps?) to the Ladder of Interpretation (by my sights, a bit more apt).[1]

One reason the tool is so popular is that it opens a window onto how your mind works when you make sense of situations. And once you see how your mind works, you can never quite see things the same way again. All of a sudden you realize that what you see isn't necessarily the way things are, and what you take to be matters of fact are actually matters of interpretation—and pretty abstract interpretation at that.

In this book, I put the Ladder of Inference to yet another use: reflecting on interactions for the purpose of mapping them. And I rename it yet again, calling it the Ladder of Reflection.

Using the Ladder of Reflection to Observe and Map Interactions

Whenever you map interactions, you need some way of ensuring (1) that you're not deluding yourself, and (2) that people can use the map to understand and change the pattern it captures. You can use the ladder in Figure 17 to reflect on interactions, starting with what people are actually saying and doing and ending with your conclusions about what it all means.

By reflecting on interactions a step at a time, you're much less likely to jump to premature conclusions and much more likely to see gaps in your views or to see alternative interpretations, especially when you reflect with other people who are also taking it a step at a time.

For the purpose of mapping, I've given my ladder five rungs: select, describe, explain, predict, and evaluate.[2] The first two steps include our *observations,* the last three our *conclusions.* I've put all three *conclusion rungs* in bold as a reminder to stop and take a closer look before proceeding, because this is where people get into the most trouble, especially if they can't climb back down the ladder to say how they moved from the bottom to the top. Unable to say what leads to their conclusions, they don't have a leg (or a ladder) to stand on.

Figure 17: The Ladder of Reflection

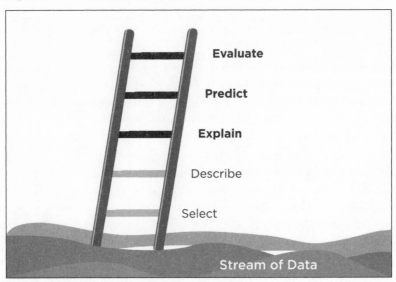

When mapping interactions, you can use this ladder to:

▸ Go from some behavior you observe to your conclusions about that behavior.
▸ Connect any conclusions you reach to the behaviors you see.
▸ Examine your conclusions to see if you're missing things that might alter your view.
▸ Discuss with others the steps you took to arrive at your conclusions.
▸ Explore any differences in what you and others see.

▶ Look at the same behavior from different angles.

▶ Inquire into any behavior that puzzles or surprises you.

▶ Consider what each person's conclusions reveal and conceal.

Going Up the Ladder a Step at a Time

Let's take a close look at each step on the ladder, using a simple example to illustrate. Next to that example I offer a counterexample to illustrate the common mistakes I see people make. Underlying each of these mistakes is the tendency to think that our most abstract conclusions are concrete facts. As you'll see, they're not.

1. Select. Anytime you observe an interaction—whether you're in it yourself or just watching—you can't possibly pay attention to everything that's happening. There's just too much going on. You have to select something. For the purpose of mapping, you want to select those behaviors that might be implicated in some pattern, even if you can't yet name the pattern or explain it very well. You've got to start somewhere, and the best place to start is with what people are actually saying and doing in *here-we-go-again moments*—moments that are easy to recognize but hard to understand or alter. To do this, *select* from your notes (or a tape recording) what people said and did during those moments.

> **EXAMPLE OF SELECTED BEHAVIOR:**
> Dick said, "See Spot! Look at Spot run!" Jane said, "Run, Spot, run!"
>
> **COUNTEREXAMPLE OF A COMMON MISTAKE:**
> Dick vied for Jane's affections by showing her something he believed she'd find interesting. She pretended to show her affection by looking at what he showed her.

Where the first example simply reports what Dick and Jane said, the counterexample skips a few steps on the ladder and rushes to judgment about what their words mean. Anytime you hear words like "vie," "believe," or "pretend," you'll know you skipped a step. These are not behaviors but explanations for behaviors, as the next sections show.

2. Describe. Once you've selected behaviors, you can *describe* them in relatively observable terms *without* speculating about motives, feelings, intentions, frames, or the like. At this step, it's vital that you stick to what you see or hear. This makes it easier for people to point out behavior you might have missed or to understand which behavior you think needs to change. Either way, it's the single most important step in mapping—and the one most people skip.

EXAMPLE OF DESCRIBED BEHAVIOR:
Dick directed Jane's attention to the running dog. Jane looked at it and exclaimed.

COUNTEREXAMPLE OF A COMMON MISTAKE:
Hoping to gain Jane's favor, Dick tried to get her attention by showing her something he believed she'd find interesting. He thought he succeeded when Jane joined in the fun, but Jane was just trying to appease Dick, who was acting like a chauvinist by dominating her attention.

As with the first step, be on the lookout for words in your description like "try," "intend," "hope," "want," "fear," "worry," "believe," and the like. Each of these words refers to what's going on inside of people (which you can't directly see), not to what they're doing (which you can directly see). In this respect, they're not descriptions as much as they are explanations for the behavior you have yet to describe.

3. Explain. If the previous step is the most important, this one is the trickiest, which is why it appears in bold. Having selected and described those behaviors you think contribute to some pattern, you must now explain what causes those behaviors by drawing on some theory. In this book I relied on the Anatomy Framework to explain behaviors (see Chapters 2, 3, and 5). In everyday life, we rely on our largely unconscious experiential knowledge. While this knowledge gets the job of framing done quickly and effortlessly, if not always effectively, it isn't up to the job of mapping—at least not as long as it stays unconscious. To be most useful and reliable, explanations must be conscious enough to state them so others can consider them and help you see things you might have missed.

Since it's widely accepted that observed behavior is caused by both internal and external factors, most theories of human behavior refer to both (external contexts, immediate situations, or triggering events and internal mental states like intentions, purposes, goals, beliefs, assumptions, and/or frames). To use theories well, you need more than just observed behavior; you need a window onto the external and internal factors that might be causing that behavior. Without them, all you can do is speculate. And who's to say whether your speculations apply in this case? Not a very solid basis for understanding behavior—certainly not for changing it.

So far, in our example, we don't have a clue what Dick and Jane are feeling or thinking, nor do we have any idea what external factors might be at play. Thus the behavior we've selected could be explained very differently depending on the external context (whether it's occurring in the midst of a dog fight or on a playground at school) *and* depending on Dick and Jane's internal thoughts and feelings (whether they're feeling warmly or resentful toward each other).

To illustrate, let's say that Dick and Jane are on an elementary school playground during recess, and let's say that Dick tells us that he likes Jane very much, that he was excited to see his own dog Spot running onto the playground, and that he was thinking to himself, "Jane likes dogs. Jane will certainly want to see my dog." Now let's say Jane tells us she also likes Dick, that she does indeed like dogs very much, but that when she turned to see the dog, she saw what she believed to be a coyote running after it, leading her to fear for the dog's life and to think to herself, "If Spot doesn't run faster, he'll surely get eaten!"

EXAMPLE OF EXPLAINED BEHAVIOR:
> *Because* Dick likes Jane and thought that Jane liked dogs, he directed Jane's attention to his dog Spot when he ran onto the school playground. *Because* Jane likes Dick as well as dogs, she looked where Dick directed her attention. And *because* she then saw what she thought was a coyote running after the dog, she feared for the dog's life. This caused her to exclaim, telling the dog to run.

COUNTEREXAMPLE OF A COMMON MISTAKE:
> *Because* Dick is a chauvinist, he made Jane look at his dog. *Because* Jane is a member of a submissive class, she felt compelled to go along. *Because* she identified with the dog—being chased as it was by a coyote, who reminded her vaguely of Dick—she tried to protect the dog from being eaten.

As silly as the counterexample seems, I've seen sillier in everyday life, and I'll bet you have too. The point is, we can make almost anything out of the behavior we see; people do it all the time, and they get away with it. Most of us are too polite to point out that it's beyond our comprehension how others reached the conclusions they reached.

In the first example, by contrast, you can connect the explanation to the description that preceded it and to what Dick and Jane were feeling, thinking, and doing. This is what makes it relatively easy for you to see how someone might reach this conclusion, whether or not you agree with it. Similarly, if you look at any of the conclusions I reached—say, about Jobs and Sculley or Dan and Stu—you can see how I arrived at them and judge for yourself whether they make sense. In the case of our counterexample, you'd be at a loss.

4. Predict. Like the previous step, this fourth step involves thinking through what causes what. Only, in this case, you're not thinking about what caused the behavior you see, but what the behavior you see causes—the consequences that behavior creates or at least contributes to.

That's why, to take this step, you again need some kind of theory that can tell you what causes what. Just as I used the Anatomy Framework throughout the book to explain what caused behavior, I also used it to predict the consequences that behavior might cause. What's more, I focused my predictions on outcomes people cared about, and I formulated them in ways that helped people avoid outcomes they didn't like and achieve outcomes they did. But to stay with our example here, consider these predictions:

EXAMPLE OF A PREDICTION:
By directing Jane's attention to his dog Spot, Dick makes it more likely that Jane will turn and see Spot. By listening to Dick and turning toward Spot, Jane will be more able to see Spot and the other animal chasing him. This will make it possible for her to do something to try and save Spot's life. If Dick and Jane continue to interact this way, they will likely continue to be good friends; they may even save a few dogs.

COUNTEREXAMPLE OF A COMMON MISTAKE:
By imposing his will on Jane, Dick will perpetuate the power dynamics that characterize the male-dominated playground so prevalent in Western society. By following Dick's unilateral directions, Jane will never learn to be self-directed and will continue to be victimized by society's paternalistic social order. Because of people like Dick, that paternalistic social order will continue to stifle seven-year-old women like Jane, and many a sentient dog like Spot will get eaten because only those Dick points out will get saved.

As these two examples illustrate, not all theories are equal. The more abstract, unconscious, or disconnected your theory is, the harder it is to scrutinize the predictions you make. This makes it more likely that your predictions won't come to pass because they're wrong or won't help much because they're so disconnected from what's happening that people can't do any-thing about them. Conversely, the more conscious and connectable a theory is, the easier it is to revise predictions (making them more powerful) and to alter the outcomes it predicts (making them more useful).

5. Evaluate. This last step draws on all the others to assess whether you like what you see. Just as the previous two steps required a theory, so does this one. But it requires something else too, something that's not always so easy to see: our values. It's not by chance that the word "evaluation" has at its core the word value.

In this last step, you look back at your explanations and predictions and say whether some behavior is "good" or "bad"—or, in business parlance, whether it's effective or ineffective, whether it's value-added or not. What-ever words you use, you're sizing up behavior relative to some value or crite-rion. If you value profits above all else, then you'll consider a hard-driving rainmaker who only sees his or her kids twice a month an effective contribu-tor. If you value a balanced life or family above all else, then you'll think the same person is deficient. It's all relative, depending on what you're looking at *and* the values you use to assess what you see.

To avoid getting caught in an endless loop of relativity, perhaps even to find common ground, you need to take into account not just your values but the values of others, and you need to search for values that are more univer-sally shared—say, justice or a sense of security.[3] Equally important, you must use the ladder to connect these values to what you now see and to what you'd prefer to see in yourself, another person, in your relationship, or in the world.

EXAMPLE OF AN EVALUATION:
>   Dick and Jane's interaction illustrates an effective way of connect-ing, having fun, and helping out a dog in need.

COUNTEREXAMPLE OF A COMMON MISTAKE:
>   Dick's behavior—boorish in the extreme—illustrates just how badly boys can behave and the difficult position in which they put good girls like Jane.

As you can see, the second example is even sillier than the first, and that's saying something. What adds to the second example's silliness is the blanket value judgment that gets woven out of a single thread of behavior, and a small thread at that. All these blanket value judgments do is smother any chance of learning or finding common ground.

Implications. Though truth and accuracy are the first casualties of sloppy reflection, they're not the only ones. Change and growth also get killed, usually in their wake. The problem with our counterexamples isn't that there's no truth to them. There *is* inequality in the world; boys do dominate girls at times. The question is whether that's the best way of understanding what's happening here. Unlikely. The leaps of abstraction taken right from the start make it hard to know whether the reflections apply in this case and, if they do, what any of us would do about it.

On Ladders, Labels, and Frameworks

The Dick and Jane example has the benefit of being simple, but if you look throughout the book, you'll see more complex examples, including Jobs and Sculley, Chris and Peter, Dan and Luke, Stu and Dan, and so on. In each case I used the ladder to analyze the interactions between these pairs and to explore how they gave rise to relationships that had a characteristic structure. In each case, you can see how I go from some "data"—what these folks were thinking, feeling, saying, or doing—to my conclusions about them and their relationships.

Though it takes time and practice, once you master the ladder, it's easier to imagine different ways of seeing the "same" behaviors and easier to see behaviors you or others might miss, because each of you will be giving the other a window onto how you climbed the ladder. Equally important, once you and others are able to connect your more abstract explanations or predictions to what people are actually feeling, thinking, doing, or saying, you'll be more able to help each other alter what you see.

Ultimately this will give you far more traction than tossing around labels or flat characterizations (he's passive-aggressive, she's a wimp, he's a control freak, she's too aggressive, he's a monster, she's a jerk). While any of these labels may be directionally true, they're not especially useful. Most of the time, they exacerbate the very behaviors they label, as people feel compelled to defend themselves and to attack back.

Even nontoxic labels like those used in the Myers-Briggs assessment, can get bandied around in ways that cut off the curiosity and empathy you're going to need to help each other change. Though the assessment is designed to help people appreciate difference, many people only end up thinking, She's *simply* an ISTJ (Introverted, Sensing, Thinking, Judging); he's *simply* an ENFP (Extroverted, Intuitive, Feeling, Perceiving). That explains *everything!*

In this case, the problem isn't so much the labels as the labelers. Most people slap them on and give no more thought to what they see. This not only cuts off the potential for growth ("I am what I am," as Popeye said), it also lops off a person's underlying complexity—making it harder for you to understand them or to spot toeholds for change. *The point is, no set of labels can explain everything, even when they're based on solid theory and evidence. All have a range of usefulness beyond which they're more trouble than they're worth.*

Even so, we can't live without them. Labels are here to stay. It's the way the mind works. But nothing about the mind requires you to use bad labels, to apply them mindlessly, or to think you've figured everything out once you've applied them. All that's up to you. The Ladder of Reflection gives you a way to connect labels to behavior and to use frameworks like the Anatomy Framework to see what no label can help you see: how something works.

As the father of renowned physicist Richard Feynman advised his son, as they puzzled together over a bird that was busily at work pecking at its feathers: "You can know the name of that bird in all the languages of the world, but when you're finished you'll know absolutely nothing whatever about the bird. You'll only know about humans in different places, and what they call the bird. Let's look at the bird and see what it's *doing*—that's what counts."

Feynman later said of this impromptu lesson: "I learned very early the difference between knowing the name of something and knowing something."[4]

Acknowledgments

For more years than my friends or colleagues would have wished, I've promised to put down on paper what I've learned about relationships in teams. Without their encouragement, I would not have started, let alone finished, this book. To all of them, I give my thanks.

Along the way, many people have influenced the way I think about relationships, but no one has more than my earliest mentors—organizational learning pioneers Chris Argyris and Donald Schön, and systems theorist and therapist David Kantor. Their ideas have not only shaped my own but everyone's. It is on their very broad shoulders that I now stand.

Among the many things these men passed on to me is an unyielding commitment to building ideas that serve practice. Sharing that commitment are the folks at the Harvard Negotiation Project, where some 20 years ago I first met Roger Fisher and my husband, Bruce Patton. I have never met anyone more committed to making complex ideas accessible than Roger or Bruce, nor anyone more successful at doing it. Their impact on my thinking and my writing is incalculable, as is my gratitude to each of them for all they have taught me.

I owe a special thanks to the two organizations that have served as my intellectual home for many years: Action Design and the Monitor Group. Ever since we met at graduate school, my partners at Action Design—Bob Putnam and Phil McArthur—have been supporting and challenging me. Most of the ideas in this book are a product of that lifelong collaboration. I thank them both for showing me that it's possible to build relationships that not only last but grow stronger with time.

For the past ten years, Monitor has provided every kind of support a firm could provide. For so generously giving me their time and thoughts, my thanks go to Steve Jennings, Bob Lurie, Bill McClements, Jim Cutler, Joe Fuller, Bansi Nagji, and Mark Fuller. To Mark, I am especially grateful; from the start, he believed in this book in that uncanny way he has of believing in things. Before you know it, you start believing too.

Through my work with Monitor I have had the good fortune to work with two other organizations that have provided invaluable support: New Profit, Inc., and the Monitor Institute. These two organizations, which are changing the way people go about changing the world, inspire me daily. For the past five years they have given me everything from a learning laboratory to moral support to constructive criticism to endearing friendship.

I wish I could also publicly acknowledge all those client organizations that have generously allowed me to study them, their efforts to change, and my efforts to help them. All the data in this book, except for those that come from public sources, come from my work with these organizations. I am grateful to them for supporting my research over the years.

That research would never have seen the light of day had it not been for those friends and colleagues kind enough to read and comment on various drafts of the book. For that arduous task, my heartiest thanks go to Chris Argyris, Hilary Austen Johnson, Bernadette Bernon, Doug Borchard, Emma Barnes Brown, Ambar Chowdhury, Rory Clark, Ruth Cherneff, Ed Cohen, Meg Flynn, Mark Fuller, Jon Hughes, David Kantor, Alan Kantrow, Sue Launsby, Jong Lee, Josh Lee, Doug Marshall, Jack May, Phil McArthur, Bill McClements, Bill Miracky, Tammy Hobbes-Miracky, Bill Noonan, Neil Pearse, Susan Podziba, Bob Putnam, Lori Russell, Peter Senge, Rajeev Singh-Molares, Geneva Smith, Rob Smith, Owen Stearns, Sameer Srivastava, Kathe Sweeney, Kim Syman, and Jeff Wetzler.

I am especially indebted to that monstrous regiment of women who not only read and commented on earlier drafts but kept me afloat while writing them. My dearest friends—Jamie Higgins, Iris Bagwell, and Amy Edmondson—were a wellspring of encouragement and constructive criticism. No matter what the circumstance, they always seemed to find the right balance between the two. Katherine Fulton, on more occasions than I can count, took her keen eye as a leader and an editor to every single draft, always giving me the kind of guidance and support I needed to make it better. With remarkably good cheer, my research assistant, Kathryn Flynn, immersed herself in overwhelming amounts of data, selected just the right passages, and offered incisive analysis and camaraderie throughout. Thanks, Nailclipper. Vanessa Kirsch, who believes in good causes and people as a matter of principle, somehow found it in her heart to believe in me and in this book, which helped me do the same. With her Southern wit always about her, Stacy McManus did a yeowoman's job of tracking down and reviewing different sources in the literature, never failing to root me on in moments of doubt. For the many times these women made me laugh and for all they taught me, I am most grateful.

Equally helpful and just as much fun were the five members of the "Brotherhood of Love," that group of young leaders in the ongoing seminar "Leading Through Relationships." For offering their emotional support, for helping me hone unwieldy ideas, for making me howl with laughter, and most of all, for serving as the audience in my head—my thanks to each of them.

For all that I have learned about myself, as a clinician and as a person, I am grateful to David Diamond, whose practice as a psychoanalyst is unparalleled. I could not do the work I do—at least not responsibly—without the kind of self-knowledge David has helped me build.

When I first began this project, I wasn't much of a writer. While I may have a way to go, I've traveled a good distance. Had it not been for my writing coach and editor, Tim Murphy, I wouldn't have gotten out of the gate. This is a guy who cares so much about making a difference that he couldn't care less how much credit he gets. Well, he deserves all the credit for whatever good writing you see in this book. The bad writing is a tribute to my slow learning. His teaching is impeccable, as is his editing. His good nature is beyond account.

To Julie Sherman of J. Sherman Studio, LLC, whose spectacular sense of design has made these ideas shine, my gratitude and my appreciation for her collaborative spirit and her impish eye.

In my next life I wouldn't mind coming back as my agent, Esther Newberg. When she's not cheering on the Red Sox from her office in downtown Manhattan, she's finding a good home for books. When I asked her how she decides which books to represent, she said in that succinct way of hers, "If it interests me." I'm very grateful that my book interested Esther enough that she found it a home at Portfolio, where the incomparable editors Adrian Zackheim and Adrienne Schultz have taken such good care of the manuscript and me.

Taking care of all things and creatures, large and small, at home and at work were my assistants-cum-friends Lisa Byrne and Scott Dyer (Uncle Scotty). Their gracious support made writing this book doable; their goodnatured ribbing made it fun.

To my husband, Bruce, I dedicate this book with love. More than any-one, he's made it possible. Throughout he was indefatigable, continually of-fering feedback on the book's content and style, reading and commenting on each draft, and not letting *me* rest until the ideas were as clear as I could make them. Much more than that, everyday he teaches me through experi-ence what it's like to be in a relationship that allows you—even lovingly asks you—to grow.

Notes

I like notes; many people don't. If you're at all like me, you may want to look at the notes in the following sections. In them, I document sources, cite those who have influenced my thinking on a topic, situate my ideas among others, and provide more conceptual nuance than some readers might want or need. Those who aren't interested in these things can happily skip the notes without losing the thread.

Chapter 1

1. I will often use the term "firm" to refer to all organizations, including those in the not-for-profit and governmental sectors—the term "organization" being a bit clunky.
2. Fictional name, actual firm and case.
3. Though we succeeded in helping the team make better and faster decisions by facilitating deliberations and reflecting on team dynamics, key team relationships kept getting in the way, making it impossible for the team to turn around the firm's performance fast enough. Had we focused on transforming those few key relationships, we'd have stood a much better chance. See Edmondson and Smith, "Too Hot to Handle?" Of the three practices discussed in this article, I focused on the second at Elite, when all three were needed. For a more detailed account of the Elite case, see Smith, "Keeping a Strategic Dialogue Moving."
4. To clarify my use of the term *relationship*, let me make two points. First, even when you use the term "relationship" to include relationships among groups or organizations, you're ultimately referring to relationships among the human beings who represent those groups—human beings who have "emotions, deeply held values, and different backgrounds and viewpoints" (see Fisher, Ury, and Patton, *Getting to Yes*,

19). Second, all two-person relationships within an organization exist as part of a larger web of relationships in some organizational context. So even if you focus primarily on two-person relationships, as I do here, it's important to remember that other people and relationships are always lurking in the background, impinging on how the people in any two-person relationship regard and behave toward each other.

5. The prisoner's dilemma is a component of game theory. In this game, two "prisoners," separated by police, have the choice to cooperate (by remaining silent) or to defect (by blaming the other). The game shows that, under conditions of uncertainty, it's rational for both people to defect, even though doing so harms them both.

6. In 1924, social psychologist Floyd H. Allport first described these circular patterns, saying: "[T]he response of each person [is] revoked or increased by the reactions which his own responses called forth from others." Cited in Weick, *The Social Psychology of Organizing*, 4. I argue that these patterns of interaction give rise to relatively stable interpretations, converting patterns of interaction into more enduring and harder-to-change informal structures.

7. In 1925, Mary Parker Follett said, "As conflict—difference—is here in the world, as we cannot avoid it, we should, I think, use it. Instead of condemning it, we should set it to work for us." See Follett, "Constructive Conflict."

8. A body of work, known as LMX theory, holds some promise for understanding leadership within the context of relationships, though it offers virtually no practical advice. See, for example, Uhl-Bien and Maslyn, "Reciprocity in Manager-Subordinate Relationships." Family therapists are more prescriptive about relationships, but their ideas don't always transfer easily to organizations. See, for example, Watzlawick and Weakland, *The Interactional View*. For a discussion of the transfer challenge, see Hirschhorn and Gilmore, "The Application of Family Therapy Concepts to Influencing Organizational Behavior."

9. This idea is similar to that first put forth by Karl Weick: "The unit of analysis in organizing is contingent response patterns, patterns in which an action by actor A evokes a specific response in actor B (so far this is an interact), which is then responded to by actor A (this complete sequence is a double interact)." See Weick, *The Social Psychology of Organizing*, 89. How pairs combine to create the larger social fabric of a team is best left for another book, so this one doesn't die of its own weight.

Chapter 2

1. Sedaris, "Old Faithful."
2. See Hertzfeld, *Revolution in the Valley*, 267.
3. This account shows how Jobs and Sculley's relationship had an adverse effect on Apple's performance. I'm not suggesting that other factors, like the decision not to open their platform, didn't also have an adverse effect.
4. I rely heavily on two sources for the case material on Sculley and Jobs. The first is Frank Rose's 1989 account in *West of Eden*. Written in the wake of the relationship's demise, this account chronicles the turmoil between Steve Jobs and John Sculley. Named by *BusinessWeek* as one of that year's ten best books, it draws on extensive interviews with Apple's executive staff, as well as solid historical research on the computer industry and the emergence of Silicon Valley. The other major source is John Sculley's memoir, *Odyssey*, which offers a rich account of what he and Jobs said and did with each other, as well as what he was thinking and feeling at the time. I use Sculley's account to look at his interactions with Jobs and at Sculley's reactions to those interactions. The only direct data on Jobs's reactions I could find come from a 1995 *Smithsonian* interview (see Morrow, "Oral History Interview with Steve Jobs") and his 2005 Stanford commencement address (see Jobs, Commencement Address). In the absence of direct data from Jobs, I rely on Rose's account, which is supported by other accounts in the public domain, including one by a core member of the Macintosh team; see Hertzfeld, *Revolution in the Valley*.
5. Rose, *West of Eden*, 16.
6. Ibid., 15–16.
7. Ibid., 70.
8. Ibid., 75.
9. In 1981, two years before Sculley joined the firm, Mike Markkula stepped down as chairman and assumed the position of CEO. At that time, Jobs took Markkula's job as chairman. All this occurred after Markkula's friend from his semiconductor days, Mike Scott, got pushed out as CEO after launching a round of firings that came to be called Black Wednesday. Scott's survival probably wasn't served by his decision to appoint John Couch, not Jobs, to lead the highly desirable Lisa division. This left Jobs to take over a small, experimental project called Macintosh. By this point, Wozniak—Jobs's original partner in founding Apple—had decided

to take a break from Apple after a plane crash that affected his short-term memory and a series of disagreements with Jobs.

10. Rose, 71.

11. Ibid., 71.

12. Ibid., 79.

13. Ibid., 108.

14. Sculley, *Odyssey*, 200.

15. Rose, 109.

16. Sculley, 157.

17. Rose, 71.

18. For more on behavioral repertoires, see Chapter 3, "Step 4: Behavioral Repertoires." Also see Appendix A: A Thinking Person's Guide to Behavioral Repertoires.

19. See Gladwell, *Blink*. Gladwell cites psychologist John Gottman's research on marital relationships to explain how "a distinctive pattern, a kind of marital DNA, . . . surfaces in any kind of meaningful interaction" (p. 26).

20. Ibid., 78.

21. Sculley, 90. During their courtship, Jobs asked Sculley, "Do you want to sell sugared water for the rest of your life, or do you want a chance to change the world?" Sculley later wrote of that moment, "It was as if someone had reached up and delivered a stiff blow to my stomach. . . . It simply knocked the wind out of me."

22. Rose tells many stories of Jobs's disdain for institutional authority, starting in high school with the Buck Fry Club—a transposition designed to rankle the principal, Mr. Bryald (Rose, 27). Years later, Apple's motto "one person—one computer" captured in one pithy expression Jobs's complex and long-standing desire to alter the balance of power between the individual and the institution (Rose, 38).

23. In one account, Rose says, "Sculley had more definite ideas about how things should be done, and he expected his managers to try them out. The organization he was creating was one in which decisions came down from above. That was a corollary to the hierarchy he was constructing" (Rose, 167). Also, in *Odyssey*, Sculley often refers to his fears of losing control and his efforts at gaining better control.

24. Rose, 139.

25. Ibid.

26. According to Rose, most of Sculley's design decisions reflected a preference for rational order and greater control. Early on, for example, after

hanging an organizational chart on his wall, he turned his attention to the network of stores that sold Apple products to the public, deciding that Apple should have its own sales force. As Rose says of that decision, "[Sculley] wasn't happy with the way some of the rep organizations were performing; he thought it was time that Apple had the prestige of its own sales organization—the prestige and control" (Rose, 166–67).

27. Sculley, 240. It was only much later, after the consequences of the decision had played out, that it seemed so misguided. At the time, Sculley thought giving Jobs more operational responsibility made good sense, so much so that he changed his title from vice president to executive vice president.

28. Ibid., 167.

29. Ibid., 198.

30. Sculley decided to fold Lisa into the Macintosh group so they would have only two lines of business: Apple II and Macintosh. This decision, which upset those working both on Lisa *and* Macintosh, made the Macintosh division more powerful than the Apple II division.

31. Sculley, 199.

32. Jobs's disrespect first emerged during a meeting at Xerox PARC a couple of years earlier. As far as Jobs could tell, no one at Xerox appreciated the dazzling technology they had right under their noses or the brilliant engineers they had working on it, some of whom Apple later recruited. In that moment, Xerox must have struck Jobs as a glaring example of the almost criminal stupidity of big institutions.

33. Sculley, 205–6. My addition identifying Adams and Glavin.

34. For a detailed account of the impact on Jobs and how he handled it, see Rose, 217–18.

35. Rose, 209.

36. Sculley, 167.

37. Ibid., 166.

38. Ibid., 166–67.

39. Ibid., 167.

40. Ibid.

41. The cover story "Apple's Dynamic Duo" appeared in *Business Week*'s November 26, 1984, issue. The Dynamic Duo label stuck at the very point that their relationship became unglued.

42. Rose, 193–94.

43. Ibid., 211.

44. Sculley, 210.

45. Ibid., 228.
46. Rose, 229.
47. Sculley, 235.
48. Rose, 252.
49. Sculley, 240.
50. Ibid., 238.
51. Rose, 247.
52. Sculley, 236–37.
53. Rose, 259.
54. Sculley, 235.
55. Rose, 254.
56. Ibid., 255.
57. Sculley, 241.
58. Rose, 282.
59. Sculley, 261.
60. Ibid., 240.
61. Sculley, 230, 231, 237, 239.
62. Ibid., p. 252. Also see Morrow, "Oral History Interview with Steve Jobs."
63. Sculley, 238.
64. Rose, 255.
65. Ibid., 282.
66. Sculley told Jobs that he hadn't been more aggressive, because Jobs hadn't created the opportunity for him to lead more aggressively. The idea that Jobs might view this statement as an illustration of Sculley's limitations as a leader does not appear to occur to Sculley.
67. Morrow, "Oral History Interview."
68. At Stanford's 2005 commencement, Jobs said of his firing: ". . . as Apple grew, we hired someone who I thought was very talented to run the company with me, and for the first year or so things went well. But then our visions of the future began to diverge and eventually we had a falling out. When we did, our Board of Directors sided with him. So at 30 I was out. And very publicly out. . . . I'm pretty sure none of this [starting NeXT, Pixar, and a family] would have happened if I hadn't been fired from Apple. Sometimes life hits you in the head with a brick. Don't lose faith. I'm convinced that the only thing that kept me going was that I loved what I did."

Chapter 3

1. See Gladwell, *Blink*, 27–29. Gladwell cites John Gottman's marital research to illustrate how patterns in relationships develop a distinctive character that arises naturally and automatically.
2. Though many details in this story have been modified to protect the confidentiality of the protagonists, most of the data on what Chris and Peter thought, felt, and said came from case material based on meetings about their relationship.
3. Also see Appendix B: The Ladder of Reflection, for the tool I used to observe and analyze behavior using this framework.
4. See Berger and Luckmann, *The Social Construction of Reality*, 29. The authors make a similar point when they argue: " 'What he is,' therefore, is ongoingly available to me. This availability is continuous and prereflective. On the other hand, 'What I am' is *not* so available. To make it available requires that I stop, arrest the continuous spontaneity of my experience, and deliberately turn my attention back upon myself." Also, see Nisbett and Ross, *Human Inference*, for a good summary of the research on the actor-observer divergence in causal attributions.
5. Different theorists from different traditions define and use the term *frame* differently. Cognitive psychologists Daniel Kahneman and Amos Tversky use the term to refer to the more conscious, analytic processes people go through when assessing risk or making choices—such as whether to fly or not to fly, or whether to buy one stock or another; see Kahneman and Tversky, "Choice, Values, and Frames." Donald Schön, a philosopher by training and an organizational theorist by trade, uses the term to refer to the process by which professionals reflect on and revise their professional knowledge by framing and reframing their roles. See Schön, *The Reflective Practitioner*. John Van Maanen, an organizational ethnographer, refers to a similar phenomenon when he writes of "situational definitions [providing] an individual with a practical theory for 'what's going on' in concrete situations." See Van Maanen, "On the Understanding of Interpersonal Relations," 64. Although Schön talks in terms of "stories" and Van Maanen of "theories," both refer to the largely tacit or unconscious processes that allow us to make useful sense of situations such that we can act *in the moment* with others. Like Van Maanen and Schön, I use the term to refer to the tacit interpretations we make in the heat of the moment in order to act. But I reserve the term for the more stable interpretations we form about ourselves in relation to

others; these more stable interpretations emerge over time out of patterns of interaction and turn those more variable patterns into more stable informal structures.

6. A number of cognitive psychologists claim that we answer these questions in a particular sequence, but little consensus exists as to what that sequence is. Carol Dweck and Ellen Leggett argue that goals come first. See Dweck and Leggett, "A Social-Cognitive Approach to Motivation and Personality." Taking a contrary view, James Shah argues that our representations of others automatically affect the goals we set for ourselves. See Shah, "Automatic for People." While we'll probably never know for sure which comes first, I suspect that goals follow from how we frame situations and ourselves relative to others. Once we've taken that step, some goals naturally spring to mind while others would never occur to us. From the point of view of the actor, however, it doesn't much matter: it feels as if it's all happening at once.

7. See, for example, Lord, Brown, and Freiberg, "Understanding the Dynamics of Leadership." The authors argue that our conception of ourselves is far from monolithic. Rather it's a "confederation of self-schemas derived from past social experiences." Van Maanen makes a similar point when he says, "While the self may be thought of as our most personal and prized possession, it nevertheless resides ultimately in the hands of others who may choose to deny it, confirm it, ignore it, or change it. . . . We can be mothers, lawyers, socialites, sisters, secret sinners, devout believers, workhorses, aggressive lovers, shy speakers, politicians, game players, and so forth. We can play several roles at the same time, change roles, fake roles, and still we tend to think of ourselves as whole and unique." See Van Maanen, "On the Understanding of Interpersonal Relations," 45. Also, James Shah summarizes evidence that suggests "our complex representations of significant others may come to influence not only how we perceive others, and interact with them, but how we come to perceive and evaluate ourselves." See Shah, "Automatic for People."

8. See Lord, Brown, and Freiberg, "Understanding the Dynamics of Leadership." The authors, who develop the notion of self-schema in the context of leader-follower relationships, distinguish between peripheral and core self-concepts.

9. Nearly everyone agrees that human behavior is purposive—that is, designed with some purpose in mind. But much disagreement exists on how to understand purposes and what kind of understanding is most useful for explaining behavior in specific situations. See Dweck and

Leggett, "A Social-Cognitive Approach." The authors argue, as I do here, that conceiving of purposes as general motives—say, for power— can't predict specific behaviors. Conceiving of purposes as specific goals solves that problem. Goals are more connectable to specific behavioral patterns and thus a more useful concept for understanding and altering those patterns.

10. See Shah, "Automatic for People."

Chapter 4

1. Kirn, "I'm OK. You're OK. We're Not OK." This *Time* magazine essay was reporting on an effort to include "relational disorders" in an up-dated edition of a psychiatric diagnostic manual.

2. Oxford American Dictionaries.

3. Fictional name, actual firm and case. All data on what Luke and Dan said, did, thought, and felt come from transcripts of voicemails, tape, recordings of face-to-face meetings, and observations of nonverbal behavior.

4. Ong, et al., "Psychological Resilience," 743.

5. Ibid.

6. For example, Jay Elliot, the vice president of human resources, told them "they were both being self-indulgent with their little power struggle." See Rose, *West of Eden*, 282.

7. Most people believe others are the cause of their problems and that they are mad or bad for causing them. A smaller number of people tend to locate the cause in themselves. Either way, blaming is the consequence, learning the casualty.

8. Steve Jobs had the formal power of chairman, the economic power that came from leading the firm's most profitable division, the power of information as an operating manager, the cultural power bestowed on him as chief product visionary in a firm that prized products above all else, the personal power of his charismatic personality, and the power of persuasion that flowed from his rhetorical skills. Yet in only two years, Jobs's relationship with Sculley managed to destroy almost all the political and social capital he'd built. By the time the board had to choose between Jobs and Sculley, they took "Sculley's side."

9. The ability to think complexly about situations and to experience a complex of emotions helps people respond adaptively to stressful events. See Ong, et al., "Psychological Resilience."

10. Metcalfe and Mischel, "A Hot/Cool-System Analysis of Delay of Gratification."

11. Also see Smith, "The Muck Stops Here," and McArthur, Putnam, and Smith, "Climbing Out of the Muck," In Senge, *The Dance of Change*, 120–28.

12. This shift is what allows leaders to get "out on the balcony," to use Ronald Heifetz and Donald Laurie's notion, where they can get enough distance to reflect on themselves and their organizations. See Heifetz and Laurie, "The Work of Leadership."

13. In reality, I doubt that Luke or Dan had this precise map in their head, even though they'd discussed it. More likely, they recalled the outlines of the map: its circular quality, the notion that patterns of interaction among people—not people alone—are the problem, and the idea that they each contributed to a pattern they didn't like. While such notions are incomplete and imprecise, they're all you need to stop a hot system from running amok.

Chapter 5

1. Clothier, *Bones Would Rain From the Sky*, 49.

2. Fictional name, actual firm and case. All data on what Dan and Stu felt, thought, said, and did came from tape recordings and observations of nonverbal behavior.

3. These characteristics—trust, commitment, approach to conflict, results orientation, accountability—correspond to those cited in Lencioni, *The Five Dysfunctions of a Team*. Thinking in these terms, you might conclude that a relationship (or a team) is functioning well (or badly) at any point in time. Whether a relationship (or a team) has the ability to sustain a high level of functioning over time and across circumstances is another question. As argued in the previous chapter, that depends on a relationship's cool system. That system determines whether and how quickly people in a relationship can shift perspective in the heat of the moment, allowing them to build relationships within a team that function well over time, even under adverse conditions.

4. The data included in all three tables are taken from meetings with Dan and Stu.

5. Many people worry that they'll be self-conscious about tape recording or videotaping, but most people forget about it as soon as they get caught up in the conversation. If taping is out of the question, though, take

careful notes on what you and others are actually saying—not your descriptions or interpretations of what you're each saying.

6. These data were excerpted from a meeting transcript.

7. For more on "behavioral repertoires," see Chapter 3 and Appendix A: A Thinking Person's Guide to Behavioral Repertoires.

8. By observing and describing behavior closely, as an anthropologist would, and asking open-ended questions, as any good researcher would, you stay curious enough to fully understand interactions *and* to uncover the factors that lead them to persist, putting you in a better position to alter patterns that get in people's way. Developing the ability to observe closely and to inquire openly depends on four things: using the Anatomy Framework introduced in Chapter 3, using the Ladder of Reflection introduced in Appendix B, adopting the relational perspective described in Chapter 4, and cultivating the relational sensibilities discussed in Chapter 11.

9. At this point, our explanation of their interaction can only be partial, because we do not yet understand all the factors that maintain the pattern, including the themes which predispose them to being triggered and the experiential knowledge they've built around those themes, such that they see things one way and not another. Our explanations become more complete as we move through the stages of change. See Chapters 6 and 7.

10. This template is derived from the Anatomy Framework and singles out for attention people's interlocking reactions and actions. For more, see Chapter 3.

11. See Nisbett and Wilson, "Telling More Than We Can Know." Also see Argyris, Putnam, and Smith, *Action Science*.

12. There are limits to each of these approaches even when done well. *Asking* gives you the most direct data but not necessarily the most reliable: people are often unaware of what they think and feel. *Speculating* based on other things people have said—for instance, in an initial assessment—can help you connect patterns to people's goals and concerns but won't necessarily capture what the person is feeling and thinking in that particular moment. Finally, *predicting* based on some theory and what people are now doing will open up possibilities people might not have considered, but it's never easy to tell whether the theory (and thus the predictions) apply in this case. This means you have to hold tentatively any statements that wind up in this box, remaining ever ready to revise them.

13. No matter how suspect we might be of an actor's ability to know or describe what she is thinking or feeling, she can still go inside herself and register some kind of feeling and notice some kind of thought. Putting aside whether this access is accurate, it is indisputably *different*. That means actors and observers will always tend to see different things in— and make different sense of—the "same" behavior.
14. See Nisbett and Ross, *Human Inference*.
15. For an engaging account of the difficulties involved in describing what we are feeling or thinking, see Spence, *Narrative Truth and Historical Truth*.
16. Nothing will close people down faster—or make them more defensive— than telling them what's going on inside their heads or their hearts. Better to be humble and to defer to their account, at least provisionally. You can always come back later and revise your understanding when people are more able and willing to explore and discuss how they're really feeling.
17. For laugh-out-loud examples of what happens when people throw a monkey wrench into everyday cultural works, see Garfinkel, *Studies in Ethnomethodology*.
18. For more on action experiments, see Argyris, Putnam, and Smith, *Action Science*.
19. Space constraints prevent me from illustrating failed experiments. But they are a valuable part of the change process, because they rule out actions that won't succeed in disrupting the pattern. To reduce the costs of failed experiments, it helps to create a context where experimentation is encouraged and to test out options under less threatening conditions— for example, by role-playing what you might actually say or do before trying it under real-life conditions.

Chapter 6

1. To get at people's reactions, it's best to ask open-ended questions like, "What's going on?" But avoid asking *why* someone did something. It's apt to yield what Paul Johnson calls *reconstructed reasoning* or what Chris Argyris and Don Schön call an *espoused theory*—a plausible explanation or justification that's often disconnected from what the person actually feels, thinks, and does. Instead, ask people to describe what's going through their minds as if they have a tape recorder in there. See Ericsson and Simon, *Protocol Analysis*. This method elicits what Johnson calls *authentic reasoning* and Argyris and Schön call a *theory-in-use*.

2. My paraphrasing here of what Dan and Stu said uses their actual language.

3. We can never know for sure all that Dan and Stu were feeling or thinking; even if we could, our ability to infer the frames embedded in those reactions would always be imperfect. Understanding this, we kept our conclusions open to revision, continually going back and elaborating them as we learned more and built even greater trust.

4. Compare Schön, *The Reflective Practitioner*.

5. See Putnam, "Recipes and Reflective Learning." Also see Weick, *The Social Psychology of Organizing*. Karl Weick argues that you must act before you know what you think.

Chapter 7

1. Conlin, "I'm a Bad Boss? Blame My Dad," *BusinessWeek*.

2. People don't ever recount events qua events. As Jerome Bruner points out in "On Perception of Incongruity," it is the storied version of events that we relay. In terms of our task here, that's not a problem. We're less interested in what actually happened, but in what people made of what happened and how that affects their ability to navigate current circumstances.

3. To capture the experiential knowledge that Stu and Dan brought to their relationship, I relied on "The Thinking Person's Guide to Behavioral Repertoires" (see Appendix A).

4. Research on learning suggests that learners are anything but empty vessels. Even young children bring their own naïve theories to learning, leading them to structure and restructure what they hear and see in their own terms. For an excellent discussion of how people learn, see Greeno, "Perspectives on Thinking." Also see Hatano and Inagaki, "Everyday Biology and School Biology: How Do They Interact?"

5. See Kets de Vries and Miller, *The Neurotic Organization*, 111. The authors make a similar argument when they write: "It is important for both superior and subordinate to become aware of the existence of dysfunctional interaction patterns, for awareness is the first step toward dissolving them. Promoting this awareness requires the cooperation of both parties." Here I am arguing that neurotic behaviors create repetitious patterns of interaction, which in turn evoke and maintain more neurotic behavior. By focusing simultaneously on changing individual behaviors and the structures they create, you accelerate the change of both.

Chapter 8

1. Conlin, "I'm a Bad Boss? Blame My Dad," 60: "[There's] a new frontier in productivity: emotional inefficiency which includes all that bickering, backstabbing, and ridiculous playing for approval that are a mark of the modern workplace."

2. At one firm, people further down in the organization looked to the head of product design and the head of sales to assess whether the firm was really serious about becoming more commercial, as their new strategy espoused. Every time these two executives fought, the word got out and spread like wildfire, even when their fights occurred behind closed doors.

3. The relationship between John Sculley and Steve Jobs springs to mind. Over time, their relationship brought out the worst in each of them. This exacerbated their liabilities as leaders and made them more evident to others.

4. See Henry Mintzberg's thoughts on "mutual adjustment" in *The Structuring of Organizations*. Also see Goleman, *Emotional Intelligence*, and Conlin, "I'm a Bad Boss?" The greater interdependence found in today's organizations has sparked an increased interest in emotional intelligence (Goleman) or emotional competence (Conlin).

5. In thinking through the formal design of an organization, experts have long advised managers to focus on information as a key design variable, determining the desired degree of interdependence required. See Galbraith, *Designing Organizations*. I'm arguing that what formal interrelationships offer in terms of information flow, informal interrelationships can quickly take away if neglected.

6. Like all strategies, when misapplied, this one becomes problematic. For example, if people start ignoring the ill effects of relationships that really are critical to a firm's success, sooner or later it will take a toll on the firm's effectiveness.

7. This approach breaks down when you feel your only choice is to impose a structural separation, no matter what the circumstances. When that happens, you end up creating wacky structural arrangements or making personnel decisions that harm a firm's performance.

8. If you use this approach to manage the ill effects of highly interdependent relationships, you'll soon run into trouble, because those effects will be so frequent and so widespread that it will fast become more costly to manage them than to change them.

9. When this strategy is overused—that is, applied when the other strategies would work at least as well if not better—it is a waste of scarce resources. Only set out to transform the critical few relationships that meet these criteria.

Chapter 9

1. Wallace, "The Capital T Truth."
2. For more on assessing the heat of a topic, see Edmondson and Smith, "Too Hot to Handle?"
3. For different approaches to facilitation, see such classic texts as Walton, *Managing Conflict*; Schein, *Process Consultation*; and Schwarz, *The Skilled Facilitator*. Many approaches to mediation are also quite effective at helping people make progress on especially difficult issues. See Susskind and Cruikshank, *Breaking the Impasse*.
4. Chris Argyris's more recent work is the best example of this strategy. Although he engages patterns when needed, he devotes most of his attention to reflecting on and interrupting behaviors that generate sloppy reasoning about substantive matters from finance to strategy to the design of human resource systems.
5. Many psychologists of different stripes till this same soil. Systems theorists like David Kantor and psychodynamic theorists like Larry Hirschhorn, Michael A. Diamond, Manfred Kets de Vries, and Danny Miller are all in the business of transforming behavioral dynamics that undermine a firm's performance, even if they go about it in different ways.

Chapter 10

1. Compare Polivy and Herman, "If at First You Don't Succeed."
2. People who lead and study change efforts often speak of the importance of creating a "felt need for change" by pointing out the gap between what people want and what they have, or what people espouse and what they do. Done well, the dissonance that results generates an "optimal level of anxiety"—just enough to motivate people to change but not so much that they get overwhelmed and give up before starting. While this anxiety will spark change, it is mostly negative energy, even when optimal. As such, it will rarely sustain change over time. To sustain change, you need to continually generate the kind of positive energy that these principles create. See Quinn, *Change the World*.

3. See Fisher and Sharp, *Getting It Done*, 45–49. They speak to the same problem I do here—namely, grand visions fail to tell us what to do today, while more sober, restrained goals don't look like they'll make much difference tomorrow. Like me, they also advise not choosing between the two poles but instead setting three different types of purposes over three different points in time: an inspiring vision, a midterm goal to use as a milestone, and some immediate objectives. I've found that the connection between these goals is more compelling at the outset and more motivating over time if, when setting each goal, you have a stage theory of change that (1) says how each goal, once met, creates conditions for meeting the next goal; (2) identifies the steps you need to take at each stage to meet the goals at each stage; and (3) tells you how to anticipate and use any obstacles you'll face, so instead of discouraging you, they help you meet each goal more quickly.

4. Recall that each stage starts with a paradox, which can only be resolved by pushing further into that stage, and ends with a dilemma, the resolution of which catapults people into the next stage. See Chapters 5 through 7.

5. Making fun of others is a tricky business and should be avoided, especially when it involves topics that are not yet discussable. Never poke fun at others unless you're sure there's no hidden, hostile meaning lurking behind it. Also see Chapter 11 note 20.

6. See Masten, "Ordinary Magic."

Chapter 11

1. Welch, *Jack: Straight from the Gut*, xi: "When you write a book like this, you're forced to use the narrative 'I' when it's really the 'we' that counts." King, et al., *A Knock at Midnight*. Goodwin, *Team of Rivals*.

2. I won't argue that these sensibilities and only these sensibilities distinguish leaders who lead through relationships. While my clinical research suggests this is the case for all practical purposes, more research needs to be done to explore if other sensibilities might also matter or matter more.

3. The *Oxford American Dictionary* defines the term *sensibility* as "the ability to appreciate and respond to complex emotional or aesthetic influences; sensitivity." Eliot Eisner, in *The Enlightened Eye*, develops this notion in much of his work as does his student and my friend Hilary Austen Johnson in *Artistry in Practice* and "Artistry for the Strategist."

The two of them have influenced my own thinking here about the limits to theory and technique when aiming to develop the artistry of any practice.

4. Goodwin, *Team of Rivals*, xvii.

5. White, *Lincoln's Greatest Speech*, 23.

6. Ibid., 48.

7. Ibid., 59.

8. Compare Goodwin's observations in *Team of Rivals*, xvii.

9. White, 179.

10. James MacGregor Burns makes a similar point in his classic book *Leadership*, when he distinguishes between two types of leadership (transactional versus transformative) based on the quality of the relationship that leaders form with their followers. In Burns's more recent book, *Transforming Leadership*, he builds on his earlier idea to argue, as I do, that transformative leaders become dynamic agents of social change.

11. Lincoln's handwritten copy of the address, included in White's book along with a typed version, includes various errors that are identified in the text by the phrase "[sic]." For ease of reading, I have corrected those errors.

12. Lincoln is a good example of what Jim Collins calls a Level 5 leader—someone who "builds enduring greatness through a paradoxical blend of personal humility and professional will." I believe it was Lincoln's highly developed sensibilities that allowed him to function at such a high level, even under stress. See Collins, *Good to Great*, 17–40.

13. I am indebted to White's account of Lincoln's Second Inaugural Address, which greatly influenced the thoughts that follow.

14. White, 143. Expressed in a letter to Eliza P. Gurney, a Quaker minister from Philadelphia.

15. Ibid., 145.

16. Ibid.

17. My italics.

18. White, 159.

19. Ibid., 150.

20. I considered including humor as one of the sensibilities, especially since Lincoln's humorous stories helped him greatly when his many losses threatened to strangle hope. But in the end, I came to believe that his humorous stories were not so much a sensibility as the vehicle through which he developed them. As I later argue, it is through these stories that Lincoln was able to create meaning and strengthen relationships—two of

three conditions that need to be in place for relational sensibilities to grow.

21. White, 142.

22. Ibid., 168.

23. The term *appreciation* can mean either (1) the recognition and enjoyment of the good qualities of someone or something, or (2) a full and sensitive understanding of someone or some situation. In the world of organizational behavior, Cooperrider and his colleagues use the term in the first sense. They argue against what they call a problem-oriented view of the world because it undermines the innovative and inspirational stance required to challenge existing social orders and to create new ones: "The action–researcher is drawn to affirm, and thereby, illuminate the factors and forces involved in organizing that serve to nourish the human spirit." See Ludema, Cooperrider, and Barrett, "Appreciative Inquiry," 189. I emphasize the second meaning of the term in order to make a different point: you can't challenge or fundamentally alter the underlying structure of any social behavior or situation unless you have a highly sensitive understanding of the experiences and circumstances that led people to create that structure.

24. White, 86. This awareness came from a steady stream of correspondence and countless meetings in which he listened to what people said of the war—its causes and its effects.

25. Ibid., 168.

26. Ibid., 102.

27. Ibid. According to abolitionist Frederick Douglass: "The whole proceeding was wonderfully quiet, earnest, and solemn. . . . There was a leaden stillness about the crowd. . . . The address sounded more like a sermon than a state paper." The quotes are from Royster, *The Destructive War*, cited by White, 78–79.

28. Ibid.

29. Whereas the South saw the North destroying states' rights, the North saw the South destroying human rights.

30. White, p. 86.

31. Ibid., 182.

32. Ibid., 145.

33. White, 170.

34. Ibid. 164–65.

35. Ibid., 184.

36. Goodwin, 47–53.

37. Ibid., 49.
38. Ibid., 173–75.
39. "Conversation" in *Harvard Business Review*, June 2007, 28.
40. Goodwin, 51.
41. Ibid., 52.
42. Ibid., 167.
43. Ibid., 167–68.
44. Ibid., 103.
45. Ibid., 280–81.
46. See advice offered by Daniel Goleman in his groundbreaking book *Emotional Intelligence*. Building on current thinking about how to offer feedback, he recommends that people say things like, "When you forgot to pick up my clothes at the cleaners, it made me feel like you don't care for me." As Goleman points out, statements like these are a big improvement over "You're always so selfish and uncaring. It just proves I can't trust you to do anything right." But they can still feel like a veiled accusation to the person on the receiving end (you're responsible for making me feel this way), and they can prevent the person feeling uncared for from seeing his or her part in creating that effect (perhaps they have been asking the other person to do so much that he or she is overwhelmed and forgot).
47. Goodwin, 49.
48. Ibid., 8.
49. Ibid., 280.
50. Ibid., xvi.
51. Ibid., xvi–xvii.
52. I created this seminar as part of my clinical research to see if it was possible to cultivate new sensibilities in adults. For the past five years, that seminar has served as a learning laboratory. In subsequent writings, I will use this research to illustrate in greater detail how to cultivate relational sensibilities and how to design activities and contexts to accelerate that development. Clearly we need to figure out how to do this more quickly and more broadly than I did. But it is a start and hopefully an informative one.

Appendix A

1. The ideas presented in this guide are cursory, because space does not permit elaboration. For those interested in learning more, the next note

includes references to authors who have explored these ideas in much greater depth. Also, for those more interested in application, see Chapters 3 and 7, which illustrate how you can use the guide to explore and capture experiential knowledge for reflective purposes.

2. Some students of human behavior focus on the more universal, less variable aspects of behavior, others on the more variable, personal aspects. Since I do both in a somewhat cursory fashion, I include references to both here for those who may wish to delve deeper:

Personal Knowledge: Personal knowledge, like cultural knowledge, takes four different forms: *narrative* (see Roy Schafer, Michael White, David Kantor); *analytic* (see George Kelly); *moral* (see Lawrence Kohlberg, Robert Kegan, Carol Gilligan); and *practical* (see Smith). Some, like Jerome Bruner, straddle the categories by exploring different modes of knowing.

Cultural Knowledge: Cultural knowledge also takes four forms: *narrative* (see Iain Mangham, John Van Maanen); *analytic* (see organizational theorists who study shared beliefs, assumptions, and theories: Sonja Sackmann, Ed Schein, John Van Maanen, Peter Drucker, Michael Tushman and David Nadler, John Kotter and James L. Heskett, Gordon Donaldson and Jay Lorsch; also see psychologists studying social cognition: Richard Nisbett, Lee Ross, Timothy DeCamp Wilson, Carol Dweck and Ellen Leggett, Daniel Kahneman and Amos Tversky, and Robert Lord); *moral* (see George Homans, Ed Schein, Chris Argyris and Donald Schön); *practical* (see Esther N. Goody, Erving Goffman, Roger Schank and Robert Abelson, Michael Cohen, Chris Argyris and Donald Schön). As you can see, a number of scholars cross the artificial but hopefully useful boundaries I create here.

3. I don't include rituals in this cell, because I'm focusing on the less conscious knowledge people use to make meaning and to take action. While rituals express or manifest that knowledge, they are conscious acts and their meaning is embedded in visible, audible forms.

4. According to psychologist Jerome Bruner, "If (children) don't catch something in a narrative structure, it doesn't get remembered very well, and it doesn't seem to be accessible for further kinds of mulling over." Quoted in Frank, "Students Discover Economics." Also see Bruner, *Actual Minds, Possible Worlds.*

5. Those who study everyday social cognition refer to this belief as the "fundamental attribution error."

6. See Kelly, *The Psychology of Personal Constructs*, for an account of how these constructs form and change.

7. For a structural view of moral development, see Kohlberg, *Essays on Moral Development*.

8. See Garfinkel, *Studies in Ethnomethodology*.

9. This is especially true when you try to use cultural scripts to handle important relationships in ambiguous or difficult situations. Bargaining routines may work well when haggling over a rug, but they rarely work well in complex negotiations in long-term relationships. See Fisher, Ury, and Patton, *Getting to Yes*.

Appendix B

1. For those who enjoy tracing the history of an idea, academic-turned-politician S. I. Hayakawa introduced a similar notion to the Ladder of Inference in 1939, building on the even earlier work of Alfred Korzybski of "the map is not the territory" fame. Hayakawa's notion, called the Abstraction Ladder, shows how we use language to create increasingly abstract categories from *Bessie the cow* to *livestock* to *farm* to *wealth*. Like the Ladder of Inference, you can use the Abstraction Ladder to analyze communications, understandings, and misunderstandings—though some people, who make finer distinctions, would beg to differ (see, for example, Walls and Waldon, "Understanding Unclear Situations"). Anyway, as Steve Stockdale explains on his Web site, ThisisNotThat.com, Hayakawa's Abstraction Ladder is especially helpful in "immunizing" against political propaganda of the kind that was running rampant in the 1930s. Stockdale explains, drawing on one of Hayakawa's examples: "a local politician attempts to drum up support by exclaiming, *'Farmer Jones, vote for me to ensure that Schmokum County serves as a beacon of forward-looking growth and prosperity!'* As this exhortation contains no specifics, only generalized, highly abstract references, you could infer that this belongs fairly high up on the Ladder of Abstraction. And if Farmer Jones recognizes this, he will likely ask the Schmokum County candidate, *'What exactly do you mean, what will you do?'* And when the candidate replies, *'Well, er, Jones, what I mean is, uh . . . we're going to build a new road right across your farm!'*" As this example shows, once we come down the ladder, there can now be no misunderstanding—or at least, a lot less. Farmer Jones now knows exactly what this politician means by "forward-looking growth and prosperity." He means a very specific, and pardon the pun, *concrete* road.

2. Depending on their purpose, different people have created different ladders, each with a different number of rungs, almost all of them going by different names. To cite a few notable ones: Argyris and his colleagues use a five-rung ladder to reflect on people's reasoning; see Argyris. In a similar vein, my colleagues and I at Action Design offer a three-rung version to help people see how they go from some "data" to their closely held "certainties" about the world; see www.actiondesign.com. In *The Fifth Discipline*, Peter Senge speaks of "leaps of abstraction" in the context of people's mental models, as he does in *The Fifth Discipline Fieldbook*, where he and his colleagues offer their own version of the ladder. In *Difficult Conversations*, Doug Stone, Sheila Heen, and Bruce Patton use a three-rung ladder to explain where people's "stories" come from. Finally, Ted Wall and David Waldon's five-step "Reasoning Cycle," which intentionally steers away from the term *ladder*, can be used to analyze "language data."

3. I'm not claiming that these values are enacted, completely shared, or equally applied. But when it comes to learning and to finding common ground, it's enough that most people hold a value, even if they don't always enact it or apply it to others. It still matters to them, usually a lot. And that can serve as the basis of a conversation that's more likely to produce learning and to discover common ground.

4. Feynman, *What Do You Care What People Think*, 14.

Bibliography

Argryis, Chris. *Strategy, Change and Defensive Routines*. Boston: Pitman Publishing, 1985.

Argyris, Chris, Robert Putnam, and Diana McLain Smith. *Action Science: Concepts, Methods, and Skills for Research and Intervention*. San Francisco: Jossey-Bass, 1985.

Argyris, Chris, and Donald A. Schön. *Theory in Practice: Increasing Professional Effectiveness*. San Francisco: Jossey-Bass, 1974. Reprint 1992.

———. *Organizational Learning II: Theory, Method, and Practice*. Reading, MA: Addison-Wesley, 1996.

Bennis, Warren, John Van Maanen, Edgar Schein, and Fred Steele, eds. *Essays in Interpersonal Dynamics*. Homewood, IL: Dorsey Press, 1979.

Berger, Peter L., and Thomas Luckmann. *The Social Construction of Reality: A Treatise in the Sociology of Knowledge*. Garden City, NY: Anchor Books, 1966.

Bruner, Jerome. *Actual Minds, Possible Worlds*. Cambridge, MA: Harvard University Press, 1987.

Bruner, Jerome, and Leo Postman. "On the Perception of Incongruity: A Paradigm." *Journal of Personality* 18 (1949): 206–23.

Burns, James MacGregor. *Leadership*. New York: Perennial/HarperCollins, 1978.

———. *Transforming Leadership: A New Pursuit of Happiness*. New York: Atlantic Monthly Press, 2003.

Clothier, Suzanne. *Bones Would Rain From the Sky: Deepening Our Relationship With Dogs*. New York: Warner Books, 2002.

Cohen, Michael D., and Paul Baldayan. "Organizational Routines Are Stored as Procedural Memory: Evidence From a Laboratory Study." *Organization Science* 5, no. 4 (December 1994): 554–68.

Collins, Jim. *Good to Great: Why Some Companies Make the Leap . . . and Others Don't*. New York: HarperCollins, 2001.

Conlin, Michelle. "I'm a Bad Boss? Blame My Dad." *BusinessWeek*, May 10, 2004.

Covey, Stephen M. R., with Rebecca R. Merrill. *The Speed of Trust: The One Thing That Changes Everything*. New York: Free Press, 2006.

Czarniawska, Barbara. *Narratives in Social Science Research*. Thousand Oaks, CA: Sage Publications, 2004.

Diamond, Michael. "Organizational Change and the Analytic Third: Locating and Attending to Unconscious Organizational Psychodynamics," *Psychoanalysis, Culture and Society* 12, no. 2 (July 2007): 142–64.

Diamond, Michael A., and Seth Allcorn. "The Cornerstone of Psychoanalytic Organizational Analysis." *Human Relations* 56, no. 4 (2003): 491–514.

Donald, David Herbert. *Lincoln*. New York: Touchstone, 1995.

Donaldson, Gordon A., and Jay W. Lorsch. *Decision-Making at the Top*. New York: Basic Books, 1984.

Drucker, Peter. "The Theory of Business." *Harvard Business Review*, September 1994.

Dweck, Carol. *Mindset: The New Psychology of Success*. New York: Random House, 2006.

Dweck, Carol, and Ellen Leggett. "A Social-Cognitive Approach to Motivation and Personality." *Psychological Review* 95, no. 2 (1988): 256–73.

Edmondson, Amy C. "Psychological Safety and Learning Behavior in Work Teams." *Administrative Science Quarterly* 44 (1999): 350–83.

———. "Framing for Learning." *California Management Review* 45, no. 2 (2003): 34–54.

Edmondson, Amy C., Richard Bohmer, and Gary Pisano. "Speeding Up Team Learning." *Harvard Business Review*, October 2001.

Edmondson, Amy C., and Diana McLain Smith. "Too Hot to Handle? How to Manage Relationship Conflict." *California Management Review* 49, no. 1 (Fall 2006): 6–31.

Eisenhardt, Kathleen, Jean L. Kahwajy, L. J. Bourgeois III. "How Management Teams Can Have a Good Fight." *Harvard Business Review* 75, no. 4 (July–August, 1997): 77–85.

Eisner, Elliot W. *The Enlightened Eye: Qualitative Inquiry and the Enhancement of Educational Practice.* Upper Saddle River, NJ: Merrill, 1998.

Ericsson, K. Anders, and Herbert A. Simon. *Protocol Analysis: Verbal Reports as Data.* Cambridge, MA: MIT Press, 1984.

Feynman, Richard P. *What Do You Care What People Think: Further Adventures of a Curious Character.* New York: Bantam, 1989.

Fisher, Roger, and Alan Sharp. *Getting It Done: How to Lead When You're Not in Charge.* New York: HarperBusiness, 1999.

Fisher, Roger, William Ury, and Bruce Patton. *Getting to Yes: Negotiating Agreement Without Giving In* (Second Edition). New York: Penguin Books, 1991.

Follett, Mary Parker. "Constructive Conflict." In Pauline Graham, ed., *Prophet of Management.* Boston: Harvard Business School Press, 1996.

Frank, Robert H. "Students Discover Economics in Its Natural State." *New York Times,* September 29, 2005.

Galbraith, Jay. *Designing Complex Organizations.* Reading, MA: Addison-Wesley, 1973.

————. *Designing Organizations: An Executive Guide to Strategy, Structure, and Process.* San Francisco: Jossey-Bass, 2002.

Gardner, Howard. *Frames of Mind: The Theory of Multiple Intelligences.* New York: Basic Books, 1983. Reprint 2004.

Garfinkel, Harold. *Studies in Ethnomethodology.* Englewood Cliffs, NJ: Prentice-Hall, 1967.

Gerzon, Mark. *Leading Through Conflict: How Successful Leaders Transform Differences Into Opportunities.* Boston: Harvard Business School Press, 2006.

Gilligan, Carol. *In a Different Voice: Psychological Theory and Women's Development.* Cambridge, MA: Harvard University Press, 1993.

Gladwell, Malcolm. *Blink: The Power of Thinking Without Thinking.* New York: Little, Brown and Company, 2005.

Glaser, Judith E. *Creating WE: Change I-Thinking to WE-Thinking to Build a Healthy, Thriving Organization.* Avon, MA: Platinum Press, 2005.

Goffman, Erving. "On Facework: An Analysis of Ritual Elements in Social Interaction." In Adam Jaworski and Nikolas Coupland, eds., *The Discourse Reader.* New York: Routledge, 2006.

Goleman, Daniel. *Emotional Intelligence: Why It Can Matter More Than IQ.* New York: Bantam Books, 1995.

———. *Working with Emotional Intelligence*. New York: Bantam Books, 2000.

———. *Social Intelligence: The Hidden Impact of Relationships*. New York: Bantam Dell Publishing Group, 2006.

Goodwin, Doris Kearns. *Team of Rivals: The Political Genius of Abraham Lincoln*. New York: Simon & Schuster, 2005.

Goody, Esther N. "Questions and Politeness: Strategies in Social Interaction." In Esther N. Goody, ed. *Cambridge Papers in Social Anthropology* 8. Cambridge, England: Cambridge University Press, 1978.

Gottman, John M., and Joan DeClaire. *The Relationship Cure: A Five-Step Guide to Strengthening Your Marriage, Family, and Friendships*. New York: Three Rivers Press, 2001.

Greeno, James G. "A Perspective on Thinking." *American Psychologist* 44, no. 2 (February 1989): 134–41.

Guttman, Howard M. *When Goliaths Clash: Managing Executive Conflict to Build a More Dynamic Organization*. New York: Amacom, 2003.

Harkins, Phil. *Powerful Conversations: How High-Impact Leaders Communicate*. New York: McGraw-Hill, 1999.

Hatano, Giyoo, and Kayoko Inagaki. "Everyday Biology and School Biology: How Do They Interact?" *Quarterly Newsletter of the Laboratory of Comparative Human Cognition* 9, no. 4 (October 1987): 120–28.

Hayakawa, Samuel Ichiye, and Alan R. Hayakawa. *Language in Thought and Action* (Fifth Edition). New York: Harcourt Inc. 1991. (First published in 1939.)

Heifetz, Ronald A., and Donald L. Laurie. "The Work of Leadership." *Harvard Business Review* (January–February 1997): 124–34.

Hertzfeld, Andy. *Revolution in the Valley: The Insanely Great Story of How the Mac Was Made*. Sebastopol, CA: O'Reilly Media Inc., 2005.

Higgins, Jamie, and Diana M. Smith. "Some Feedback on Feedback." *Harvard Management Update*, June 1999.

Hirschhorn, Larry. *The Workplace Within: Psychodynamics of Organizational Life*. Cambridge, MA: MIT Press, 1990. Reprint 2000.

Hirschhorn, Larry, and Tom Gilmore. "The Application of Family Therapy Concepts to Influencing Organizational Behavior." *Administrative Science Quarterly* 25, no. 1 (March 1980): 18–37.

Homans, George. *The Human Group*. New York: Harcourt College Publications, 1950.

Hughes, Marcia, L. Bonita Patterson, and James Bradford Terrell. *Emotional*

Intelligence in Action: Training and Coaching Activities for Leaders and Managers. San Francisco: Pfeiffer, 2005.

Jobs, Steve. Stanford University commencement address, delivered June 12, 2005. http://news-service.stanford.edu/news/2005/june15/jobs-061505.html.

Johnson, Hilary A. *Artistry in Practice.* Palo Alto, CA: Stanford University School of Education (doctoral thesis), 1998.

Johnson, Hilary A. "Artistry for the Strategist." *Journal of Business Strategy* 28, issue 4 (2007): 13–21.

Johnson, Paul E. "What Kind of Expert Should a System Be?" *Journal of Medicine and Philosophy* 8 (1983): 77–97.

Jung, Carl Gustav. *Psychological Types* (In *The Collected Works of C. G. Jung*, Volume 6). Princeton, NJ: Princeton University Press, 1971.

Kahneman, Daniel, and Amos Tversky. "Choice, Values, and Frames." *American Psychologist* 39 (1984): 341–50.

Kantor, David. "Critical Identity Image: A Concept Linking Individual, Couple, and Family Development." In John K. Pearce and Leonard J. Friedman, eds., *Family Therapy: Combining Psychodynamic and Family Systems Approaches*, 137–67. New York: Grune & Stratton, 1980.

———. "Couples Therapy, Crisis Induction, and Change." In Alan S. Gurman, ed., *Casebook of Marital Therapy*. New York: Guilford Press, 1985. Reprint 1991.

———. *My Lover, Myself: Self-Discovery Through Relationship*. New York: Riverhead Books, 1999.

Kantor, David, and William Lehr. *Inside the Family: Toward a Theory of Family Process*. San Francisco: Jossey-Bass, 1975.

Kantor, David, and John Neal. "Integrative Shifts for the Theory and Practice of Family Systems Therapy." *Family Process* 24 (March 1985): 13–29.

Katzenbach, Jon R., and Douglas K. Smith. *The Wisdom of Teams: Creating the High-Performance Organization*. New York: Collins Business Essentials, 2003.

Kegan, Robert. *The Evolving Self: Problem and Process in Human Development*. Cambridge, MA: Harvard University Press, 1982. Reprint 2006.

Kelly, George A. *The Psychology of Personal Constructs*. New York: Routledge, 1955.

———. *Theory of Personality: The Psychology of Personal Constructs*. New York: W. W. Norton & Company, 1963.

Kets de Vries, Manfred F. R., and Danny Miller. *The Neurotic Organization: Diagnosing and Revitalizing Unhealthy Organizations.* New York: HarperCollins, 1991.

King, Martin Luther Jr., Peter Halloran, ed., and Clayborne Carson, ed. *A Knock at Midnight: Inspiration from the Great Sermons of Reverend Martin Luther King, Jr.* New York: Warner Books, 1998.

Kirn, Walter. "I'm OK, You're OK, We're Not OK." *Time,* September 16, 2002.

Kohlberg, Lawrence. *Essays on Moral Development: The Philosophy of Moral Development.* Volume 1. New York: Harper & Row, 1981.

Kohlberg, Lawrence, and Thomas Lickona, eds. "Moral Stages and Moralization: The Cognitive-Developmental Approach." *Moral Development and Behavior: Theory, Research, and Social Issues.* New York: Holt, Rinehart and Winston, 1976.

Kohlreiser, George. *Hostage at the Table: How Leaders Can Overcome Conflict, Influence Others, and Raise Performance.* San Francisco: Jossey-Bass, 2006.

Kolb, Deborah M., and Judith Williams. *The Shadow Negotiation: How Women Can Master the Hidden Agendas That Determine Bargaining Success.* New York: Simon & Schuster, 2000.

Kotter, John P., and James Heskett. *Corporate Culture and Performance.* New York: Free Press, 1992.

Lakoff, George, and Mark Johnson. *Metaphors We Live By.* Chicago: University of Chicago Press, 1980. Reprint 2003.

————. *Philosophy in the Flesh: The Embodied Mind and its Challenge to Western Thought.* New York: HarperCollins, 1999.

Lax, David A., and James K. Sebenius. *3-D Negotiation: Powerful Tools to Change the Game in Your Most Important Deals.* Boston: Harvard Business School Press, 2006.

Lencioni, Patrick. *The Five Dysfunctions of a Team: A Leadership Fable.* San Francisco: Jossey-Bass, 2002.

————. *Overcoming the Five Dysfunctions of a Team: A Field Guide for Leaders, Managers, and Facilitators.* San Francisco: Jossey-Bass, 2005.

Lord, Robert, and Douglas J. Brown. *Leadership Processes and Follower Self-Identity.* Mahwah, NJ: Lawrence Erlbaum Associates, 2003.

Lord, Robert, Douglas J. Brown, and Steve Freiberg. "Understanding the Dynamics of Leadership: The Role of Follower Self-Concepts in the Leader/Follower Relationship." *Organizational*

Behavior and Human Decision Processes 78, issue 3 (June 1999): 167–203.

Ludema, James D., David L. Cooperrider, and Frank J. Barrett. "Appreciative Inquiry: The Power of the Unconditional Positive Question." In Peter Reason and Hilary Bradbury, eds., *Handbook of Action Research: Participative Inquiry and Practice*, 189–200. Thousand Oaks, CA: Sage Publications, 2001.

Mangham, Iain L. *Interactions and Interventions in Organizations.* New York: John Wiley & Sons, 1978.

Martin, Roger. *The Responsibility Virus: How Control Freaks, Shrinking Violets—and the Rest of Us—Can Harness the Power of True Partnership.* New York: Basic Books, 2002.

———. "How Successful Leaders Think." *Harvard Business Review*, June 2007.

Masten, Ann S. "Ordinary Magic: Resilience Processes in Development." *American Psychologist* 56, no. 3 (March 2001): 227–38.

Matheson, David, and Jim Matheson. *The Smart Organization: Creating Value Through Strategic R&D.* Boston: Harvard Business School Press, 1998.

McArthur, Philip, Robert Putnam, and Diana McLain Smith. "Climbing Out of the Muck." In Peter Senge, et al., eds., *The Dance of Change*, 120–25. New York: Doubleday, 1999.

Metcalfe, Janet, and Walter Mischel. "A Hot/Cool System Analysis of Delay of Gratification." *Psychological Review* 106, no. 1 (1999): 3–19.

Mintzberg, Henry. *The Structuring of Organizations.* Englewood Cliffs, NJ: Prentice-Hall, 1979.

Morrow, Daniel. "Oral History Interview with Steve Jobs." *Smithsonian*, April 20, 1995.

Myers, Isabel Briggs. *Gifts Differing: Understanding Personality Type* (reprint edition). Mountain View, CA: Davies-Black Publishing, 1995.

Nisbett, Richard E., and Timothy Wilson. "Telling More Than We Can Know: Verbal Reports on Mental Processes." *Psychological Review* 84 (1977): 231–59.

Nisbett, Richard E., and Lee Ross. *Human Inference: Strategies and Shortcomings of Social Judgment.* Englewood Cliffs, NJ: Prentice Hall, 1980.

Noonan, William. *Discussing the Undiscussable: A Guide to Overcoming Defensive Routines in the Workplace.* San Francisco: Jossey-Bass, 2007.

Ong, Anthony, Cindy Bergeman, Toni Bisconti, and Kimberly Wallace. "Psychological Resilience, Positive Emotions, and Successful Adaptation to Stress in Later Life." *Journal of Personality and Social Psychology* 91, no. 4 (2006): 730–49.

Patterson, Kerry, Joseph Grenny, Ron McMillan, and Al Switzler. *Crucial Conversations: Tools for Talking When Stakes Are High.* New York: McGraw-Hill, 2002.

———. *Crucial Confrontations: Tools for Resolving Broken Promises, Violated Expectations, and Bad Behavior.* New York: McGraw-Hill, 2005.

Perlow, Leslie. *When You Say Yes But Mean No: How Silencing Conflict Wrecks Relationships and Companies . . . and What You Can Do About It.* New York: Crown Business, 2003.

Polivy, Janet, and Peter Herman. "If at First You Don't Succeed: False Hopes of Self-Change." *American Psychologist* 57, no. 9 (2002): 677–89.

Putnam, Robert. "Recipes and Reflective Learning: What Would Prevent You From Saying It That Way?" In Donald Schön, ed., *The Reflective Turn: Case Studies In and On Educational Practice.* New York: Teachers College Press, 1991. Also available at www.actiondesign. com.

Quinn, Robert E. *Change the World: How Ordinary People Can Accomplish Extraordinary Results.* San Francisco: Jossey-Bass, 2000.

Reiss, David, with Jenae M. Neiderhiser, E. Mavis Hetherington, and Robert Plomin. *The Relationship Code: Deciphering Genetic and Social Influences on Adolescent Development.* Cambridge, MA: Harvard University Press, 2000.

Rosch, Eleanor. "Prototype Classification and Logical Classification: The Two Systems." In *New Trends in Conceptual Representation: Challenges to Piaget's Theory?* Hillsdale, NJ: Lawrence Erlbaum Associates, 1983.

Rose, Frank. *West of Eden: The End of Innocence at Apple Computer.* New York: Penguin, 1989.

Royster, Charles. *The Destructive War.* New York: Alfred A. Knopf, 1991.

Sackmann, Sonja. *Cultural Knowledge in Organizations: Exploring the Collective Mind.* Thousand Oaks, CA: Sage Publications, 1991.

Schafer, Roy. "Action and Narration in Psychoanalysis." *New Literary History* 12 (1980): 61–85.

———. "Narration in the Psychoanalytic Dialogue." *Critical Inquiry* 7 (1980): 29–53.

Schein, Edgar H. *Organizational Culture and Leadership*. San Francisco: Jossey-Bass, 1985.

———. *Process Consultation: Its Role in Organization Development* (Second Edition). Englewood Cliffs, NJ: Prentice Hall, 1988.

Schön, Donald. *The Reflective Practitioner: How Professionals Think in Action*. New York: Basic Books, 1982.

———. *Educating the Reflective Practitioner*. San Francisco: Jossey-Bass, 1987.

Schwarz, Roger. *The Skilled Facilitator: A Comprehensive Resource for Consultants, Facilitators, Managers, Trainers, and Coaches*. San Francisco: Jossey-Bass, 2002.

Sculley, John, and John A. Byrne. *Odyssey: Pepsi to Apple: A Journey of Adventure, Ideas and the Future*. New York: Harper & Row, 1987.

Sedaris, David. "Old Faithful." *New Yorker*, November 29, 2004. Also available at www.newyorker.com.

Senge, Peter. *The Fifth Discipline: The Art and Practice of the Learning Organization*. New York: Currency, 1990.

Senge, Peter, Art Kleiner, Charlotte Roberts, Richard Ross, George Roth, and Bryan Smith. *The Dance of Change*. New York: Doubleday, 1999.

Senge, Peter, Charlotte Roberts, Richard Ross, Bryan Smith, and Art Kleiner. *The Fifth Discipline Fieldbook*. New York: Doubleday, 1994.

Shah, James. "Automatic for People: How Representations of Significant Others Implicitly Affect Goal Pursuit." *Journal of Personality and Social Psychology* 84, no. 4 (2003): 661–81.

Shank, Roger, and Robert Abelson. *Scripts, Plans, Goals, and Understanding*. Mahwah, NJ: Lawrence Erlbaum Associates, 1977.

Smith, Diana McLain. "Different Portraits of Medical Practice." In Russell Sawa, ed., *Family Health Care*, 105–30. Thousand Oaks, CA: Sage Publications, 1992.

———. "The Muck Stops Here." In Peter Senge, et al., eds., *The Dance of Change*, 125–28. New York: Doubleday, 1999.

———. "Keeping a Strategic Dialogue Moving." In Peggy Simcic Brown and Roberta Wiig, eds., *Corporate Communication: A Strategic Approach to Building Reputation*. Oslo, Norway: Gyldendal Norsk Forlag, 2002. Also available at www.actiondesign.com.

Spence, Donald P. *Narrative Truth and Historical Truth: Meaning and Interpretation in Psychoanalysis*. New York: W.W. Norton & Company, 1982.

Stone, Douglas, Bruce Patton, and Sheila Heen. *Difficult Conversations: How to Discuss What Matters Most.* New York: Viking, 1999.

Susskind, Lawrence, and Jeffrey Cruikshank. *Breaking the Impasse: Consensual Approaches to Resolving Public Disputes.* New York: Basic Books, 1987.

Torbert, William R. *Managing the Corporate Dream: Restructuring for Long-term Success.* Homewood, IL: Irwin Professional, 1987.

Tucker, Anita L., and Amy C. Edmondson. "Why Hospitals Don't Learn From Failures: Organizational and Psychological Dynamics That Inhibit System Change." *California Management Review* 45, no. 2 (2003): 55–72.

Tushman, Michael, and Charles A. O'Reilly. *Winning Through Innovation: A Practical Guide to Leading Organizational Change and Renewal.* Boston: Harvard Business School Press, 1997.

Uhl-Bien, Mary, and John M. Maslyn. "Reciprocity in Manager-Subordinate Relationships: Components, Configurations, and Outcomes." *Journal of Management* 29, issue 4 (August 2003): 511–32.

Van Maanen, John. "On the Understanding of Interpersonal Relations." In Warren Bennis, John Van Maanen, Edgar Schein, and Fred Steele, eds., *Essays in Interpersonal Dynamics.* Homewood, IL: Dorsey Press, 1979.

Wallace, David Foster. "The Capital T Truth." *O, the Oprah Magazine,* December 2006.

Walls, Ted, and David Walden. "Understanding Unclear Situations and Each Other Using the Language Processing Method." *Center for Quality of Management Journal* 4, no. 4 (Special Issue, Winter 1995).

Walton, Richard E. *Managing Conflict: Interpersonal Dialogue and Third-Party Roles* (Second Edition). Reading, MA: Addison-Wesley, 1987.

Watzlawick, Paul, and John H. Weakland, eds. *The Interactional View: Studies at the Mental Research Institute, Palo Alto, 1965–1974.* New York: W.W. Norton & Company, 1977.

Weber, Max, H. H. Gerth, ed., and C. Wright Mills, ed. *From Max Weber: Essays in Sociology.* New York: Oxford University Press, 1958.

Weick, Karl. *The Social Psychology of Organizing.* Reading, MA: Addison-Wesley, 1979.

Welch, Jack. *Jack: Straight from the Gut.* New York: Warner Business Books, 2001.

White, Michael, and David Epston. *Narrative Means to Therapeutic Ends.* New York: W. W. Norton & Company, 1990.

White, Ronald C. Jr. *Lincoln's Greatest Speech: The Second Inaugural.* New York: Simon & Schuster, 2002.

For further reading, see the Action Design bibliography at www.actiondesign.com; click on "bibliography."

Illustration Credits

Index

Page numbers in *italics* refer to illustrations